D0712772

WASHO SHAMANS AND PEYOTISTS

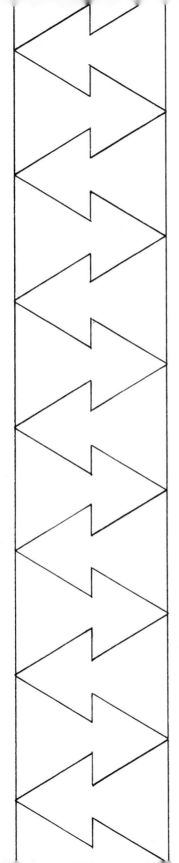

WASHO
SHAMANS
AND
PEYOTISTS

Religious Conflict in
An American Indian Tribe

EDGAR E. SISKIN

UNIVERSITY OF UTAH PRESS
Salt Lake City, Utah

Library of Congress Cataloging in Publication Data

Siskin, Edgar E., 1907–
    Washo shamans and peyotists.

    Revision of the author's thesis (Ph. D.—Yale Univer-
sity, 1941) which had title: The Impact of the peyote
cult upon shamanism among the Washo Indians.
    Bibliography: p.
    Includes index.
    1. Washo Indians—Religion and mythology. 2. Shamanism
—Nevada. 3. Shamanism—California. 4. Peyotism—
Nevada. 5. Peyotism—California. 6. Indians of North
America—Nevada—Religion and mythology. 7. Indians
of North America—California—Religion and mythology.
I. Title.
E99.W38S59   1983   299'.78   83–14573
ISBN 0-87480-223-7

To Lillian

CONTENTS

Illustrations

Dresslerville Indian colony
George Snooks • Water babies' pool
Blind Mike Dick • Charlie and Susie Rube
Long Pete • Brush enclosure for peyote meeting
Sam and Ida Dick • Henry (Moses) Rupert
Ramsey Walker • John Frank

INTRODUCTION

In the late summer of 1981 I drove through the foothills of west-central Nevada, over Kingsbury Pass in the high Sierras and along the eastern shore of Lake Tahoe, a geographic area I knew well, for it was here that I spent several summers, beginning in 1937, as a graduate student in anthropology at Yale University. This was traditional Washo Indian territory, and for three summers I lived among the Washo as a field ethnologist.

Forty years ago the valleys east of Lake Tahoe were virtually empty of people except for those living in the scattered ranches and thinly populated townlets. Now, they were the site of a chain of dormitory communities built for a spreading urban population. Then, the eastern shore of Tahoe commanded an unobstructed view of the blue lake circled by pine forests and the white peaks of the high Sierras—what Mark Twain described as "the fairest picture the whole earth affords." Now, the eastern side of the lake was a medley of high-rise gambling resorts, motels, stores, restaurants, and all the satellites of a thriving pleasure haunt.

In 1937 Washo families would make their traditional spring trek westward over the mountain passes and summer around the mountain lakes. There I would spend time with them. But that is a tribal pattern which has vanished. As I drove the car slowly along the crowded highway of Tahoe's eastern shore, stopping and starting at the frequent traffic signals, I was left to ruminate on what changes the hand of man had wrought.

The suggestion to study the Washo in the field had come from Edward Sapir, who was chairman of the department of anthropology and linguistics at Yale. Sapir was himself interested in the Washo because of his work on Hokan, one of the North American

Indian language stocks. As the only Hokan-speaking tribe between the Rockies and the Sierras, the Washo are a linguistic oddity—a Hokan island in a Uto-Aztecan sea. This intrigued Sapir as it had other linguists; two years before one of his graduate students, Walter Dyk, had gone out to work with the Washo on their language. Dyk was one of the brilliant young linguists who had come with Sapir from the University of Chicago in 1932 to establish at Yale what in a few years became a leading center for linguistic studies. Later, Dyk worked with the Navaho and wrote the classic, *Son of Old Man Hat: A Navajo Autobiography*, the life story of Left Handed.

No ethnography of the Washo had as yet been written, although Alfred L. Kroeber, Robert H. Lowie, and Samuel A. Barrett had published short monographs after spending brief field sessions with the tribe. Before I left for Nevada that summer, Dyk gave me the name of his chief linguistic informant, whom he highly recommended as an interpreter. Sapir had suggested that I go over to Berkeley and speak with Kroeber and Lowie before venturing into Washo territory. They might have information which would be useful in making the first approaches to the tribe.

Once in Berkeley I made my way to the university campus and to the jerry-built structure with a corrugated tin roof which then housed the department of anthropology. As I entered this flimsy, shed-like barracks, the first thought that struck me was, Kroeber and Lowie—here? Kroeber was away but Lowie received me with a formal, if somewhat stiff, graciousness that suggested his Viennese origin. He proposed that we go for a walk, and we made for the football stadium. Lowie was a big lumbering man who breathed heavily as he walked. We began circling the empty arena, and he talked about his field trip of a few weeks with the Washo, excusing himself now and again for the leanness of his information. He recommended one informant he had worked with, Bill Cornbread, who was said to be the oldest living Washo.

Later when I read Lowie's monograph I could not but admire the amount of information he had gathered in so short a stay and the cogency with which he had ordered it. As for Bill Cornbread, he turned out to be quite deaf, merely nodding his head at my shouted questions. But he introduced me to Long Pete, who became my best Southern Washo informant.

Lowie suggested that I see Edward W. Gifford, a faculty colleague, whose office was in a somewhat sturdier building where the university publications in anthropology were stored. I knew of Gifford through his ethnography of the Miwok, southwestern neighbors of the Washo, and found him all quiet affability. We talked for a while, and I left loaded down with what may have been copies of most of the university publications in ethnology. These were to provide reading more than sufficient for the next three summers.

The train ride from San Francisco took me across the Sierras to Reno, Nevada. When I got off the train, I walked to the first used-car lot I saw and bought a Model A Ford for $50. That left the $250 fieldwork grant from Yale somewhat dented, but in those days of scanty funding I had no complaints. I drove south, bound for Gardnerville, largest town in Douglas County with a population of two hundred. Gardnerville was less than five miles from Dresslerville, the main Washo settlement located in the geographic center of Washo territory. I knew I would be spending a lot of time in Dresslerville.

The main highway south, U.S. 395, was unpaved and the rains had left it corrugated like the roof of the Berkeley anthropology building. I was soon bumping and rattling along as the road made its way through the sagebrush desert interspersed with irrigated ranchlands. On my right the towering peaks of the Sierras rose steeply from the 6,000 feet elevation of the plateau floor, on my left a range of low hills hovered on the horizon. The scent of sage, raised by the rain that falls like clockwork every early afternoon, was in the marvelous crystalline air. Washo country — and I thought with Mark Twain that there could be no landscape more fair in all North America. After an hour I reached Gardnerville, where I rented a room for five dollars a week. This would serve as the base from which I would travel to the sparse Washo settlements to work with the people.

So began my first season in the field, which together with the two following summers are sketched in the Preface. On the basis of this fieldwork I wrote my Ph.D. dissertation, *The Impact of the Peyote Cult upon Shamanism among the Washo Indians*, submitting it in 1941. George Peter Murdock, John Dollard, and the late Clellan Ford were the readers, and there was a recommendation that it be considered for publication in the *Yale University Publications In Anthropology*. But it was the first year of World War II, Yale went on a wartime footing, and I went out to the Pacific to join the First Marine Division. Three years later when I returned, other activities supervened and the dissertation remained unpublished.

During the decades that have passed since my last extended field trip, I have kept in touch with the Washo — in earlier years through fitful correspondence with George Snooks, my first interpreter, and Sam Dick, shaman and early peyote leader, and then later through contact with anthropologists who worked with the Washo and wrote about them. On two occasions I visited the Washo — in 1961 when during a trip west I stopped to see George Snooks in Dresslerville, and in 1974 when I spent three weeks in Carson Valley renewing ties with the people. The oldsters I had known were gone, most of the remaining adults had been children when I first met them. I talked at length with a number of individuals and kept notes of our conversations.

Through these channels I was made aware of the changes taking place in Washo life, particularly in the religious culture of the people. My study of the Washo had its focus in their religious life, notably in the conflict between shamanism and peyotism, which developed and reached its violent climax precisely during the years when I was in the field. From time to time it was suggested by colleagues familiar with my field studies that the doctoral dissertation be published, but I felt that before publication it should be augmented by more recent fieldwork. In any event, for all the reasons that came readily to hand when loath to revive an aging venture, I did nothing about the intermittent notion to publish.

Two years ago the University of Utah Press informed me of their interest in publishing the dissertation. When I suggested that I write a supplementary section — the Epilogue — that would bring the study of Washo religion up-to-date, the Press agreed. Before commencing to write, I went out to Nevada in the late summer of 1981 to revisit the Washo and to inquire into the general life of the people and particularly into their religious life. At the end of my stay I was ready to begin writing the additional chapters. My objective was to portray the religious life of an Indian tribe as it has adapted itself to the profound and persistent changes taking place around it.

Since my first field trip to the Washo, both shamanism and peyotism have emerged from the obscurity they once shared to become subjects popularly associated with movements of protest and revolt, mainly by the young, against many of the cherished institutions and hoary values of Western society. Because of this embattled context, shamanism and peyotism have been both extravagantly lauded and sternly denounced. At the same time, the American Indian, whose way of life has long included both religious complexes, has taken his place in the forefront of national attention.

Shamanism has come to excite the interest of a young, non-Indian generation seeking a new, expanding consciousness. It is the nonintellective consciousness of feeling and imagination which, spurning science, technology, and the objectively rational, embraces the occult and the mystical. In this perspective, shamanism is a paradigm of the expanding consciousness, and the shaman the wise master who roves magically through the transcendant wonders and ineffable mysteries of a world beyond our own.

Peyote has meanwhile achieved a notable topicality for its divergent uses. Pharmacologists at work in their laboratories have experimented with mescaline, the psychotropic agent of peyote, as a possible specific in psychotherapy. At the same time peyote has become a shining star in the firmament of the drug culture. Mescaline was sampled approvingly by Havelock Ellis in 1898 and pronounced the perfect anodyne in Aldoux Huxley's *The Doors of Perception*. This revelation has since been acted upon with considerable enthusiasm by an assortment of individuals, many in quest of the expanded consciousness, others in search of kicks.[1]

Concurrent with the vogue of peyote and shamanism in chosen circles has been the rise of American Indian chic.[2] The American Indian, discovering a refurbished self-image born of ancestral pride, began to be regarded with "romanticism-ensorcelled eyes," to use La Barre's memorable locution, by many whites. Under the banner of native tribal movements, Indians pressed forward in the struggle for rectification of ancient wrongs. Raised to a new level of ethnic awareness, they saw the federal government disbursing unprecedented sums of money in settling land claims. To the dismay of the white community, they began asserting themselves with unaccustomed militancy; and even anthropologists, long their champions, were surprised, not to say taken aback, by the Indians' new posture.[3]

Thus were the central subjects of my early field investigation—shamanism and peyotism in the experience of an American Indian tribe—lifted in the span of a few decades from the dim regions of dusty academic burrowing into the bright lights of pop culture. It is relevant to the times that all three subjects were conjoined in the spectacularly popular books of Carlos Castaneda, a university Ph.D.[4] These best-selling amalgams of fact and fancy purport to recount Castaneda's experiences after he placed himself under the tutelage of a Yaqui shaman/sorcerer; ate hallucinogenic plants, including peyote; and entered into the vast inner space of a separate reality. A debate has ensued over the authenticity of Don Juan and of Castaneda's writings; but whether fantasy or science fiction, fabrication, or work of art, his books have been acclaimed a "Bible for the young" and their author a "folk hero." Beatification for Castenada was bestowed when his surrealist face appeared on the March 5, 1973, cover of *Time*.

Forty-five years ago no one could have foreseen that some of the main foci of my original study would within the short span of a few decades create such a commotion on the American cultural scene.

Chapters 1 through 5 of this work are based on the three field trips to the Washo undertaken in 1937–39. They were originally written in 1941 as my Ph.D. dissertation. The Epilogue is based on the field excursions to the Washo in 1974 and 1981, and was written in 1982. Relevant source material on shamanism and peyotism written since 1941 has been utilized.

Occasional changes, mainly stylistic, have been made in the original text of the dissertation chapters. Recent sources have sometimes been added to correct those anachronisms and errors inevitable in a document written more than four decades earlier. But in retaining the essentially original version, written close to the events recorded, it is hoped that something of the dramatic immediacy of the religious conflict which disturbed the tribe so deeply may be conveyed.

Regarding two items of usage: "shamanistic" rather than "shamanic" has been used; and the designation "Northern Paiute" used here has for some time superseded the tribal name, Paviotso, preferred by R. H. Lowie and W. Z. Park. In some cases the names of Washo individuals have been changed. Because of typesetting contingencies most of the Washo words phonetically transcribed in the original text have been omitted and those retained are rendered in Anglicized spelling.

I acknowledge a debt to those who have helped at various times to facilitate the long journey of this study from idea to published work.

Edward Sapir, who suggested that I study the Washo, decisively shaped the development of my intellectual life. A scholar of prodigious range who embodied rare artistic and human gifts, he was a brilliant and inspiring teacher, whose lamentably premature death robbed anthropology of one of its finest creative minds and his students of a peerless mentor. He died while I was in the field and therefore to my lasting regret did not get to read my dissertation. The one-hundredth anniversary of Edward Sapir's birth will be observed in 1984. This book pays tribute to his memory.

George Snooks, my first interpreter and friend, gave me an understanding of shamanism that no written record can convey. Sam Dick, shaman and peyote leader, my friend and brother, led me to a knowledge of peyote, betokened by his gift to me of peyote songs and a sacred rattle.

Don Handelman of Hebrew University, who has done fieldwork with the Washo on shamanism, read the Epilogue and discussed it with me in Jerusalem to my great benefit. Weston La Barre, a fellow graduate student of Sapir's at Yale, who in 1938 wrote a classical work on peyotism, *The Peyote Cult*, has been kind enough to answer some questions on the text.

Omer C. Stewart studied Washo-Paiute peyotism in 1938, and in an interesting illustration of the theory of convergence, was in the field with the Washo when I was, although we never met. He generously shared his manuscript material with me. No one studying peyotism or the Great Basin can fail to be grateful for Stewart's contribution to the field.

Grace Dangberg, historian of early Nevada settlement and recorder of Washo texts, has placed her valuable field material at my disposal, and since my first field excursion has been gracious and helpful.

Over the years many Washo have shared with me knowlege of their way of life, ancestral and modern. I am grateful for the kindness and friendship given during the seasons in the field.

Lillian, my wife, has been a steady and constant help. Her encouragement together with an exceptional skill as editor and typist, brought all the strands together, making the completion of this work possible.

Jerusalem, Israel
1982

PREFACE

While engaged in general fieldwork among the Washo in the summer of 1937, I was presented with the opportunity for making an intensive study of shamanism. The agent of this opportunity was my chief interpreter, George Snooks. Snooks was the sort of interpreter one is tempted to call ideal. Intelligent, widely familiar with both native and white culture, fluent in both languages, interested in the student's task and actively helpful in its realization, he possessed the additional merit of having become acquainted with field disciplines as principal linguistic informant for Walter Dyk when the latter was working on the Washo language. There was no difficulty in establishing rapport, and the task of obtaining a picture of shamanism in an area where this phase of culture had long been neglected proved equally challenging to us both.

It was through Snooks that friendly and effective contact was made with Mike Dick, recognized as the most powerful shaman in the tribe. Dick was at first unwilling to give information about shamanism. He shared the reluctance of every member of the tribe in this respect. A frontal attack having failed, my next approach was through myths. For several weeks, Dick, the authority in tribal lore, narrated Washo myths and disclosed other relevant aspects of the culture. At the end of that period, he was ready to talk about shamanism.

Most of the data gathered in 1937 came from him. It was valuably supplemented by Snooks's own knowledge, gained not only through close association with his father, who was in the process of becoming a shaman at the time of his death in 1936, but also through his personal experiences as a lay dreamer. From Charlie

Rube, once an antelope shaman, and Susie Rube, both well over eighty but hale and alert, additional information was obtained. Dick lived in Sheridan, Nevada, until late in the summer when he removed to Myers, California, near Lake Tahoe. Similarly, the Rubes divided the summer between Minden, Nevada, and Bijou, California. It was traditional Washo practice to move westward from the Nevada valleys to the high Sierra lakes. I lived in close proximity to both Dick and the Rubes during this time and Snooks was my constant associate.

The division of the Washo into three geographic and dialectic groups — Northern, Central, and Southern Washo — having been determined, approved ethnological method called for investigation of the cultural scene in all divisions.[1] Informants mentioned thus far were Central Washo. To learn something of Southern Washo shamanism, a trip was undertaken to the territory immediately south. For three weeks at Coleville, California, we received information from Long Pete, then over seventy years of age and as a lifelong Southern Washo, qualified to speak with authority on the local culture.

The opportunity to visit the Northern Washo did not come until the following summer. George Snooks had left Nevada the previous winter and was no longer my interpreter. Will Christensen, premedical student at the University of Oklahoma, was acting in that capacity. Together we journeyed to Loyalton, California, scene of a small Northern Washo settlement and home of Bill Wilson, a shaman of some note. During our stay in Loyalton, we made friendly contact with Wilson and his wife, who was also a shaman, until eventually we were invited to witness a curing ceremony. We attended a séance at which Wilson, assisted by his wife, officiated.

During the rest of the summer, the association with Mike Dick, begun under Snooks's aegis a year before, continued. Frequent meetings together bore fruit and finally we gained permission to witness one of his ceremonies, a privilege hitherto denied. This was the first of three full four-night sessions presided over by Mike Dick that we attended. We were allowed to take notes. Christensen took down the spoken part of the séance, I chronicled the incidents.

It should be mentioned that a factor which undoubtedly con-attributed to Mike Dick's progressive cooperation was the advent of peyote, which by the summer of 1938 had become a powerful force in the tribe. The ready communicativeness of the peyotists must have done much to break down his reticence. In the conflict between shamanism and peyote, he could not afford to be indifferent to any interested individual, least of all to one who had been hospitably received by his rivals.

Mike Dick's interest stimulated the support of other shamans. Subsequently—during the remainder of the summer of 1938 and for part of the summer of 1939—Sam Dick, Henry Rupert, Dick Bagley, Ruth Calley, and Tom Mitchell were all interviewed. Information gained from them, though not so full as that derived from weeks spent with Mike Dick and George Snooks, was nevertheless valuable in that it served as a check on the more comprehensive data.

It was in this second summer of fieldwork that the presence of peyote began to loom on the ethnological horizon. Introduced in the fall of 1936, it had quite casually come to my attention the following summer. Snooks had attended a meeting, a description of which I recorded at the time. None of my informants esteemed it of any importance. By the summer of 1938, however, peyote had achieved a considerable popularity and was causing a disturbing ferment in the tribe as a whole. The shamans were especially voluble in their denunciations of the new religion.

The movement had as its pivotal character Ben Lancaster, a Washo returned from extensive wanderings for twenty years to his Nevada home. Lancaster was the peyote proselytizer. It was not difficult to meet him. After some preliminary conversations, he, always anxious to create the correct impression, invited me to a peyote meeting. I attended, was seated next to the chief himself as guest of honor, and ate the sacred cactus.

That serious conflict was brewing was all too clear. It occurred to me that such conflict was part of historic culture process, that what I was witnessing was a contemporary example of culture change in a primitive society. I determined to investigate as best I could the forces set in motion by the introduction of the new cult.

My task was not difficult. I already had the confidence of the shamans. The peyotists, leaders and laymen, were only too eager to talk. Invitations to attend meetings were pressed on all sides.

When I returned the following summer, 1939, more far-reaching changes had taken place. Peyote's star had declined. Lancaster was seldom to be seen in Washo territory. Dresslerville Indian colony had expelled the peyotists. Resentment and rancor were everywhere left in the wake of the social upheaval. Sam Dick, Lancaster's earliest convert and chief disciple, was conducting the only meetings in Washo territory—in Coleville on the Washo-Southern Paiute boundary. Sam Dick had by this time broken with Lancaster, the rupture a consequence of intracult hostilities.

It was with Sam Dick that I spent most of the 1939 field session. I attended meetings, was accepted into the cult as a brother, was given songs and a sacred rattle. He was a particularly valuable informant for a number of reasons. He had been a shaman himself and thus constituted a bridge between the old and the new; in him were epitomized the conflicts in the culture—he was their embodied expression; he was occupied with nothing but peyote and was willing to talk about it endlessly.

At intervals, I journeyed to Dresslerville and interviewed leaders of the opposition, Steve Earl, Martinez Kyser, and John Mack. There I also spoke at length with Willie Smokey, tribal leader and an early convert, but as the result of the local tumult forced to withdraw from the cult. Other tribesmen wherever encountered had their word to say about peyote.

From these several sources I obtained in time a rather comprehensive picture of the contemporary cultural scene. With a knowledge of the aboriginal background gained in the early field experience, it appeared possible to elaborate a cogent explanation for the changes which had occurred. Such a study, it seemed, should meet the objection, valid enough, that "studies of culture transfer and culture change . . . focused mainly on what happens to new elements" are not altogether satisfactory since "it is only one half of the picture." Through familiarity with the aboriginal setting, there might be achieved in the assessment of one culture that "true perspective regarding the processes involved" for which anthropologists justifiably plead.[2]

New Haven, Connecticut
1941

WASHO SHAMANS AND PEYOTISTS

1. SKETCH OF WASHO CULTURE

The Washo occupy a territorial area of approximately 3,400 square miles falling in west-central Nevada and east-central California (Figure 1). Two physiographic provinces are shared by the terrain, the Great Basin and the Sierra Cascades, and it is in terms of this marginal physiographic position that Washo subsistence economy can best be understood.[1] In the fall and winter, the western margin of the Great Basin is the tribal domain; in the spring and summer, the wooded eastern slopes of the Sierra Nevadas, which bisect the territory, become their habitat. Boundaries are roughly defined by Pine Nut Range on the east, the crest of the Sierras on the west and south, and Long Valley in the north.

Three divisions of the tribe are demarcated by boundaries running east and west. The Northern Washo *(welmelti)* divide from the Central Washo *(pauwalu)* at the northern end of Carson valley; the Central Washo separate from the Southern *(hangalelti)* at the present California-Nevada border at Woodfords, California. Parallel westward and eastward movements are carried on by each of the three divisions in accordance with seasonal food-questing migrations.[2] Tribal kinship is recognized by all groups, the difference between them limited to slight cultural and dialectic variation. The name Washo (sometimes spelled Washoe), is derived from the name they give themselves, *waju. Waju* is the name of a seed gathered annually by the women.

Two distinct types of natural environment yield for the Washo a more varied and perhaps fuller subsistence than that secured by neighboring tribes confined to the arid Great Basin. The desert range of hills produces the piñon *(Pinus monophylla)* trees whose nuts

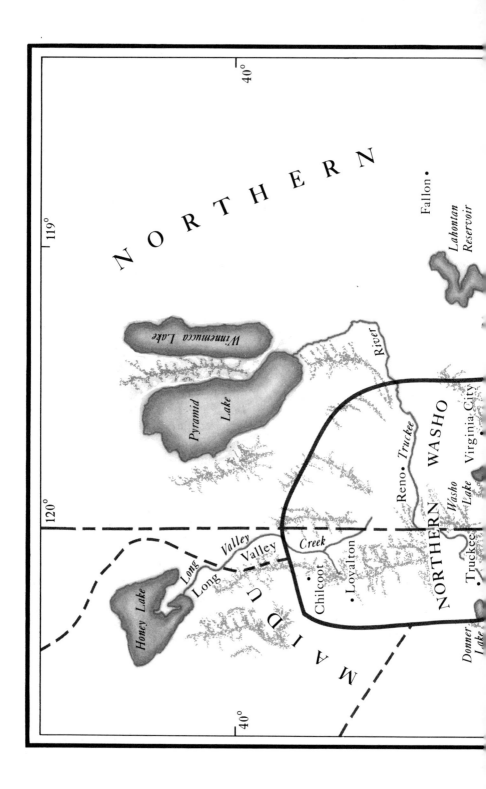

NORTHERN

119°

120°

40°

40°

Fallon •

Lahontan Reservoir

Winnemucca Lake

Pyramid Lake

River

Truckee

WASHO

Reno •

Virginia City

Washo Lake

NORTHERN

Truckee

Creek

Valley

Valley

Loyalton •

Chilcoot •

Long Valley

Long

Honey Lake

MAIDU

Donner Lake

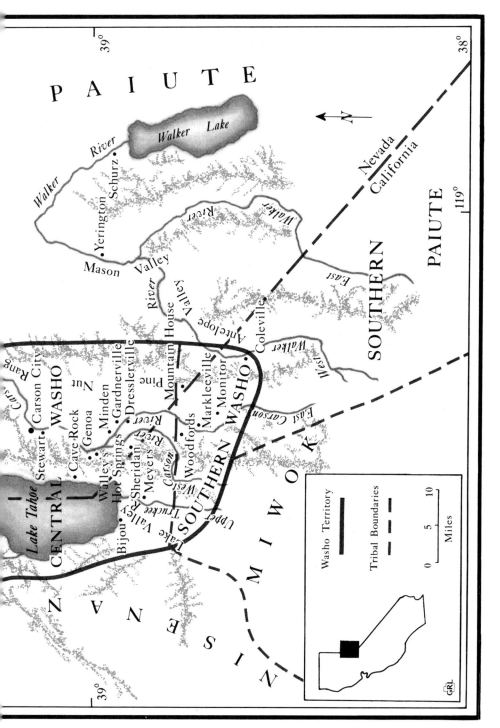

Figure 1. Map of Washo and contiguous territory. Cartography by Robert E. Wood.

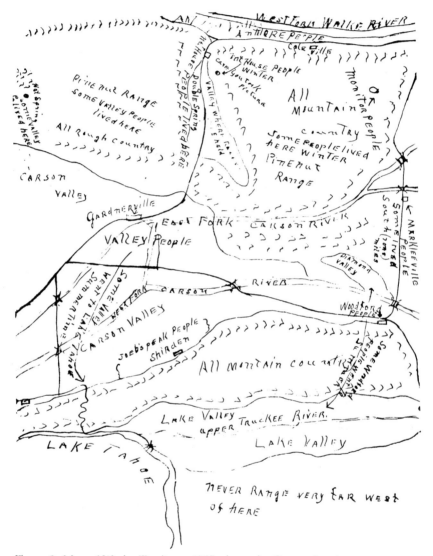

Figure 2. Map of Washo Territory, 1937, drawn by George Snooks.

are staple food for the tribe. The dry Basin valleys grow little more than sagebrush, grass, and edible seeds that the women seasonally gather. There is no agriculture. Small game, especially rabbits, are taken in this fall and winter habitat. Deer, principally, and antelope, mountain sheep, and bear, secondarily, are hunted. The streams of the river drainages north and south of Lake Tahoe brim with a plentiful supply of fish, which becomes the main summer food. Acorns gathered on the forested slopes of the Sierras provide an important food item, and crickets, grubworms, and insects a minor one. However, although the resources are somewhat larger than for the average Great Basin tribe, food shortage is an ever-present fear. Sometimes late snows will prevent access to mountain rivers, and as a result, communities will starve.

The consequences of the intermediate physiographic position of the Washo spread, as we shall see, into every phase of the culture. Thus the density of population (16.10 per 100 kilometers) is much higher than that of the Basin generally, but a good deal less than that of the adjacent California province. Kroeber lists the total population as amounting to approximately 1,000 individuals.[3] (More recent population estimates vary from Freed's 600 to Downs's 2,000.)[4]

Linguistically the Washo do not affiliate closely with any neighboring stock. Their tongue is said to be aberrant Hokan.[5] But whatever their linguistic associations, the Washo remain the only tribe in the Basin—except for some Yuman-dialect speakers on the southern periphery—which does not speak a Uto-Aztecan language.

Contact with neighboring tribes is more often than not pacific. Intertribal visiting is done with the Paiute to the east, Southern Paiute to the south, Miwok to the southwest. Trade is carried on and these contacts sometimes result in marriage. Warfare, provoked usually by trespass or theft, breaks out occasionally but consists of nothing more than a stereotyped skirmish. If someone is killed, everybody will scurry home, the death to be avenged at some future time. With the western and northern Nisenan and Maidu, relations are more hostile, fighting and killing more common. D'Azevedo comments: "The legends of 'war' involving the Washo are essentially accounts of skirmishes between small hunting or gathering parties. There are more numerous legends of Washo hiding in the hills and watching intruders pass by their hidden camps."[6]

During the winter, the people live in permanent settlements which are named, the location fixed with reference to such desirable features as nearness to water, shelter from climatic rigors, accessibility to deer runs. Dwellings are built anew each year when the migrants return from summer and fall haunts, usually in the latter part of September. Settlements consist of a number of dwelling clusters, each composed of two or three houses, each house harboring a family. Distance between houses depends roughly upon closeness of relationship.

The house itself is the typical Great Basin subconical structure with circular ground plan. Two pairs of slanting sideposts of pine or juniper, joined at the top by a connecting ridgepole, form a frame against which poles are leaned. Overlapping pine-nut boughs or tule mats bound to the frame with willows constitute the covering. In the southern wooded area, cedar bark is used as roofing material. Provision is made for a smoke hole, and entrance to the house is through a vestibule. Pine needles or tules cover the floor, in the center of which a fire burns. House furniture is scanty, pine needles or sagebrush bark serving as beds. Basketry, clothing, rabbit-skin blankets, and hides will be stored along the periphery of the house. Houses are ten feet high, thirteen to fourteen feet in diameter.

Accessory to winter dwellings are food storage pits and pine-nut granaries, the latter of two types—a bowl-shaped bark container built in a tree and a structure of poles and interlaced willow branches set in the ground. Rude sweat lodges stand a short distance removed. Dance-houses of the generalized east-central California type are found in each Southern and in some Central Washo settlements.

A typical household is composed of the father, mother, unmarried children, and younger married daughters whose children are still infants. The son-in-law's parents often live nearby in the same settlement. But when the daughter's family grows larger and the children reach the age of puberty, she and her husband move out and either set up their own residence nearby or go to another community.

No fixed rules of residence prevail, although there is a bias toward matrilocal establishment. Mobility characterizes family life, consequently membership in any settlement tends to fluctuate. Among the principal factors which contribute to this fluidity is the sparse food supply. Scarcity sometimes makes it necessary for whole families to move to more favorable localities. Basic economic anxiety also tends to reduce the size of the family unit. Feeding the household is an onerous task, made more difficult by lack of animal transportation. Other factors making for mobility are the abandonment of houses, which takes place whenever death occurs, and brittle monogamy.

Rudimentary social and political organization might also be termed a force making for simple and fluid community life. There are no sibs, no exogamous moieties. Households with a community are not necessarily related, and choice of settlement is no determinant of kinship organization. Nor is there any political hierarchy. The closest approach to chiefship is seen in the nonhereditary office of community headman, a person chosen for individual capability. Tribal activities of various kinds—hunting, pine-nut gathering, antelope driving—fall under the random leadership of men of proved merit, most of whom possess some supernatural power derived through dreaming. (A fuller discussion of chiefship is presented in chapter 3 in the section on "Shaman and Layman.") In Washo society, the nuclear and transitory extended family emerge as the basic social units.[7]

Lacking unilateral kin organization, the Washo have no rule governing marriage except an extension of the incest taboo to all near kin and, of course, to all individuals classed as siblings (i.e., cousins). There is no preferred primary marriage, and although the levirate and sororate are frequently made effective, they are not compulsory. Marriage occurs within the settlement as well as out of it. The seasonal subsistence movements, and the larger get-togethers at "big times," give adequate opportunity for young people to meet potential spouses from other communities.[8]

Cutting across the loose bilateral organization of Washo society is one unilinear social grouping which unites men and women of all communitites — a quasi-moiety[9] organization which functions not as an institution but solely in sports and games held at the "big times." The moieties are called *peulelel tayadi* ("those who camp on the eastern side") and *tanglelel tayadi* ("those who camp on the western side") because of the camping arrangement at tribal gatherings. A third division, *dachilgas tayadi* ("those who camp at the end of a line of camps"), is intermediate between the two, joining sides with one or the other of the main divisions. Affiliations with these divisions is patrilineal.

Social activities during the winter are limited to games, of which there is a profusion, various shamanistic activities, such as curing séances, demonstrations of prowess and novice performances, and ceremonies—the girl's puberty rite and an annual mourning ceremony.[10]

The feeling for bilateral family connections is reflected in various aspects of economic, social, and ceremonial life. Before marriage economic exchanges are undertaken between the families involved, and these connections continue as the young couple becomes established and begins rearing children. Maternal grandparents assist at childbearing and are an influence in the bringing up of children. Matrilocal residence is more common, yet patrilocal residence is by no means uncommon, and couples not infrequently shift their residence from wife's parents to husband's. Often, too, the presence of paternal grandparents in the same community confers on them an important function. At childbirth and on other festive occasions relatives of both parents gather. At the important girl's puberty rites, both families assist in gathering food and arranging for the dance. At funerals the same cooperation is in evidence.

Bilaterality is also mirrored in the kinship system. Four grandparent terms are used reciprocally for grandchildren. Parents' siblings are designated by separate terms (father's brother, father's sister, mother's brother, mother's sister). Older brother is distinguished from younger brother, older sister from younger sister. The sibling terms are extended to both cross and parallel cousins, although here the use of older and younger sibling terms depends on the relative age of the parents, not on the relative age of cousin and ego. (When an English-speaking Washo refers to a cousin, he uses the term "cousin-brother," or "cousin-sister.") Affinal terms equate father's brother with mother's sister's husband and mother's sister with father's brother's wife. There is but one term for parent-in-law, but separate terms for son-in-law and daughter-in-law. A single term refers to wife's brother and husband's sister.

A number of the affinal terms of address are teknonymous. The term for husband's brother means "my child's father's brother"; the term for sister's husband, "my sister's child's father"; the term for brother's wife, "my brother's child's mother." Such terms are used in address, and indeed all kinship terms for near relatives are regularly transformed into teknonymous terms by the addition of an appropriate suffix when used as terms of address. This practice dovetails with the Washo tendency to avoid the use of personal names.

As might be expected where communities are small and the residency shifting, there is a minimum of formalized kinship usages in Washo society. There is no mother-in-law taboo. Parents-in-law, however, must be treated with respect. The only usage reminiscent of the joking relationship is the preferred, if unsanctioned, status of wife's sister as additional sex partner.

The economic activities of the winter settlement are divided among men and women in keeping with the customary division of labor. Men hunt deer, mountain sheep, antelope, rabbits, bear. Women prepare food, make baskets, dress and tan skins, fashion clothing. Both men and women trap small game.

Subsistence during the long winter months is based partly on stored pine nuts, acorns, and seeds, partly on meat. Hunting is the main auxiliary subsistence activity. The bow is the chief weapon. Arrow points made of flint will sometimes be smeared with poison taken from a rattlesnake and mixed with pitch. Headless arrows are used for small game. Rabbits are taken in huge nets which sometimes achieve a length of three hundred feet. Almost all hunting is invested with religious overtones. Leaders will dream or will possess efficacious medicines.

As many as twenty hunters will participate in a rabbit drive. Antelope are also hunted communally, driven into a corral through a sagebrush chute. Deer are killed either by small groups or individuals and remain the most desired prey of Washo hunters.

In the fall when the deer are fat, individual hunters venture forth; but during the winter, parties of men go out at the instigation of one who had dreamed of deer. When hunted cooperatively the deer are driven into a narrow pass by fires kindled along a runway. There is a prescribed method for butchering and apportioning the parts. Individual hunters cunningly stalk deer with simulated deer headdress, their knowledge of the terrain and of the animal standing them in good stead. Stereotyped rituals calculated to ensure success punctuate the hunt.

Rabbits constitute with deer the principal winter meat. A rabbit boss calls together a number of men, each of whom brings a net. These would be attached to each other and hung from sticks planted in the ground. At a signal from the leader, the rabbits are driven into the nets and dispatched with either bow and arrow or with a stick. The skins are cut into strips, rolled into a rope, and woven with continuous warp on a simple frame into blankets.

Bear hunting is of less importance economically but carries significant religious implications. Mountain sheep are found and caught at water holes. Woodchucks are hunted with dogs, the only domesticated animal. Prairie dogs are taken in noose snares. Ground squirrels, porcupine, lizards, birds such as sage hen and grouse are also taken. The eggs of the latter are eaten. Insects and worms are gathered.

Besides gathering and taking small game, the women busy themselves with various domestic occupations. They are excellent basket makers, the product of their skill comparing favorably with the finest baskets in North America. Many kinds are fashioned in both coiled and twined technique.[11] Since pottery is unknown, food is cooked, stone-boiled, in baskets. Pine nuts and acorns yield a variety of soups, gruels, and biscuits. Meats are roasted in hot ashes. Nuts, seeds, insects, and worms are placed on a basketry tray with live coals and, through skillful manipulation, parched. The scant clothing is made of buckskin or woodchuck hide. To guard against the severity of winter, rabbit-skin blankets are worn as robes. Footgear consists of moccasins — of two types — and sandals. As has been noted, clothing manufacture is woman's work.

As the end of winter approaches and the food stores dwindle, it is time for the community to break up. Traveling in family groups, the people begin the climb through the steep Sierra passes to summer fishing grounds near Lake Tahoe. But first the snows must melt. Sometimes when the thaw is late the people will hunger and, in extremity, chew rabbit-skin and deer-hide blankets. Transportation is on foot, consequently belongings are reduced to a minimum. Snowshoes facilitate passage through deep snows.

The mountain ascents negotiated, the people move to family-owned fishing grounds situated on the banks of streams flowing into Lake Tahoe. On their way to the mountains, the women will gather seeds, an activity which will claim much of their time during the months ahead. In the mountain forests they will also collect acorns, bringing them back to the valley at the end of the season for storage.

Locations occupied in the mountains vaguely relate geographically to valley residence patterns. Families own sections of the riverbanks, and this suggests another reason why settlements maintained during the winter break up with summer migrations. Ownership of such sites is vested in the male, inheritance being patrilineal. A permanent fishing platform marks each preserve.

Fish are caught by a variety of methods. Large trout are speared with harpoons and single- and double-pronged spears, which commonly reach a length of twenty feet. Fish are also caught in weirs, traps, and baskets. These methods would be resorted to either by those who had unfavorable fishing locations or by those who had no inherited sites. (Every informant spoke of fifty- to sixty-pound trout.)

All summer the people remain in the mountains. They are housed in simple brush shelters, sometimes on the underside of a large boulder. While the men fish, the women continue with their traditional work—gathering vegetal products, dressing skins, making baskets, preparing food.

Toward the end of August, the summer camps will disband for the eastward migration to Pine Nut Range. Here the pine nuts are gathered. As with fishing sites, pine-nut strips, running northwest to southeast, are individually owned.

Before the pine nut picking actually begins, camps from every part of the tribe will converge on a large flat near Mountain House. This is the only occasion of the year when what might be called a tribal gathering takes place. People camp in accordance with affiliation in the quasi-moiety organization mentioned before. Football, hockey, and other games are played and foot races run. There is much feasting and socializing. When the time is ready for pine nut picking, the assembly breaks up and families move on to their strips. A first pine-nut-picking ceremony, rich in ritual symbols, is always held.

Men and women cooperate in the picking. The men will knock off the burrs with a long pole, the women will gather them in large burden baskets. When night falls men and women gather around fires and dislodge the nuts from the combs. The nuts will be roasted and eaten, but by far the greater part of the crop will be packed and hauled back to the winter settlement, where the family will arrive toward the end of September to begin again the yearly round of activity.

A pregnant woman is hedged in with certain restrictions. She may not eat what young hunters kill, since that would bring bad luck. Therefore, no man under fifty would knowingly give a pregnant woman game or fish that he had killed. The only restriction placed on the husband during the period of his wife's pregnancy is the prohibition of sexual intercourse.

In winter the child is born in the winter-house. At other seasons a special dome-shaped shelter of pine boughs is built shortly before the woman's confinement. When the first labor pains are felt she retires to the hut to await delivery. Relatives and old folk from neighboring camps, especially women experienced in midwifery, gather to attend the delivery, passing the time inside the hut. Although men are not generally present, there is no taboo on their entering the hut. In difficult cases a man might even assist by lifting the woman to ease parturition. With the mother in a sitting position, encouraged by the oldsters surrounding her and aided by relatives, the delivery takes place. The child's umbilical cord is tied about three inches from the body to prevent bleeding and is then cut. To hasten delivery of the afterbirth, the woman will sometimes stand.

The baby is immediately washed. Meanwhile the close relatives mark the event by giving away a fine basket, placed on the ground and taken by the first comer. This is said to insure the child's future welfare. A poultice of meal prepared from a root is applied to the umbilicus and a buckskin band tied around the child's belly. In three to five days the band will be removed and the cord falls off.

After delivery, a bed of hot ashes is prepared and covered with blankets. On this the mother sits. Later she will lie down on it. From time to time the "hot-bed" will be renewed to prevent the blood from cooling and clotting. The mother remains here for an indeterminate period, ranging from a week—when the umbilical cord drops off—to a month. She may eat no meat, fat, or salt. She must use a scratching stick. Infusions of hot water and pine sugar will be taken to promote the easy flow of blood.

The afterbirth is buried by the maternal grandmother and the manner of its burial is thought to control future births. If buried "face down," the woman will not conceive. Only the mother and the maternal grandmother know where the afterbirth is buried and they may manipulate it in accordance with their desire for children. Should its whereabouts be discovered by someone else, serious embarrassment might arise.

During this period, the father's activities are also governed by certain regulations. Immediately after the birth of his child, he bathes. He dips a branch of sagebrush in the water and sprinkles himself with it. While he is bathing, the people of the community are privileged to take his clothes and money, and he may not object. If he has a four-point deer head in his possession, he is instructed to place it on the ground and crawl between the antlers without touching them at any point. To succeed in this assures good fortune for the child; to fail would bring bad luck to all. Food taboos must also be observed by the father until the sloughing off of the umbilical cord. As long as the mother is in seclusion, her husband is forbidden to do any running. Neither mother nor father may gamble. The taboo on sexual intercourse between the parents is effective for eleven months after childbirth.

At the expiration of the seclusion period, a ceremonial feast is held in the evening. Prior to this, the woman's hair is cut, and both she and the baby are given a ceremonial bath. This rite is again the occasion for giving away a fine basket, a buckskin, or some other prized objects. Relatives and nonrelatives from other camps are present and anyone may receive a gift. A generous feast will be provided followed by the customary gambling games. There is no dancing or singing.

After the newborn child is washed, usually by the maternal grandmother, it is wrapped in a rabbit-skin blanket and placed in a seed-beater basket which has been newly made. This is its first cradle. In three or four days it is transferred to a hooded cradle basket and the first basket thrown away. As the child grows, it is provided with a series of larger baskets, the previous one being always discarded. No child may lie in a basket which has been used before. Should the child die during the two years in which it sleeps in the cradle, the cradle is buried with it. Again as in the treatment of the afterbirth, the position of the basket will determine the mother's future fertility. If the basket is buried in an inverted position, the mother will not again become pregnant.

The baby is kept in a cradle for about two years. When it grows restive and at night, it will be taken out. Diapers of sagebrush bark softened by rubbing with the hands are placed between the legs. The bark is simply thrown away when soiled. Children are not expected to control themselves until they learn to speak, at about the age of two. Although the child begins to walk when about a year old, he continues to sleep in his cradle basket for another year. Nursing continues until the child is ready to leave the cradle. There are no supplementary foods. When the child cries day or night, it will be fed. The first food after weaning is nut soup. From weaning until about nine years of age, it is fed such tender portions of game as kidney, heart, liver, brains. But once past this age, these foods become taboo and may not be eaten until the age of forty or fifty. It is explained that if an active hunter eats these parts, his luck will spoil. There is no restriction on other meat either for child or adult.

When the child learns to talk he is given a name suggested by some amusing mispronunciation of a word, by a bright saying, or by some personal idiosyncrasy. His "real" name is never used in address; a nickname serves the purpose. No two persons ever have the same name. There are no inherited or family names. Children are taught to respect their elders, to avoid fighting among themselves, to play quietly, and to refrain from boasting, lying, or stealing. Whipping is seldom resorted to. Approved disciplinary technique is to "tell them to behave and talk kindly to them." When stronger measures are necessary, children are frightened into obedience by the threat of being carried off by a wild beast or of having their eyes pecked out by an owl. Respectful behavior toward people outside the family is required lest an offended person punish the child by witching. Myths related by the grandfather at night before the household retires not only provide an acquaintanceship with tribal lore but also instill a knowledge of native values.

As soon as a boy is old enough his father teaches him subsistence techniques. When he is six or seven, he will have his own bow and arrow, practicing marksmanship on targets and small game. From the age of ten he will begin to accompany hunting parties, equipped with his toy bow. His role is to observe rather than participate in the actual hunting. Not until his middle teens is he ready to use a man's weapons and become a hunter in his own right. At a somewhat earlier age he begins participating in fishing. Here the chief requirement is that he overcome fear of large fish.

A girl's participation in women's work begins when she is six or seven. In a short time she is helping her mother in gathering, food preparation, clothing manufacture, and caring for younger children. As soon as she can manipulate the splints, she begins weaving her little baskets, and even as a young girl she is likely to be quite proficient in the craft.

At the onset of the girl's first menses, she immediately informs her mother and begins a four-day fast. Should she delay a day in giving the information, she is punished by the addition of a day to her fast period. She is not kept in seclusion; rather she is required to keep active lest she become lazy. Use of a scratching stick is obligatory. Relatives provide her with an eight-foot staff of elderberry wood painted red which she carries about with her.

Two dances are held in connection with the occasion. On the fourth night after the beginning of the menses a preliminary dance is held. Before the ceremony begins, one or two relatives, usually women, run up a nearby hillside, kindling fires on their course. If the runners make fast progress, the girl will be alert and lively. If the line of fire is straight, the girl will have erect carriage. Occasionally the menstruating girl herself accompanies the runners but usually she is too weak from fasting.

The ritual itself finds the girl dancing with the aid of the tall red staff. A young woman who has already been through the ceremony supports the celebrant and a group of older women stands behind them and sings an accompaniment.

When the preliminary dance is over, a big dance is held in a nearby clearing. Within the circle of dancers moving clockwise, the girl herself dances. She holds the painted staff, occasionally handing it to a relative. From time to time members of the family will enter the circle and after brief and appropriate speeches present objects of value to the dancer. A man who is giving away valuables will sometimes act as clown, making funny and unexpected, but not obscene, remarks. Donation of gifts is said to protect the girl from sickness. The dance continues throughout the night, the girl keeping constantly active. At midnight a feast is held, the dancers taking turns so that the dance will proceed without interruption. It is a mark of pride to make the feast as lavish as possible with enough left for old folks to take home after the ceremony.

When the morning light appears, the girl is taken to the house, stripped, and doused with cold water. People leave the dance, gather round her, and distribute more valuables. The girl's hair is cut, her body coated with red paint and she is led away to the house to sleep. (The only mutilations, it should here be noted, are face-tattooing for women, and septum-piercing for shamans.) The red staff is hidden away in a thicket.

For one moon after the ceremony, the girl is restricted to a vegetable diet. She must use the scratching stick. Just before the conclusion of this fasting period, food is accumulated for a feast. On the day of the feast in the presence of relatives, the girl is washed ceremonially. She chews sagebrush leaves and rinses her mouth with water. Now she is ready to eat meat for the first time since the beginning of the fast. All then join in the feast but there is no dancing or gaming.

When the second menses occurs the puberty ceremony is repeated in its entirety. A new staff is used but all the features of the first rite are repeated. At the conclusion of this second ceremony, the girl enters the status of womanhood and is ready for marriage. Henceforth she is subject only to the ordinary menstrual regulations — taboo on meat, cold water, cold foods; use of the scratching stick; sleeping on a hot-bed.

The average age of girls at marriage is fourteen or fifteen. Boys do not usually marry until about seventeen. In the premarital period chastity is expected of girls but infractions are common. There are no penalties. A boy who wants to marry a girl might go into her house in the evening and lie down. If the girl's mother has no objections to him as a son-in-law, he is allowed to sleep with the girl. But should the mother object, she simply keeps the fire going until the boy becomes discouraged and leaves.

Marriage negotiations are most frequently undertaken by the parents with the consent of the son or daughter. The boy's father or the girl's mother might initiate negotiations by taking a gift of food to the parents of the prospective spouse. Acceptance of the gift and a return gift validate the marriage. The young man then usually goes to live with the girl's family. Gift exchange is not absolutely necessary but is customary. Reciprocal exchanges between the in-laws of the young couple may continue indefinitely if the parties involved in the exchange are on good terms with one another. Polygyny is practiced but is not common. Polyandry is never encountered. The selection of one's wife's sister as occasional supplementary sex partner has been mentioned.

Divorce is a simple matter of agreement and may occur for a variety of reasons. The offended party may simply ask the other to pack up his or her belongings and leave. Residence determines the custody of all except nursing children. If the couple is living at the camp of the husband's family, he keeps the children; if at the wife's family camp, she keeps them. Older children are allowed to exercise their own choice, sons usually going with the father, girls with the mother. Divorced women seldom remarry, although there is no rule against it. Men usually remarry unmarried girls. When either spouse dies, the survivor is expected to remarry within a year. The levirate is not compulsory but frequently follows. The sororate is generally observed. The chief determinant in both is the need to reestablish the nuclear family in order to care for growing children. Such marriages are not accompanied by negotiations or gift exchanges.

When a death occurs, relatives are summoned to wail over the body. Disposal of the corpse takes place no later than two days after death. Both cremation and burial are practiced, the former more commonly among the Southern Washo. In cases of cremation, property is burned on the pyre. The house in which death has occurred is always abandoned.

2. THE NATURE OF WASHO SHAMANISM

WASHO WORLD VIEW AND THE SHAMAN

The Washo view their world as pervaded with supernatural power. This power is a vague, vast force which finds embodiment in a multitude of spirits. The incarnate forms of such spirits are lodged in the realms of the natural and the supernatural — birds, animals, reptiles, water babies. Communion with these spirits comes in dreams. Rapport with one's power provides a key with which to exercise a possible measure of control over the fortunes and hazards of life. When properly wooed, it confers prosperity, good luck, health. When offended, ritually desecrated, or pitted against superior power, then misfortune, sickness, death result.

Power is not formally quested. Almost always it comes involuntarily. It is not inherited, although the predisposition toward shamanistic calling in certain families is apparent. The possession of supernatural power is not confined to a limited class of religious professionals, but is diffused through many individuals. There are some, however, who through assiduous cultivation of a spirit come to have an especial degree of power. These are the shamans. A shaman may be defined as a person who has more power than a layman, who has demonstrated his capacity to employ his power, and who is recognized as a religious practicioner.

The shaman's principal function is to cure the sick. There is remarkably little specialization among Washo shamans. Weather clairvoyance and general prognostication are not practiced. Hunting, be it of antelope, deer, or bear, does not call for special shamanistic ministry. Warfare finds the shaman a member of the war party, but as a surgeon, not as supernatural intermediary. To cure disease is practically the sole occupation of the shaman.

Full-fledged shamans are clearly recognized. Both men and women are shamans — theoretically in equal number. Ten individuals were designated as full-fledged shamans during my stay with the tribe: Dick Bagley, Mike Dick (commonly called "Old Blind Mike"), Sam Dick, Becky Jack, Ruth Calley, Henry (Moses) Rupert, Tom Walker, Bill Wilson, Emma Wilson and Harry Wilson.[1] In this enumeration there are only three women, which might indicate that whereas in theory the number of men and women shamans might be evenly balanced, in actuality men outnumbered the women. Diligent questioning failed to elicit any knowledge or recollection of berdaches.

SPIRITS

Spirits, source of power among the Washo, assume a wide variety of forms. Native theory, indeed, allows for limitless possibilities. Actually, however, they fit into certain well-defined categories. Thus by far the greater number of spirits are animate, and of these the most common are birds, animals, reptiles, and water babies. Inanimate objects are seldom encountered as spiritual powers, and natural phenomena, it would seem, just as seldom. The contradiction between the actual composition of the supernatural world and the theory which supposedly undergirds it is reflected in the evidence of George Snooks: "The dream might come in any form—skeleton, eagle, bear, or any animal or human form. It must have life. I never heard that it came any other way, like a tree or arrow."

Spirit is both ideologically and verbally synonymous with dream, the term used by Snooks. The reason for this terminological identity is seen in the circumstances under which spirit visitation takes place. The communion occurs in dreams. To the Washo the spirit and the dream are one. Interpreters used the terms interchangeably, although manifesting a preference for "dream." (Dream is used as synonymous with spirit and power hereafter.)

Lowie's observation that "the nature of the familiar remains obscure"[2] finds little support in my data. My informants experienced no difficulty in describing their spirit helpers. Often, indeed, such descriptions were vivid in the extreme. It might be noted that no familiars of the vague and obscure character depicted by Lowie's informants were ever mentioned specifically.

Another interesting dichotomy between conceptual theory and manifest expression is seen in the notion of comparative spiritual potency. More than one informant explained that degree of power inhered not in a particular spirit but in the spirit's human host. "Power," said Mike Dick, "depends upon how powerful the doctor will become in time." Yet despite theory, spirits were placed in a loose hierarchy of puissance. It was the same Mike Dick who at another time said, "The dream comes in different forms — eagle, bear, rattlesnake, water baby. These are most important."

Eagle is said to be the most powerful dream. It is the only spirit capable of restoring a lost soul. "Eagle brings back the spirit of a person who has died. He is the only one who will do it. . . . Eagle can go after a departing spirit and bring it back. That's why eagle is good. He helps people."

Water babies loom large in the constellation of Washo supernaturals. They are accounted very powerful, albeit benevolent. The Washo regard them with a peculiar mixture of affection and awe. When a shaman, or anyone who dreams, sees a water baby, he loses consciousness, such is the power of this spirit. "Once," related George Snooks, "my grandmother saw a water baby as she sat making a big winnowing basket, and she passed out. Blood ran from her nose. When she came to, she had crushed and broken to pieces the basket she had been making." Even shamans whose dream is water baby lose consciousness when they encounter this familiar.

Water babies are graphically envisaged. They are small, about two and a half feet tall, are either male or female. Their hair is long, reaching the ground "but somehow not touching it." Girl water babies are pretty, their complexion "reddish—the same color as Indian paint." Their hands are large and broad. They talk like any human—in Washo. They live in the water. They are heard in many places since they travel about a good deal. The mountains also seem to be a favorite habitat. People sometimes see their tracks, which are "like small human tracks." They are conceived as anthropomorphic. Dick Bagley said, "Doctors claim that water babies have everything—clothes, baskets, shell-beads—just like the Indians. They also have families, children." On one occasion George Snooks carefully examined the ground around a lagoon at Myers, California, for water baby tracks. With all his sophistication, he could not

conceal his belief in these supernaturals. This was characteristic of
practically every Washo. The spirit world is a reality, with water
babies an especially vivid part of it.

Cave Rock, a high promontory on the eastern shore of Lake
Tahoe towering majestically over the water, an important site in
Washo spirit lore, is a favorite abode of water babies. From a point
at the base of Cave Rock, a road in the form of a path of white sand
runs along the bottom of the lake, emerging at the northwest shore
of Tahoe. "It is their road." "In Cave Rock water babies have been
seen (by the doctors) attired in white man's clothes — ribbons, high-
heeled shoes, and everything," said Snooks.

Depending upon their willingness to help humans, water babies
are classified as either good or bad. "The good ones will help you
when you're sick. They'll be on your side. The bad ones won't help
you. But they won't injure you. The good ones are your friend."
Water babies are never malevolent.

Bagley once had an interesting experience with water babies.
The narrative, related by Snooks, will further illustrate the Washo
conception of these spirits. Moreover, the entire experience contains
elements which strikingly parallel power-contact phenomena in contiguous areas.

Dick Bagley was returning home one morning from Genoa,
where he had been doctoring. He had fallen into the fire at the end
of the session and his pants had been practically burned off,
although his flesh was unsinged. He improvised a skirt out of his
coat. On the way home, he intended to stop at Walleys Hot Springs
and take a swim in a tule patch, a "kind of slough." He sat down to
take his clothes off. Suddenly he lost consciousness. A water baby
came and took him down into the slough. They dove down together,
arriving shortly in another "country" where the water babies live.
Having emerged from the water, they started to walk along the path
to a water baby settlement. In the distance were houses made of
obsidian. The water baby, who was a girl, was leading him and
pointing out places of interest. "The farthest house over there," she
said, "is where the chief lives. The big house." They reached the
house for which they were bound but found that the owner ("maybe
Dick's dream") was gone. There were twenty girl water babies
there. One of them spoke up and said, "We know some songs.
We'll sing them to you." Dick sat in the middle of a circle formed
by the water babies and they sang to him. After singing, when they
thought he was about ready to go back, the water baby who had

brought him took him down to the spot from which they had emerged. She dismissed him with the words, "Go back the same way we came. You won't get lost now." He dove in and came up. "He didn't notice that he came up." He awoke and found himself under the overhanging tules. "Probably water baby had left his body there so that he shouldn't be discovered [i.e., found missing]. He was dead while his body was lying there, there was no life in it." He got up, put on his clothes, and went home.[3]

Lowie obviously has reference to water babies when he speaks of "a species of evil water-beings."[4] They are described in exactly the same terms as water babies; and the story recounted of the Washo who fished up a tuft of hair from a water baby while out fishing, causing the unwitting fisherman to lose consciousness, is almost identical with an account I recorded. However, it is questionable whether these supernaturals are as grim as Lowie suggests. Although imbued with great power, water babies are withal benevolently "friendly."

Two instances of an inanimate source of power were recorded. The two cases offer several interesting parallels: The source of power was a gun, the possessors were dreamers but not shamans, the instances involved events which transpired twenty and more years ago. One of the dreamers was Tom Walker's father, the other was a certain Jim Lew. Lew had a cracker box in which he used to keep his sacred outfit. Among the articles in the box was a .38 caliber revolver. This was his *dewgeleyu,* his power. Lowie cites the case of a Washo whose dream of bullets, power, and a gun miraculously rendered him invulnerable to them.[5] In this instance, too, the dreamer was not a shaman.

The assignment of spirits is predetermined according to Henry Rupert. "It was discussed in the spirit world beforehand which spirit would guide a certain person." The Washo term for the spirit world means "land of the dead," "dead people's home."

A shaman may have more than one spirit helper and his power increases in accordance with the number of familiars. However, his principal helper remains the first one dreamed. According to Susie Rube:

All shamans have more than one dream. They usually have four or five. This increases the doctor's power. But doctors have one main dream, which is the first one dreamed. Others come in as help. The more helpers, the more power. The longer the practice, the more helpers. In doctoring all dreams work together.

Sometimes more than one familiar would contend for the privilege of being a person's chief power. Thus, after dreaming of fish duck over a period of time, Emma Wilson dreamed about the sun, which "wanted to become her power." This she did not wish. There ensued a period of stress during which she prayed to the sun, evidently to make it cease its importunings. This finally happened but only after she had gone into the sun one day and become blind. After that her power was fish duck.

A shaman will never disclose the identity of his own spirit helper but he will freely reveal that of another shaman.[6] From Mike Dick I learned that Bill Wilson's dream was rattlesnake. George Snooks did not know who his father's dream helper was, although they lived together during the father's brief experience as shaman. No dire consequences are said to follow a shaman's disclosure of the nature of his own dream helper. "Nothing will happen if they tell," remarked Snooks. "They just won't tell."

If a person dreams of a normally dangerous animal, he will never be harmed by that animal. "I heard where they catch rattle-snakes and it won't bother them at all," Snooks said.

It is generally felt that the dream, the source of power, is not a passive but an active, dynamic agent possessed of typically human emotions. This is true not only of water babies but likewise of super-naturals drawn from the animal and natural realm. Thus the dream will demand "payment" if the shaman "doesn't do right," that is, if the shaman, hitherto benevolent, kills with sorcery or violates some ritual requirement. Susie Rube warned, "The dream will begin looking for a life—maybe the doctor's." Again it is the dream which deliberately puts a sickness into the neophyte dreamer.

It is also believed that it is not the shaman but the dream that is paid for shamanistic service. Moreover, the dream has preferences in this regard. "The dream is more satisfied with the payment of a basket than of money." Mike Dick refused to talk about his own spirit unless paid his regular fee, which the spirit shares with him. "It would be unfair to the spirit to tell without being paid," he explained.

Mike Dick's spirit understood four languages: English, Paiute, Washo, and the spirit's own language with which he spoke to his shaman host. "This [i.e., the last] is the only language he speaks. He doesn't speak much—only once in a while when everyone [present at the séance] hears."

A familiar may direct its possessor to undertake seemingly pointless, to say nothing of arduous, tasks. "Dream will tell you to do anything." Apparently such directions are invariably carried out. According to Charlie Rube, "Once the dream of Mike's Uncle Joe told him to row around the lake [Tahoe] in one day. He did this. It is seventy-two miles." With the guidance of the dream helper, doing the normally impossible is not beyond accomplishment.

THE ACQUISITION OF POWER

The acquiring of shamanistic power among the Washo is almost wholly involuntary. It is the spirit that determines who shall be visited. As Mike Dick put it, "It depends on the spirit. If the spirit wants to help, you become a shaman." "The dream has to come to him—even though he wants it bad," said Henry Rupert. Here again is manifest the doctrine basic to Washo shamanism, namely, that the spirit is an independent, unpredictable, even capricious agent, working its will in manifold and mysterious ways. Once visited, however, it is usually for the individual to decide whether he will undertake the disciplines that lead to full-fledged shamanistic practice.

Moreover, the spirit is exacting in the extreme. The whole phenomenon of spirit possession is something to be feared, and many will strenuously avoid it. Others will seek to limit its power, which can be done through the intercession of a veteran shaman. When the spirit has been favorably received, there follow grave responsibilities which must be met in the last detail lest sickness and death ensue. There is a tyrannical compulsion about the practice of shamanism which cannot be shaken. Thus Sam Dick: "I kept on doctoring. You can't get out of it. The only way to get out of it is just to die after four years. So I kept on." For these reasons children who dream are taken in hand by an older shaman, who will strive to discourage the spirit from further visitation. Mike Dick explained:

> A child as young as seven can dream. But it will not know what it is all about. A shaman will know that the child is dreaming even though the child shows it in no way. The shaman will not want the child to continue dreaming because a dreamer [i.e., prospective shaman] has to do everything exactly as he is told in the dream. There must be no slips. Sometimes he is told to do hard things like going out in the snow in the dead of winter. If the dreamer does not do as he is told, he will get sick and die every time. he will pass away quick

with it. So the doctor will talk to the spirit while washing the boy's face and will ask the spirit not to trouble the child. He can persuade the spirit to go away for good or he can persuade the spirit to stop for a while until the child grows up [i.e., hold the spirit in abeyance]. But the spirit can do as it wants.

If the spirit keeps on troubling the child [i.e., if the child continues to dream], relatives will hire a doctor for four nights to doctor him.

There is a close connection between acquiring power, and sickness. The latter almost always accompanies the former. The case just cited of a young boy who dreams is one instance. George Snooks said: "When you become a doctor, you always get sick." The dream, however, is not identical with the sickness. "The sickness is put in a person by the dream." According to Snooks:

> The dream, or spirit, which he dreams about puts something in him — whatever the spirit thinks is best. It goes to one spot in the child's body — like telephone wires going to central — a concentration in one spot. It is too strong for the child. He is not able-bodied, strong enough. He gets sick.

There follows a typical example of curing carried out by a shaman who seeks to expel the dream "concentration" in the same manner as a sickness object. Expulsion of the dream token may be temporary or permanent, and it is for the shaman to decide. If he feels that the dream will "help" the child some day, he will remove it only temporarily. In any event, the child recovers from the distress caused by the visiting spirit, and although he may henceforth dream occasionally, he will not be harried. Much later, at the age of thirty-five or forty, the dream will visit him in earnest, "will start to work on him." Now he is ready to assume the full and arduous responsibilities of the period of apprenticeship which prepares one for the office of shaman. "It is not before this age," said Mike Dick, "that a person knows what to do, even if he would follow it up."

A prospective shaman would dream often. The dream must find a ready and receptive host. Indeed, the power must be cultivated. In Mike Dick's picturesque words, "If you are friendly with it, it will return—like a dog." The dream gives instructions and it is of the utmost importance that these be carried out without the least deviation. Such instructions are not limited to the period of preparation but will be given for an indefinite time in the future, for as long a time as the shaman is under the guidance of a familiar.

What directions the dream will give are infinitely variable in theory. "The dream will tell you to do anything," said George Snooks again and again. However, the endless possibilities in theory become, according to recorded testimony, a recognizable set of rituals limited by a traditional pattern. (This is another interesting example of the manner in which the culture pattern regulates what is conceived as being beyond regulation — "anything." There are many instances of the operation of this cultural principle in Washo shamanism.) Thus the dream would instruct the visitant to rise early, bathe, and pray during the period of trial. It would further direct that no meat, salt, onions, fat, or greasy foods be eaten during this same period. There was also to be abstention from sexual intercourse. The dream world, moreover, teaches the songs and specifies the items of paraphernalia to be used in subsequent curing.

The nature of the call to shamanistic office, the age of the recipient, the character of the period of preparation and the other circumstances relevant to the assumption of a shaman's role among the Washo may, perhaps, best be described in the personal histories of several contemporary Washo shamans.

Emma Wilson is the wife of Bill Wilson, a powerful shaman living in Loyalton, California—Northern Washo territory. She too is a doctor, although not very powerful. She assists her husband in shamanizing.

Fifteen years ago she had the first encounter with her power. (She was sixty-seven at the time of the interview, which would have made her fifty-two at the time of the first visitation.) It happened one night when she was walking toward Chilcoot, California, with a party of friends. Near a body of water, she heard a fish duck calling. She imagined it to be "a spotted bird, beautifully colored," crying in a loud voice. All the members of the party fainted. Blood ran from her nose. She knew what was afoot, having heard many times what such episodes signified. She knew fish duck was her power. She did not see the fish duck; she just heard it.

This was at the beginning of the summer. All summer long she did not dream of fish duck. It is unusual for a period as long as a whole summer to elapse before dreaming begins. But in the fall she did. These dreams were caused by her power. She was directed to pray to it and to feed it fish. She had to go to the body of water where the vision had appeared (i.e., where the call was heard) and throw in fish.

Sometime later she dreamed about the sun. It wanted to become her power. This she did not want, for although "the sun is a good thing, it makes people thirsty and dries them up. You can't spit any more.'' Her mother told her to pray to the sun, according to the old Indian tradition.[7] However, Emma Wilson refused.

One day when she was in Johnsontown, California, she went out into the sun and became blind. From then on she dreamed no more about the sun. But she would get sick fairly often. She was treated by an old shaman, who told her that she was sick because she had not tried to please the sun. He instructed her to pray to it, to wash early in the morning, to carry out all the required rituals. She complied and has not since been bothered with sickness.

She was now ready to enter upon the period of preparation for shaman's office. She dreamed often. The dream would tell her to get up early in the morning, bathe, and pray. She ate no meat, salt, or fat. This was done for four successive mornings. She was also told to feed fish to fish duck. Fish duck taught her the songs which were later to be used in curing. Then she became a shaman.

Sam Dick, about forty-six years of age, received his first visitation at the age of eighteen. He had been a shaman for fourteen years. Thus he had entered upon his practitioner's career at the age of thirty-two, fourteen years having elapsed between the first dream and the time of active shamanship. He described his call to sacred office:

> When I start in, something come and whisper in my ear. I couldn't see anything. It got me started and I didn't know it. It talked to me and told me to do that, to do this, to help my friends. I do it and follow along.
>
> I took a bath in the river. I lay on the sand alongside the river. I saw I was dreaming, in my imagination. Water baby came to me out of the water and told me: "You sing this song." I sing the song. It was a funny song. Water baby was like some little baby, yellow looking with a small round face, long hair, and naked. I don't know whether it was a boy or a girl. I didn't see everything. It didn't show me. I didn't really see it with my eyes. It showed me that way, like imagination. I lay down this side of Dangberg Bridge, Home Ranch [Carson Valley]. Water baby then left me and went to Lake Tahoe, to the cave in Cave Rock, in the water like ice all the way up the rock.
>
> After a while I got sick with it. My uncle Monkey Pete[8] told me, "What do you monkey with these things for? You got to keep up, you can't get out of it unless you die." I had to keep on. I got sick — down every once in a while.
>
> Six years later I was up at the Lake — a quarter of a mile this side of Glenbrook — near the water. There were some flat rocks close to the lake, and I went that far. Then large hail fell and it held me back. Then I ran back to the old cabin there. I was all alone. I rubbed my eyes because sand was in them. I couldn't see. I was blind. My eyes swelled up. Water baby didn't want me to see where he lived. He put me out of the way.
>
> Joe Mack, my friend, brought me back to where my mother was. I still couldn't see. For three days it lasted. Then the swelling came down. I was all right again.

Afterwards Monkey Pete told me I should have gone down to the flat rocks, dived off into the water, and come up to the cave. Then I wouldn't have gone blind. I don't know why I didn't do what Monkey Pete said.

I never heard water baby again. I kept on doctoring. You can't get out of it. The only way to get out of it is just to die after four years. So I kept on.

I had six songs. I learn them from what I hear in the air. Water baby taught me just one song.

Bill Wilson is seventy years old. He began shamanizing just five years ago, although he had dreamed as a young man. He maintained that he did not know the exact nature of the dream, nor its significance, but Mike Dick revealed that Wilson's familiar was rattlesnake. In remaining vague about his dream, Wilson was merely conforming to the practice of not disclosing the identity of one's own power.

Mike Dick was an "ordinary man" until his father died. As a boy he had no power, but after his father died, power came to him. It told that it wanted him to be a good doctor, to cure people. That happened when he was fifty. For one year after he first dreamed, he worked all by himself—praying, washing, smoking. He ate no meat, salt, onions, fat, or greasy foods. Eating these foods would have interfered with his work, with his patients. Then after a year, people "from all over" began coming to him. His experience in not receiving aid from an older shaman while preparing for the office is not typical. Possibly he had been prepared by his father, who was also a shaman.

There is no fixed span of time for shamanistic preparation. Three to five years would be the usual period of "dreaming." However, "sometimes they dream for years and years and they'll never come through, because they don't do right." Violations of the rigid ritual regulations ordained by the dream are considered the chief cause of such failure.

The role of the full-fledged shaman in the task of bringing the neophyte to a complete assumption of power is of great importance. This has already been illustrated in the case of young boys for whom spirit visitation is deemed unwelcome because of the dangers involved. In practically all cases of shamanistic aspiration the practicing shaman acts as intermediary, either aborting, holding in abeyance, or bringing to full fruition the manifest potentialities of the aspirant.

A neophyte usually hires a shaman to expel the object put into him by the dream which he himself is not powerful enough to remove. Both the neophyte and the shaman will prepare for this for four nights beforehand. It is to be noted that the object has been placed there so that it can be removed. Until it has been expelled from his own body, the neophyte cannot remove anyone else's sickness-object, that is, he cannot cure successfully. He may try to remove it himself, and if he can, he becomes a shaman that much more quickly, since the ability to do so would indicate possesson of sufficient power to cure others. But if he cannot remove it, he hires a shaman for the purpose. No one witnesses this procedure. The whole process of preparation, of "fixing up," as it is invariably termed by the interpreters, is private, with the participants seeking quiet and solitude. According to the testimony of George Snooks, "When a doctor, either a beginner or a regular doctor, is fixing himself over, he will be alone. He will be alone in his house or he may go off to the woods."

The demonstration of control over sickness by a novice may also be a public affair. Such demonstrations, discussed more fully later, are held in the dance-house. The dance-house seems to have been more common among the Southern than among the Central and Northern Washo; hence, the novice's public inaugural was described only by Southern informants. Some Central Washo informants knew nothing of the dance-house, others had a vague recollection, none could give a clear picture. It seems proper to infer, then, that the dance-house and the novice's public inaugural, which invariably took place there, are characteristic only of the Southern division of the tribe.

Tom Snooks's account of his experience in shamanistic preparation is valuable for a number of reasons. First, he worked in close relationship with Mike Dick. Secondly, he never became a full-fledged shaman. Thirdly, during his period of training, he lived with his son, George, who had the opportunity of observing him closely and who, as one of my chief informants, gave a full account of what transpired.

After an initial spirit visitation, Tom Snooks continued to dream. He received instructions which he proceeded to carry out. He bathed every morning before sunrise. ("You must do just what the dream says. You might wash early in the morning or bathe your whole body. Which you did depended on the dream. The dream might tell you to give a feast of meat. It might tell you to do other things.") He abstained from hot foods as much as possible. (George

Snooks added: "But if he eats a mouthful once in a while, it won't hurt him." This suggests that the ritual restrictions and food taboos were not so stringent as one had been led to believe. The answer is probably to be found in the difference between the Washo understanding of strict adherence to ritual form and our own.) Meat and salt were not touched. He was sexually continent. Ritual regulations of this order were observed over a four-day period. These are "fixing-up" periods, which might come at any time. The power, it is thought, is wooed, refurbished, renewed during these sacrosanct intervals.

In time, Tom Snooks's dream gave him songs. These came to him at night at the rate of one a year. At his death he had four or five. The dream also told him to get a cocoon rattle (described below in the section, "Paraphernalia").

Tom Snooks was assisted by Mike Dick during this preliminary period of training. Dick came to live with him. "He got him to doctor his way." (George Snooks said at this point: "He got him in his clutches.") Tom Snooks did not know how to "fix himself up." "He wasn't quite sure." So, according to custom, he got a shaman who "knows," one who had more power, to help him. They would sing together, each rendering his own songs, to the usual rattling accompaniment. They would also smoke. But whereas Tom Snooks danced, Mike Dick did not.

Neophytes could engage in limited shamanistic practice, and Tom Snooks did so. In keeping with tradition, his curing efforts were confined to simple cases and his fees were accordingly less than those of a full-fledged shaman. "In the old days, 'new' doctors would charge as little as twenty-five cents a night. Regular doctors would charge five dollars." It seems that such practice was usually carried out under the direction of the guardian shaman. During this time Tom Snooks never doctored without Mike Dick.

The two men subsequently had a falling-out and henceforth avoided each other. Not long afterwards Tom Snooks died, never having attained the full status of shaman. Mike Dick's testimony in this connection is significant. Tom, he said, was ready to become a shaman but did not know how to go about it. He was "puzzled." He, Mike, "straightened him out." But Tom was killed because, insufficiently experienced, he removed diseases from patients and then could not remove them from himself. (Tom Snooks's family, on the other hand, believed that death had been caused by sorcery.

Becky Jack was held responsible.) Dick had counseled him against curing seriously so soon. Obviously the direst fate awaited neophytes who presumed to undertake major shamanistic cures. Henry Rupert went into great detail about the preparations for becoming a shaman.[9]

> A doctor starts to work when he is about forty-five, but he may be older—over sixty. Some take four years to prepare, some sixteen years. Anyway, it is a lifetime study. Fasting is the main thing. Meat, salt, and onions must not be eaten.
>
> Doctoring is not taught. If you seek advice, you can get it from an older doctor. It is naturally developed, like clairvoyant power.
>
> Some individuals who are being visited by a power don't want to be a doctor. Then a doctor is hired to get rid of the power working on the unwilling person. This is different from doctoring somebody. You work on the person differently. You pray and talk to the power asking it to leave the person. You also cover yourself with ashes early in the morning and bathe with cold water. This is not done in curing sickness.
>
> Some used to wander around the mountains in preparation for becoming a doctor. Here they would get inspiration, seek advice.
>
> Novices get advice from a spirit, a certain one. They get the spirit anywhere, right where they are, with their own will. It is discussed in the spirit-world beforehand which spirit will guide a certain person.
>
> Although doctors develop themselves naturally, older doctors boost along younger ones giving advice and direction. If a younger doctor is coming along well and the older one didn't like it, the older would kill, not the novice, but the power. He would be afraid that the younger would take away his trade or become greater, so he would get rid of his power. A novice can never prevent this on his own, although he might, perhaps, by calling in another doctor.

Ritual procedure during the novitiate is specified by the dream but adheres seemingly to a prescribed pattern.[10]

A cycle of thirty-two days, made up of eight four-day periods, seems to be basic. (The four-day period, indeed, the number four, is the pattern number for Washo shamanism, as it is for all phases of Washo culture.) It is a period of strict discipline and rigid ceremonial conformity. Four four-day periods of "doing nothing" alternate with four four-day periods of activity, each of the latter being assigned to a specific task or cluster of tasks connected with preparing a sacred object. Each item of paraphernalia is acquired over a thirty-two day cycle.

For example, the novice will dream that he must obtain a rattle. Here is the schedule of procedure:

(1) Four days of fasting—"no meat, strong drink, salt, fat, eggs"—preliminary to gathering necessary materials.

(2) Four days for gathering materials for the rattle.

(3) Four days interval of "doing nothing."

(4) Four days in which rattle is made. (These objects are not necessarily made by the neophyte. Any person may be given the commission by the dreamer. Such a person, man or woman, is paid one dollar per object. Sometimes a person would refuse out of fear, a legitimate enough reaction in view of the ominous potency inherent in the shaman's properties.)

(5) Four days of "dedication." During this period, the novice places the rattle in front of him, prays to it, saying, "You will not give me headache, you will not bring me trouble or sickness, you will help me."

(6) Four days of "placing it outside." The novice will not touch it during these four days. It is placed outside his house. When this period is passed, he may take it and keep it.

(7) Four days of "dedication." During this period, the novice again places the rattle in front of him and prays to it saying, "You will not give me headache, you will not bring me trouble or sickness, you will help me."

(8) Four days of "doing nothing."

Water is sprinkled on the materials as soon as they are assembled. This consecrates them for sacerdotal use and none but the possessor may touch the object once it is rendered holy. Members of the family know where it is but they will not take it.

There is an injunction against touching anything that is alive during the thirty-two days. There are also prohibitions against building a fire and eating forbidden foods.

PARAPHERNALIA

The shaman's paraphernalia vary in accordance with mandates received from one's dream. There is no correlation between the size and extent of the sacred outfit and the degree of power possessed. Becky Jack's was not nearly so impressive as Mike Dick's, yet at one time her power was said to have been greater. Mary Andrews, a powerful shaman at the time of early white contact, doctored without any paraphernalia at all. Nevertheless, potency does reside in the sacred articles and one does not treat them lightly. The shaman will guard them closely and attend to them diligently. (After Sam Dick discarded his paraphernalia, he described his feelings: "I make up my mind to get rid of it. It was just like my whole life going to be destroyed.") Although the objects are not graded with respect to relative sanctity, some are encountered more commonly than others. Always present in the shaman's kit are eagle feathers, rattle, pipe, headdress, and miniature baskets. A minkskin appears to be almost as indispensable an item. It has no special function—it is merely displayed conspicuously throughout the ceremony. Whistles, necklaces, paint, beaded bands, and other random accessories may or may not be found.

All shamans are equipped with eagle feathers. No item is of greater importance in the practitioner's paraphernalia. It is not necessary to dream of eagle in order to use them in curing. Feathers are taken from the tail of a young eagle. The number which the shaman may possess is not limited. According to George Snooks, "Some doctors have as many as five or six sets." Neither is the form in which they are bound and used restricted to any prescribed pattern. One informant described one such form as consisting of two feathers, each about one foot in length, bound together loosely at the quills with buckskin thongs. Beadwork sometimes decorates the junction of the quills. The feathers may be smeared with red paint and hung on a wall behind the patient during the entire curing séance—day and night. They are said to be in communication with the shaman and to possess such power as to enable him or her to track down the sickness. ("If it sees anything, it tells the doctor.") Sometimes the feathers will be clenched in the shaman's hand or hung around his neck. Sometimes they will be bound to a willow stick and stuck in the ground at the patient's head. This last may link with the prayer-stick complex widespread among the tribes of western North America.[11] Still another form is that used by both Mike Dick and Bill Wilson in performances I witnessed. Four feathers are tied to two small baskets (one, a miniature winnowing tray; the other, a shallow bowl basket) by a buckskin thong. The whole is brandished in the left hand, while with the right a rhythmic rattling is maintained.

Almost as indispensable in the curing séance is the shaman's rattle. Most shamans had one or more. The principal type found among the Washo is the cocoon rattle, whose occurrence extends widely through California. Cocoons taken for a rattle are of the moth variety found on willows or (rarely) on sagebrush and must "grow in a certain way." Those "growing head down" may not be used. The belief exists that the cocoon must be taken when first seen. If one returns to take a cocoon seen but a short while before, it will be gone. A rattle will consist of three or four cocoons filled with pebbles found in the gizzard of a grouse or sage hen and bound to a shaft about eight inches in length by deer sinew. Aboriginally the shaman's rattle was decorated with hummingbird feathers wrapped to the shaft with sinew and sticking out between the cocoons. A strip of weasel-skin was also wrapped around the shaft. Reminiscent of the aboriginal model are Mike Dick's rattles, each of which has a feather attached. Nowadays beads are substituted for pebbles.

The deer dewclaw rattle was formerly employed by Central Washo shamans. An indeterminate number of dewclaws—"a bunch the size of a man's fist"—were singly bound by thongs to the top of a willow stick about eight inches long. That this rattle was not used by the Southern Washo is plain from Long Pete's testimony that the cocoon rattle was the only form used by the tribe. "Only Paiutes had them [i.e., dewclaw rattles]." In view of the closer geographic as well as cultural proximity of the Southern Washo to the California tribes, as reflected in a considerable number of traits, one might have expected to find among them the dewclaw rattle, extensively encountered in California. Found again among the Southern Paiute and their congeners, its absence among the Southern Washo forms an interesting hiatus in its distribution.

Other forms of rattle are known to the Washo. George Snooks stated that the Paiutes living to the east have a rattle made of a horse's scrotum, dried, stretched and shaped, filled with pebbles from the gizzard of a grouse or sage hen.[12] The dream will ordain which type of rattle shall be employed by the shaman.

The tobacco smoked at every shamanistic session grows wild in the region. It is usually kept in a pouch fashioned from a whole mink-skin. Stripped down from the head of the carcass, the skin is cleaned, dried, and softened by rubbing between the hands. The finished pouch is about ten inches long and six inches wide. Tobacco is drawn through the mouth of the skin. This pouch is used only on sacred occasions, at other times folded in two and kept in the kit with the rest of paraphernalia. A mink-skin is favored for this purpose but the skins of other small animals can be used. Dick Bagley has a pouch made from the skin of a squirrel. George Snooks said: "It talks just like a live squirrel. Dick knows what it says. During his doctoring, it makes a whistling noise just like a squirrel." It is believed that the various items of paraphernalia communicate with the shaman during the curing séance.

A tubular stone pipe ("smoke rock") is used for smoking. The stone is found near Topaz, California, and a harder variety is used to hollow out the bowl. The stem is of either elderberry or rosewood. The pipe is six or seven inches in length, the bowl about four inches. It is held loosely in the palm of the hand and pointed diagonally upward so as not to spill.[13] Such pipes were formerly owned by anyone who smoked, although "a doctor smoked it more than ordinary people."

A variety of headdress is worn. Mike Dick's consists of a network of beaded buckskin bands worn as a cap, with a fringe of rectangular abalone beads hanging from the back. Bill Wilson's is a black fur cap studded in front with abalone, white feathers sticking out at each side. Among the Southern Washo, headdress consists simply of a number of eagle or hawk feathers stuck in a band of mink-, weasel-, otter-, or buckskin. Woodpecker feather headbands, similar in form to Miwok flicker-quill headbands, are reported for both the Southern and Central Washo.[14] Again the dream dictates the form. Whenever the shaman goes outside in the course of the séance, he removes his headgear.

Miniature baskets, especially made and employed on no other occasion, find several uses. Flour or seeds sprinkled in the directional offering will be contained in a tiny winnowing tray two and a half inches wide and three inches long. The shaman's fee will be deposited in a small bowl-shaped basket, coiled on a three-rod foundation.[15] Both Mike Dick and Bill Wilson have as part of their equipment two of these miniature baskets, one a winnowing tray and one a shallow bowl basket, tied to four eagle feathers, all of which they would hold in their left hand. Skilled basket makers are asked by the shaman to weave the baskets, for they must be finely made. The payment will be from three to five dollars. There is no compulsion to carry out the shaman's request.

Beaded bands, much in evidence in shamans' regalia, are probably of recent origin. "In the old days," said George Snooks, "we didn't have much beads of any sort." Hence, the beaded belt, arm, neck, and pipestem bands are in all likelihood late elaborations of the native feeling for ceremonial finery. Great care is obviously taken with the decorative designs. Mike Dick's belt alternates intricate bird and geometric figures. Tom Snooks had a belt that alternated blocks of black and sky-blue, a diamond-shaped abalone shell sewn on each blue square. Abalone shells are often suspended from the beaded bands. Designs carried no supernatural significance.

The whistle used for drawing out sickness is distinguished from an ordinary whistle. Made out of two wing bones of a wild goose, it is two and a half to three inches long, the two bones wrapped together at both ends with buckskin, and hung from the neck by a buckskin string. (Henry Rupert's whistle had no such string.) As the shaman circles the fire, he blows a series of sharp four-note whistles. The possibility exists that the sickness will "go" to the whistle. This object is used only at long sessions and never by day. Another kind of whistle formed an interesting item in Dick Bagley's paraphernalia. Shaped like a molar tooth (three inches by one inch) with a hole in it, it was said to be able to "whistle by itself." "That's how I found it," he reported. "I was walking along and it whistled at me." It could not, however, draw out sickness.

Necklaces of two kinds are worn. One of wildcat claws is undoubtedly aboriginal. Claws taken from the animal are rasped and rubbed down, and the resulting half-inch thin tubular beads are strung on a deerskin thong long enough to fit around the neck. The beaded neck band of contemporary shamans has already been mentioned. It fits snugly around the neck, its bottom edge decorated with suspended abalone shells, its one end shredded into a fringe.

Body painting is aboriginal shamanistic practice. On occasion the patient's body is also painted. The paint is sometimes given the patient to drink. It is prepared from "chalk" taken from deposits found above Markleeville, California, near the east fork of Carson River. Both red and white "chalk" deposits are located there—the only colors employed. White paint is also prepared from "chalk" taken from some springs near Pyramid Lake in Northern Paiute country.

One informant reported that all doctors wore a nose ornament consisting of a horizontal piece of bone stuck through the lower septum.

No drums are found in the tribe.[16] However, in the shaman's dance of the Southern Washo, the singer will beat a split stick on the palm of his hand.

Suitcases are today used as repositories for the shaman's sacred articles. Formerly a whole fawn-skin was fashioned into a bag for this purpose.

Certain invariable routines connected with the paraphernalia have a ceremonial flavor. Thus the sacred objects are always removed from their repository and replaced there in the same order at the beginning and end of each night during the séance. Each piece is carefully sprayed with water by the shaman. This is done at the time of initial removal and at intervals thereafter. After removing the ritual objects from the suitcase, Mike Dick hung them on a rope fastened along the ceiling, where they remained until needed. Some shamans keep their outfits outdoors when not in use so that they should not be contaminated by meat and fat odors. "Old-time doctors" are reported to have carried their kits with them wherever they went since they were afraid to leave them unguarded lest they be stolen. The serious consequences of losing one's outfit are seen in the story of Jim Lew recounted by Dick Bagley.

> Jim used to carry his outfit with him all the time. One day he went fishing and lost the cracker box in which he kept the outfit. He became terribly frightened. He couldn't speak. After that he didn't last very long. He died.

The sacred accessories require care at all times. Periodically every object is "given a drink"—sprayed by the shaman with water in his mouth. Occasionally they are "given a bath"—liberally sprinkled either by mouth or by hand. George Snooks once saw his father give his eagle feathers a thorough washing. When a shaman dies, his paraphernalia is buried with him. When this happens his power is gone.

DANCE-HOUSE CEREMONIES

Among the southern Washo, the dance-house becomes the locus for important shamanistic ceremonies. The dance-house, according to present data, occurs in only one other Great Basin tribe, the Southern Paiute. Since it is found prominently among east-central California groups, cultural connection is indicated.[17] The dance-house figures prominently in Southern Washo religious life, less so, apparently, as one proceeds north in the tribe.

The structural form is the generalized type found in the region. (Said Long Pete, "It's the same as the Miwoks make only smaller.")[18] A circular shallow excavation about three feet deep and thirty feet in diameter is scooped out. Two pairs of poles are set in the ground six feet apart, each pair lashed together near the top, the distal ends forming a thirty-five to forty degree angle. Upon the small forks at the junction of each pair, a ridgepole is laid. Braced by auxiliary poles, a framework is formed upon which are laid other poles, willows, tules, grass, and earth. At the top a three- to four-foot opening is left as a smoke hole. The fireplace is a shallow pit within the excavation. The entrance always faces "the downhill side," that is, east. The completed house is about ten feet in height, its shape subconical. It is employed solely for ceremonies associated with shamanism: rites attending the induction of novices into shamanistic office and exhibitions of power by veteran practitioners.

The induction of novices involves the same procedure described previously except that they take place in the dance-house in the presence of any and all interested witnesses. The ceremony is called "making a doctor," based on the idea that before one can cure— that is, remove sickness-objects from others—one must have sickness-objects, planted by the dream and token of spirit posses-sion, removed from one's own person. And if not powerful enough to do so on one's own part, a shaman must be called in to help.

A candidate would order the dance-house built in accordance with a command received in a dream. The ensuing ceremony lasts the customary four nights, but during this period the novice does not remain inactive. He becomes a participant in the proceedings, singing his own songs, smoking, praying, and dancing—carrying out, in a word, the pattern prescribed in preliminary dreams. The full-fledged shaman busies himself with the novice's sacred para-phernalia, "making it right," perfecting its ritual efficacy. Finally he removes the sickness-object. Now the aspirant has sufficient skill and power to remove sickness-objects himself, and although they have received no tangible evidence of his prowess, the people know that he can cure. "It is like getting a doctor's degree," said Long Pete, "with the old doctor telling him what he doesn't know." When the rites are ended, people will betoken the "graduation" of the new shaman by saying that he can "spit out objects through his mouth," referring to the manner in which the shaman removes pathogenic objects, invariably drawn into his own body before be-ing expelled. On the morning following the conclusion of the ceremonies, a feast for all present is provided by the novice.

Another ceremony held in the dance-house relating to shaman-istic preparation is a "doctor dance" lasting four nights in the course of which novices are given instruction. Such dances, con-fined apparently to the Southern Washo, are in no wise initiations. They constitute a stage in the training of the shaman which precedes actual installation into sacred office. A full-fledged shaman will hold such a dance at the behest of a dream. He takes charge of the proceedings, sometimes alone, sometimes jointly with a colleague. Anyone who wishes may witness the ceremonies. Dancing is the main activity but only those specifically invited by the supervising shaman may participate. These are usually the pre-initiates and the shaman (or shamans), although nondreamers may on occasion take part. The dance itself, a description of which could not be obtained, was said to be different from any other Washo dance, a fact interesting enough in view of the paucity of dance forms among the tribe. George Snooks said, "It's something like 'paving the way.' " And according to Long Pete, "It is pretty near the same kind of dancing the Miwok do. But it is the Washo's own dance. They didn't take it from the Miwoks. It wasn't like any other dance the Washo did." The comparison with the Miwok is significant because of the geographic proximity of the two and, further, because of the existence of the ceremonial dance-house among them.

The actions of the supervising shaman are worth remarking, since they assume the pattern of a public demonstration. He oversees everything, even the audience. If a sickness-object should be lodged in a member of the audience, the shaman will remove it right there and then without charge. If someone among the dancers should be overcome with the spirit, he will revive him by washing his face and talking to him. The entire ceremony is reminiscent of the public exhibitions carried on by shamans among Plateau and California tribes. Park has noted the absence of such demonstrations in Basin shamanism, a conclusion which, in the light of Southern Washo practice, must now bear revision.[19] (See "Feats of Prowess" below.)

THE NATURE OF DISEASE

Disease is considered to come mainly from supernatural causes, and it is the shaman's task to deal with such sickness. However, some disorders of a minor character are diagnosed as springing from natural causes, and these may or may not be referred to the shaman. The women of the tribe are familiar with native herbal remedies—"A woman won't pass a medicine plant without picking it"—and if a person falls sick of a minor ailment, the services of some female relative will be sought. It is when the herbalist fails that you go to a shaman. One informant maintained, however, that one went to a "herb doctor" when one lacked sufficient money to engage a shaman. Sometimes a shaman will administer herbal remedies either upon request or in the course of a curing session.[20] In the former instance, a greater efficacy will accrue than if given by a layman because of the accompanying words uttered by the shaman. Quite outside the shaman's province also are women's ailments like "blood-sickness" — difficulty with the menses. Such cases are handled by certain old women of established reputation as herbalists — the women who also serve as midwives. A sickness which is serious, however, derives from supernatural sources and it can be successfully dealt with only through the special skills of the shaman.

The Washo, in consonance with a widely held primitive belief, conceive of disease as materialized in an object lodged in the body which can be expelled only through a shaman's ministrations. These disease objects assume a wide variety of forms — arrowheads, stones, lizards, tobacco, hair. "Sickness comes in any form," one informant succinctly stated. The causes for disease-object intrusion are various. Most common are sorcery, violation of ritual specifications in activities governed by religious precept such as shamanism and hunting, dreams, ghosts, contact with the dead, "medicines," and soul loss.

Sorcery is a major source of disease. It is the shamans who practice sorcery, and all shamans are either sorcerers or potential sorcerers. There is no native terminological distinction between shaman and sorcerer. The designations "good" and "bad" are applied to shamans to indicate whether or not they witch, but the decisive factor is obviously the designator. If you are on friendly terms with a shaman, he is "good"; if you suspect a shaman of having witched a member of your family, he is "bad." A Washo, however, will make the distinction between the two. "A bad doctor cannot cure," he says. Nevertheless, George Snooks admitted that people went to Becky Jack to be cured in spite of her being a "bad doctor." "They are mostly her close relatives," he added deprecatingly, "and she doesn't really cure. They get well for a time but they always come back." Conversely, Mike Dick, whom Snooks deems a "good doctor," is held by some to be a "bad doctor," according to Snooks's own incredulous testimony. Still, some shamans are widely reputed to be dangerously malevolent, and these are feared and avoided.

A "good doctor" can turn "bad." When a shaman kills, he turns "bad." If he neglects to follow the ritual regulations laid down by his power, he is also likely to become maleficent.

There are many witching techniques. Usually a shaman will first go through the four-day period of ritual preparation, requirement for all shamanistic activity, whereby his power is refurbished and replenished. The usual abstinence from salt, meat, hot foods, and sexual intercourse is observed. The intended victim is the target of concentrated thought. Sometimes in cases where a particularly potent spell is desired or deemed necessary the four-day period is doubled. Again, witching may be accomplished without any preliminaries.

George Snooks said, "A doctor who doesn't like you can shoot his power at you when you are passing by. He doesn't have to fix up. Maybe he never saw you before. He just doesn't like you. As he shoots his power into you, he flicks his fingers and [with sibilant] blowing] says: *hussa.* He might add: 'Get lame in your leg,' or 'Get a headache,' or anything. Some object will enter you and you'll become sick."

Although it is not imperative to witch a victim immediately after undergoing the preliminary ritual preparation, it is usually executed as soon as possible. If the intended recipient is away, the spell will wait. But the first time he is seen, "they let him have it."

Certain renowned sorcerers could cast their destructive spell over long distances, "shooting" their power for scores of miles. Desolation would be left in its wake. Susie Rube reported:

> A long time ago before the white man came, a bad doctor [a Southern Washo] living in Monitor, went to Walley's Hot Springs [Central Washo territory] to visit. His name was Detutudi. He wasn't liked by the people in Hot Springs. (He lived in another part of the country. The same reason as people didn't like those Germans in war time.) He left to return to Monitor, but before leaving, warned the woman who had fed him what was going to happen. He told her that she and her daughter would be spared but that after it happened they should move away. Back in Monitor, he fixed up. Within a week, he shot his power to Hot Springs, a distance of thirty miles, and all the way from Monitor to Hot Springs, all vegetation—trees, weeds, grass—withered in the path where his power traveled. In Hot Springs when evening came it killed everybody except the woman and her daughter.

Spittle flicked in the direction of an adversary is a potent method of witching. Since one's power bears the spittle on its ominous course, this technique can be performed at a considerable distance. The force of the arriving spittle is such that the victim is often knocked down, sometimes rendered unconscious. George Snooks said:

> Sometimes blood will flow from your nose. Then you will come to, get up, and go on your way. If you don't get a doctor to take it out in good time, you are doomed. Sometimes the place where this sickness enters your body is marked by a black and blue spot, just like a black eye.

Dried mucus, or conceivably other bodily excretions, may be used instead of spittle.

A sorcerer may witch a person by giving him food into which he has previously spat. Money or any object into which malevolent power has been projected will, when presented to an individual, cause sickness. By spitting on a person's footprint as he passes by, or by touching his body or one's own in a desired part, a sorcerer can bring on illness.

Pismires are an extremely potent agency of witching. It is the only medium which will have any effect on a white man. When ground up and flicked by a shaman, they will knock a white man unconscious. Of course, an Indian will be killed "without any trouble."

The reasons that motivate witching are those normally encountered in sorcery-ridden cultures. Hatred, jealousy, and greed often provide the impulse to witch. Someone whom he dislikes or who is prosperous is selected by the sorcerer as a victim. The procedure which is then followed represents a circuitous kind of malevolence. It is not the original object of ill-feeling who is dealt with but those who surround him, usually his children. "They kill them off one at a time until just the father and mother are left. They usually leave the father and mother."

Jealousy would incite a shaman to witch a temporal or professional rival. It was said that because Becky Jack coveted Captain Jim's position as leader she killed him. "She wanted to be captain herself." Tom Snooks, who gave promise of becoming a successful and popular shaman, was believed killed by her for similar motives. Sorcery will sometimes be practiced at shamans' contests. In such cases, the victim will either be bereft of power or sicken and die.

When a sorcerer witches for money he will not kill; he will cause his victim to sicken—and he will keep him sick as long as possible. He brings illness to a person for the express purpose of being called in to cure. In such cases, he doctors for a long time. He will tell the patient, "My dream told me to do this, and you must do that. The dream said you must give me so much money and I'll take it [the sickness] out of you." This procedure was characterized as a "skin-game." It was said that some shamans, knowing you have money, will "bleed you to death."

The *lex talionis* which governs the realm of supernatural power provides an important impulse for the practice of witchcraft. A sorcerer's dream will exact payment in kind. Thus if an evil shaman has killed someone, the latter's dream will demand compensation in the form of another life, preferably that of the evil shaman's child. If there is no child, the shaman's own life is demanded. The shaman, however, will attempt to satisfy the mortal claims of the dream by rendering substitute payment in the form of someone else's life, which he proceeds to take. In the interval between the two deaths, during which the dream is clamoring for retributive payment, the evil shaman will fall ill. People recognize this as a signal of impending death for someone in the tribe. When such a death does occur, the shaman recovers. We see here how a "good doctor" can turn "bad," how once a shaman kills through witchcraft his malignity begets further malignity.

Sorcery causes serious illness, which can be cured only through the agency of a powerful shaman. Not every shaman possesses sufficient power to cope with witchcraft. One informant remarked that "witching is cured only once in a while." The procedure is the familiar one of extracting a pathogenic object. Once the object is removed, the curing shaman may follow one of two courses. He may dispose of it in the usual way, mixing it with dirt and throwing it away, in which case matters remain *in statu quo*. He may, however, have been hired to retaliate, to witch the witching shaman. He will then, having determined the identity of the sorcerer, burn the disease object. Such action is bound to have its effect. The sorcerer will fall sick and, if not powerful enough, die. He may forestall his doom by undergoing the process of ritual preparation, in which case he expects to recover after a brief siege. But if his professional adversary is indisputably more powerful, nothing will avail. He will die, "and there won't be any two ways about it." There is always the possibility, of course, that a shaman will refuse to burn a pathogenic object—to engage in reprisals—for fear of becoming himself a "bad" doctor.

A curious feature of Washo shamanism is the hiring of sorcerers from neighboring tribes for witching purposes. There is no reason to believe that this is not aboriginal practice. The belief exists that "Paiute" methods are more effective than Washo. Alien sorcerers are more likely to succeed "not because they're more powerful but because they treat differently." Not infrequently accounts of shamanistic practice will mention such doctors, especially Paiute practitioners. Similarly, Washo shamans are sometimes engaged by non-Washo neighbors. For example, Mike Dick was in much demand by the Southern Paiute.

Sorcerers are much feared. Those of established notoriety are given a wide berth. Care will be taken to avoid all contact, for one can never tell when the evil power, working clandestinely, will strike. It is best to take no chances. Merely to talk about witching is to flirt with danger and most Washo will refuse to be drawn into any discussion of the subject. None will speak without reluctance and then only in lowered voice accompanied with many furtive glances. Names will seldom be articulated. The feeling of apprehension and anxiety with regard to sorcery may be said to permeate the culture. Even those individuals who have achieved varying degrees of sophistication feel the compulsions of sorcery anxiety. This was true of both my chief interpreters, George Snooks and Will Christensen, the latter a premedical senior at the University of Oklahoma. Snooks would never pass near the camp where Becky Jack lived. He carefully avoided encounters with members of her family. When telling of witches and witching he spoke in brief, muttered phrases. He would never mention names, but when pressed would reluctantly write them down. Details of this kind could be multiplied.

Means for coping with sorcerers are available within the cultural fabric. There are two methods of curtailing shamanistic malevolence. The first, described above, is through the agency of another shaman. The second is through homicide. A close relative of a witched person will kill the sorcerer. Fear of the latter or of his relatives, however, limits the incidence of physical reprisals. But when it does occur it receives social sanction.[21]

The following accounts are typical of witching practice and its consequences.

About thirty years ago (circa 1910) a young woman living about a mile above Gardnerville on the east fork of Carson River, was bewitched by a powerful woman shaman whose name was Wedukleklek. She was believed to have killed a great many people.

As the victim lay dying, her husband, Jack James, went over to the sorcerer's camp—about a mile and a half away—for the express purpose of killing her. Another shaman, Jack Arnot, had told him who had caused his wife's sickness. A younger brother tried desperately to dissuade him from going, "crying and hanging on," but eventually he went along after James "gave him a little hell." Twice James circled the tent in which the sorcerer, her husband and daughter were eating supper, ascertaining their positions inside. He then shot through the tent with a .38 automatic, killing the woman and wounding her husband in the knee. He had intended to kill the husband also.

That night James and his brother walked to Carson City, a distance of fifteen miles, and the following morning he was arrested. The next day his wife died. "People said he saved the lives of many people by killing this woman." They obviously approved of his action. According to Charlie Rube, several years later his throat was cut from ear to ear by the woman's son bent on avenging his mother's death.

Indicative of the feuds engendered by witching, as well as of the belief mentioned before, namely, that not the primary object of malevolence but his children are killed, is the story told of Joe Ryder's grandfather, Degumbuyinga. When an old man he was accused of witching and killing children. The accusation was made by the father of a child who had recently died, John Lancaster (Ben Lancaster's uncle). One evening when the old shaman was sitting in his camp, the aggrieved father stole up behind him with a sledgehammer and crushed his skull. When John Lancaster eventually died he was "crazy." He had been "crazy" for several years before his death. Hounded by the fear of being killed, he had secluded himself. When anyone appeared he would sneak away. People said that Joe Ryder, the murdered man's grandson and himself a shaman, had done this in reprisal. "He made him insane and killed him" was George Snooks's statement.

The brutal pitch that reprisals reached is revealed in the following incident. Almost fifty years ago (circa 1890) a Northern Washo from Truckee, California, named Tsigasha, accused a shaman living near Sheridan of witching and killing a relative. The shaman was a woman, known for her malevolence. One day he came to the settlement where she was living. He tethered his horse out of sight and approached the camp. He pulled out a gun and shot two people, one the witch. He made no attempt to get away. The shaman's sister and her husband fell upon the murderer, and while the man held him, the woman split his head open with an axe. As Charlie Rube described it, "She hacked him all up, mixing him with dirt and cutting him all up."

White men, as we have seen, are not seriously affected by sorcery. The recognition of this fact will not, however, prevent a shaman from trying to witch a hated white.

When they were cutting timber for the Virginia City mines in the 1880s, some Washo women were annoyed by a Frenchman who lived in Markleeville, California. He would come into the camp looking for a woman who happened to be the wife of a shaman named Detugibil. The intruder would stand displaying his penis in full view of the women and of the shaman himself. ("White people used to do this. They didn't care what they did to Indian women in those days.") One day the shaman took some dried mucus from his nostril and "shot" it at the Frenchman's penis. The white man felt something hit him and grasped his organ. But this was all the effect it had. It did not hurt him. A moment later he left.

About twenty-five years ago (circa 1935) Joe Ryder, "who was a pretty good doctor then"—presumably before he turned "bad" through employment of witchcraft—wanted to witch a white woman who lived in Woodfords, California. His resentment had been aroused by her practice of taking the paychecks that the men got for highway construction work (her son was the superintendent) and applying them to the bills run up in the general store she operated. For eight days Ryder ritually fortified himself, anxious to render himself especially powerful. When ready, he walked down to the store and waited. When the woman appeared, he put his index finger in his ear. "He was shooting her there." She felt it, quickly lifted her hand to her ear, looked up at the sun, sneezed three or four times, and walked away. George Snooks remarked, "It made him [Ryder] laugh. Then he knew it couldn't be done to white blood."

Violation of ritualistic procedure in activities considered either religious or as possessing implicit sacrosanct features may result in sickness.

We have already noted how the whole process of power acquisition, permeated with ritualism, was loaded with apprehension for the aspirant lest he fail to fulfill the meticulous ceremonial requirements. He had to "do right," execute the demands of the dream no matter how capricious or severe, else sickness and death might result. Even individuals who are well advanced in shamanistic preparation are not immune from the sickness which comes with incorrect practice. When Tom Snooks began handling cases for which his insufficient training had not qualified him, he fell ill and died. That is how Mike Dick explained his death.

Hunting carries certain religious overtones and is surrounded with ritual ordinance. (My data indicate that this would be true only of large animals—deer, bear and, of course, antelope. Small game might be taken by anyone without ritual formalities.) If the ceremonial proprieties are ignored, sickness will follow. One of George Snooks's serious illnesses was diagnosed by Joe Ryder, who attended him, as having been caused by Snooks's neglect of the regulations governing the killing and butchering of deer. Said Snooks: "I used to kill deer any way." The disease-object that Ryder extracted was the eyeball of a deer. At a curing session that I witnessed, the patient's lameness was likewise attributed to breach of deer-hunting formulas. Consequently, deer had entered his body and made him sick.

Related to the demand for strict observance of ritual in important tribal activities is the necessity for respecting the paraphernalia associated with them. Fishing tackle, basketry materials, hunting equipment must not be roughly handled, whether wittingly, as in a fit of temper, or not. Sickness is the penalty for failure to exercise due restraint.

The following account by George Snooks illustrates this concept.

> Tom [Snooks] was sick. He had pains all over his body. The doctors he went to around here couldn't do anything for him. So he went to Jack Wilson, a Northern Paiute, who doctored around Yerington in Mason Valley.[22] He was a powerful doctor and a very good friend of Tom's. Jack doctored him only a short while one night and removed a fishing tackle with copper wire, swivels, rings, spoon, leader, and hook. He removed it with his cupped hands without sucking. (Shortly before he started doctoring, he placed in the ground in front of him an eagle feather about a foot long. As soon as he put it in, it sank down about half way [a token of prodigious power].)
>
> After he took out the tackle he told Tom he became sick with it because a couple of years or so before in a fit of anger he had handled the tackle roughly, tearing up the wire and everything and throwing it away. Tom then remembered he had done this. Jack told him exactly what he had done.

It will be noted that when sickness follows "rough handling," the pathogenic object removed is directly connected with the cause of the disease. Fishing tackle caused Tom Snooks's illness in the foregoing narrative; it was the disease object removed by Wilson. Sickness occasioned by irreverent treatment of basketry materials will find the attending shaman extracting willow or fern root.

Contact with the dead is fraught with the danger of sickness. Such contact may take a number of forms. Dreaming of ghosts, usually of dead relatives, is a common form.

The ghost is visualized in various ways—sometimes as the actual individual, often as a skeleton, at times as a "devil," "light noise," "bluish-purple flame," and "light." If the ghost assumes the form of a dead person, the dreamer will rise early the following morning and go through the ritual of washing the face and praying. "You tell them [i.e., the ghosts] to leave you alone and not to let you dream of them anymore." This might forestall the sickness. When the ghost is not seen as a dead person, its lineaments are described by the shaman called in when the individual becomes ill, and when defined, will engender terror in the patient. "It makes shivers run up your back and your hair stand on end." The ghost will make demands, and these must be fulfilled under penalty of sickness.

What the demands are is clarified by the shaman. The visitant may be told to deposit some object on the grave of the deceased. Or he may be instructed to bury some prized article in a riverbed. "The sickness might ask that something be offered to a dead relative—dress goods, basket, tobacco—to be buried on top of the grave." The cause of such ominous dreams may derive from having once offended the deceased. It sometimes happens that the ghost of an offended person will haunt not the offender but his close relative, and it is the latter who will get sick. Demands made during these dreams must be discharged by the visitant. (Coins are now placed over the eyes of the dead when ready for burial. This is a gesture of conciliation, a payment which will keep them from visiting the living. It will also prevent the dead from seeing their relatives and thus making them sick.)

Although a common cause of sickness, visitations by ghosts[23] do not result in such serious illness as does the practice of sorcery. Only a shaman of considerable power could hope to stem the swift doom dispatched by a witch. But the malaise that comes through ghosts could be relieved by any shaman. Neither does he have to utilize all the resources of shamanistic craft—imperative in dealing with sorcery. Indeed, it is not always necessary to remove a pathogenic object. As Mike Dick put it, "In this devil business, the doctor can tell you what to do and make you well without taking out any object."

The shaman has ready access to ghosts because he is "friends" with them. In his dreams he visits their abode, the "dead people's home." Consequently he is immune from their morbid influence.

There are other forms of contact with the dead which cause disease. Walking in an abandoned camp where someone had died will make a person sick. "Something will enter you, and when you return to your camp, you will fall sick." A shaman must be summoned at once. Stepping on the bone of a dead animal will also have consequences whose seriousness only a shaman can mitigate.

"Medicines" that bring good luck in such pursuits as hunting, gambling, and love may produce sickness. These agents of good luck are obtained largely from the neighboring Miwok, and are much prized by the possessor.[24] They are charged with power and will induce dreams of potent significance. After such dreams, say of hunting, it is necessary to rise before sunrise and wash ritually. Possession of a "medicine" confers a certain amount of power, for we find owners periodically undergoing the four-day rites of supernatural replenishment, always the token of rapport with the spirit world. It is here that dangerous contingencies arise. Should one "do wrong," transgress ritual mandates, sickness will come. The "medicine" is conceived as "turning into sickness"; it becomes the pathogenic object and is extracted by the ministering shaman.

Soul loss may result in death. It is believed that before a person dies the soul leaves his body for either the south or the east. Good spirits go south; bad spirits start south but soon turn east. The soul is the vital principle, a concept revealed by the native term *kesheh*, which also means "life." "A person's spirit leaves him before he passes out. He is still breathing but he is really dead." It is possible, however, to recapture the soul, to bring it back to its former physical vesture. The shaman, who knows when the soul has taken flight, will dispatch his power and commission it to fetch back the departed "life." Eagle, it was said, was the only power capable of succeeding in this difficult mission.

When shamans go into a trance, their souls are thought to leave them, and for the duration of the trance they are counted dead. When Dick Bagley had the encounter with water babies and visited their submarine abode, his body, which remained on the bank, was dead.

It is perilous to touch a shaman when he lapses into unconsciousness after removing a sickness-object. To touch him is to court death. So binding is this injunction that one informant said, "Even if he falls into the fire, you don't dare touch him."

THE CURING CEREMONY

The curing ceremony is not a fixed and undeviating set of rituals. Two factors are all-important determinants — the shaman's dream and the seriousness of the sickness. A shaman will cure according to instructions received from his power; no two shamans will perform in exactly the same way. The seriousness of the ailment will dictate the length, hence the nature of the ceremony. The graver the sickness the longer the séance. Some cures take only a few minutes and obviously involve a limited ritualism; others take the maximum four nights during which the full stock of techniques is exploited.

Brief treatments are given for various conditions. Emergency mishaps like wounds and snakebite require immediate but unprolonged curing. Walking in the abandoned camp of a dead person or stepping on some source of sickness call for similar attention. Abbreviated treatments always involve blowing smoke on the patient's body — a constant element in all curing — and usually washing the face with cold water. As one shaman said, "Smoke and cold water are the most important things in this doctor business." The essentially impromptu nature of such curing is revealed in the lack of specific ceremonial ordinance. Treatment may be administered anywhere — inside the house, outside, or "by the trail"; the patient may face in any direction; the rattle is not used. Another interesting context in which the brief attentions of the shaman are sought is thus reported by one informant: "If you meet a doctor on the road and you get a notion you want him to doctor you, he can do it right there. He pulls out his tobacco and doctors."

The characteristic Washo curing ceremony, however, is the four-night session. In it are found certain features which, if not constant, are nevertheless prominent and common. Typically the séance combines primarily religious and incidentally social elements, in which the visitors play an inconsequential role. It is held at night in the home of the sick person. The shaman sings, dances, smokes, prays, washes the patient, makes an offering to the disease, and sucks out a pathogenic object. Granted the variables of capricious dream revelation, these are the important items in curing ceremonialism.

The general atmosphere of the séance is one that mingles religious ecstasy with suppressed apprehension and easy informality. One moment the shaman will be singing, dancing, and rattling in tense and rapt concentration; the next he will be conversing with patient, family, and visitors. There are no formalistic barriers between practitioner and laymen. The sociability of the event, with the midnight repast on the fourth night, in a setting of sickness and anxiety provides another discordant contrast to the witness from another culture.

Although the shaman is customarily brought to the house of the patient, it sometimes happens that the patient is taken to the shaman — provided the distance is not too great and the patient's condition not too serious. The formula used in hiring a shaman is *la bankush shana,* "You blow smoke on me." There appear to be no special preparations for the séance. The shaman arrives and makes ready to begin the ceremony when it is dark. Although there is no compulsion about attending, the immediate family is usually present. Visitors come, sometimes from distant camps, and no one is excluded. In the four-night ceremony, with which we are here chiefly concerned, the sessions for the first three nights last until midnight and for the fourth, all night. (It might be noted that time observance is a loose and elastic affair. There is no feeling for punctuality.)[25]

During the four days of shamanizing, the usual taboos against certain foods and activities are observed. Meat, salt, and hot foods may not be eaten. Sexual intercourse is proscribed. There is no necessity for the shaman to remain with the patient between the evening sessions. There are, however, certain rituals to be performed by the shaman in the morning such as ceremonial washing of both the patient and himself. The shaman may also desire to spend the day concentrating on the sickness, on the pathogenic object, prior to extraction. The patient remains quiet, but if he is able to walk about he may do so. No special regulations govern the conduct of family and visitors during the intervening days.

Payment for a shaman's services must be made in advance, either at the moment when he is hired or when he is brought to the sick person's house. The length of the session will determine the remuneration. In aboriginal times, a large basket was the most acceptable recompense for a four-night session. Such a basket must be of the three-rod-foundation coiled type.[26] The shaman's power considers these baskets more valuable than anything else, a belief that persists even today. They would eventually be given to relatives, "turned over to the women folks." In lieu of the favored basket, two buckskins together with a shell-bead necklace would be acceptable. For briefer curing sessions, something of lesser value would be given — a piece of buckskin, a small basket. Shamans were never paid in food.

Nowadays payment is in money and the customary fee for a four-night session is ten dollars. When a shaman doctors with his wife the fee is doubled. When additional practitioners are called in, as happens in critical cases, fees will increase proportionately. For shorter sessions the standard payment is two and a half dollars a night. The especial desirability of payment in baskets is evidenced in the practice still current of including a finely made basket with the cash fee. As Mike Dick said: "They pay good for their life."

The person who hires the shaman, usually a close relative, pays. If a man has no close relatives, distant kin will pay. A shaman will never doctor for nothing,[27] and he will return a fee only if the patient dies while receiving treatment. Should the latter die a few days after treatment, the fee will be kept. Even if the shaman acknowledges his failure to cope with a powerful sickness — a gesture sometimes made at the conclusion of the session — he will retain the fee. Payment is standardized, all full-fledged shamans receiving the same amount. Beginners and those who have not completed their novitiate charge correspondingly less.

One or even two additional shamans may be called in to assist the ministrant initially engaged. Two shamans might be asked simultaneously to treat a patient, the theory being "the more doctors, the better." The chief deterrent to such practice, is, of course, the increased expense. But auxiliary doctors are usually summoned for emergencies when the first doctor is encountering difficulty. In such emergencies distant relatives would defray the extra expense if close relatives could not. Bringing in an additional practitioner during treatment (more than one was seldom asked and never more than two) is an admission on the part of the first shaman that the sickness is too powerful for him. The function of the auxiliary shaman, as a rule, is to "chase" the sickness in the patient toward his colleague. However, sometimes he may be expressly hired to extract the disease-object himself. In such an event, he is paid more than the initial shaman; otherwise, less. It is the first practitioner who decides exactly which role the invited colleague is to fill, the choice expressed in the invitation. He will say, "Go hire so-and-so *to help me* take out the sickness," or, "Go hire so-and-so *to take it out.*" Both shamans would officiate together, each employing his individual techniques ("style"). Their combined efforts would greatly weaken the sickness.

The seating arrangement of the chief participants and guests at a shamanistic séance conforms to no established pattern. Usually, however, the patient will lie or recline on a bed situated at the northern end of the room, his head pointing west. Since south and east are the "roads to the dead," it is important that he not be oriented in those directions. Close by is the shaman, seated most of the time but jumping up and dancing about the room whenever so moved. West of the patient will be grouped the patient's family. Along the western and southern periphery will be found the visitors. (See Figure 3.)

Since the ceremony's main purpose is to expel the disease-object, which has been lodged in the body by some source of sickness and which can be removed only through supernatural agencies, the shaman devotes himself to the double task of invoking his power to lend assistance and of appealing to the disease to leave and cease troubling the sick person. All the ensuing rites hinge upon these two pivotal ideas. Whatever is done is directed toward the achievement of this double mission.

Treatment does not begin at once. Having removed his shoes, arrayed his paraphernalia before him, and ritually sprayed each article, the shaman will sit silently before the patient smoking his pipe. Now, as during almost the whole ceremony, his eyes are closed. No one may make any noise lest his "thinking" be interfered with. "It's like taking the ball away from him." He is "concentrating" on his dream, establishing rapport with his power. "He telephones to it." Sometimes he will give four low, moaning calls. (The shaman also calls to his dream in this manner when the patient's life [soul] has left the body. He is communicating with his dream to go and bring back the departing soul.) He will not have to wait long for contacting his dream. He addresses it and states his

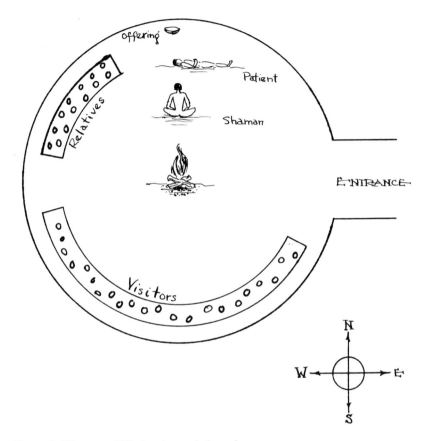

Figure 3. Diagram of Washo shamanistic curing ceremony.

desire for help in the task before him. Now he must discover the cause of the disease. In this he will be assisted by his songs, of which he may have anywhere from three to five. While singing he rattles rhythmically. A song will sometimes last as long as fifteen minutes, increasing in vigor and intensity as it proceeds. Suddenly the singer will stop and in the quiet that follows relate to the assemblage what progress he has made.

He may announce his diagnosis, describe the difficulties he is encountering in discerning the cause of sickness, or present a graphic narrative of incidents in that supernatural realm he has just glimpsed. These interim reports punctuate the entire proceedings, and the comments they engender lead to general conversation. Sometimes the company will join in the singing, and this is counted an aid to the shaman. Between songs the shaman will smoke his pipe, and this too is considered as assisting in the progress of the treatment. He may pass the pipe to the company, each individual in clockwise order taking a puff or two. Then just as suddenly the shaman will begin singing again.

As the séance continues through its appointed four-night span, other ceremonial features will be introduced. Although there is no fixed ritual order, certain items do arrange themselves in a pattern of relative importance, and in a general way it may be said that the more important rites are carried out as the curing progresses. Thus the songs accompanied simply by rattling will be succeeded by songs accompanied by both rattling and dancing. It is the shaman who dances, not the company. It is a dance characterized by a series of short, jerky jumps with both feet together. Mike Dick described it as a "crow hop." The dance may be formless in design or it may be a four-fold clockwise circuit about the fire. The shaman will not blow smoke on the affected parts of the patient's body until the ceremony has been proceeding for some time. Mike Dick said, "If you're not very sick, smoke blown on you will go right through you. If you are very sick, the smoke will hit the skin and bounce right back." The patient's face will be ritually washed each morning, but it is not until the end of the séance that the shaman will bathe him thoroughly from head to foot. Sickness-objects will not be extracted until the third or fourth night. The midnight repast takes place on the fourth night, and the ritual offering to the disease is timed to end at the conclusion of the entire ceremony. In general, the first three nights are much the same. "They keep doctoring the same way." It is the fourth night which contains important practices not occurring earlier. Hence, it looms as the most significant period in the séance. Let it be said again, however, that there is no neatly defined order of service. The shaman's dream is the final arbiter with regard to order and content.

The extraction of the disease-object is the real climax of the ceremony to which all other aspects are ancillary. Actually, the disease-object is not a tangible phenomenon; it becomes objectified only when extracted by the shaman. Henry Rupert put it this way: "It's not a material object but it's materialized that way." (Then he went on to explain that "will power" accounted for the transformation.) It is conceived as possessing sentient qualities. It sees and hears. Sometimes it talks to the shaman. It is "almost human." It manifests baffling caprices such as hiding behind the joints and wandering elusively through the body. In its peregrinations it eats up the blood and the saliva. "That's why a sick person gets thin," explained George Snooks. The shaman's custom of mentioning every part of the body in the course of curing, beseeching the sickness not to seek sanctuary there, is also explicable in terms of the sickness's sinister wanderings.

All the shaman's arts must be employed to maneuver the sickness into a position where it can be readily extracted. To this end cajolery and wiliness are most effective. The singing, dancing, smoking, and talking are all contrived to lure the sickness from its lair. The communal singing further aids the shaman by weakening the disease and enabling him to locate it more easily. For his part, he addresses the object of his quest in polite and friendly phrases, exhorting it to leave its present host and never to return. Some typical exhortations follow:

> You might leave your young ones or your dirt-odor or some other trace of you in the patient. Don't do that. Go away. Keep going. Don't look back. Let the patient get well behind you (Mike Dick).

> If you don't leave, I'll be forced to take you out, spit you into the palm of my hand, and show you to the people here, and they'll all laugh at you (George Snooks).

> You who are about this one's shoulder, make yourself ready to leave. Do not try to hide from me. You understand me, you know me, and I know you (Bill Wilson).

> Leave nothing behind you—spit, blood, piece of bone, toenail, hair, or anything (Joe Ryder).

It should be remembered that the shaman is on familiar terms with the world of the supernatural, and sicknesses, part of that unearthly realm, are no exception.

Eventually the sickness is concentrated in one spot—"like telephone wires going to central." The shaman knows when this occurs. Indeed, he has been aware of every move the sickness has made. He sees the concentration—"not with his eyes but with his thinking." Mike Dick said: "I can see it when the X-ray can't." And now it dislodges itself from the interior and comes to the surface of the body. "It gets light, floats up to the surface of the body just like through water."

Extraction is by two methods: through a whistle or by mouth. The latter, which is the more common, is the sucking technique. It is always done from a kneeling position. It may take the form of actually applying the lips to the affected part by holding the mouth close to the flesh and drawing in the breath. The whistle is used only for the long four-night treatments; sucking may be used at either short or long sessions. When in the course of the séance the shaman walks around the fire blowing his whistle, the disease will sometimes leave the patient and "go" to it. It will be recalled that Jack Wilson, famed Northern Paiute shaman, removed a disease object from Tom Snooks by another method related to sucking but somewhat different, namely, "with cupped hands." No other case involving this technique was encountered. It may have been localized Northern Paiute practice.

The pathogenic object is conceived as fixed in a matrix of malodorous dirt. This dirt must be extracted before and after the actual object is removed. Hence, the sucking will be done in installments. It normally takes repeated operations to draw out the tangible source of illness. The dirt that is drawn first enters the shaman's body, and he spits or vomits it out into his hand or onto a woodchuck hide. (Nowadays a can is used.) At the end of the session this is put in a wet, muddy place, customary repository for articles containing an ominous potency. When he finally succeeds in drawing out the object itself, he spits it into his hand. Sometimes before he can eject it, it passes into his own system. A powerful sickness "going right clear through him" can make him flatulent, and he may urinate or defecate on the spot. He cannot control it. When that happens, he usually falls down unconscious. He dare not be disturbed. Death may befall anyone who touches him. After a while, he regains consciousness and gets up.

He will then light a pipe. The smoking will soon weaken the sickness within him, and although it may seek to elude disgorgement by traveling all over his body, three or four coughs will bring it up. The shaman regards the bare object in the palm of his hand. A very small speck at first, it becomes larger as he holds it. "It grows, expands in the hand of the doctor after he spits it out. You can see it." He laughs at it to fill it with shame. It is exhibited to everyone present but none may touch it. (As has been previously noted, however, a disease-object projected by sorcery is not necessarily exhibited. Neither are its source and nature described. To do so would "make trouble.") Then he takes some dirt and together with the object mashes it in his hand. He is "killing the sickness." If it is a "weak one," he throws it into a trash receptacle in the house. If it is a "strong one," however, he goes outside and throws it away in a northerly direction.

Sickness-objects are of infinite variety. The following sickness-objects were recorded: small unshaped piece of obsidian, white quartz, pebble, piece of bone from a dead person, bone of a dead animal, arrowhead, piece of willow, fern root, string bean, small conical reddish burr-like vegetal object, green worm-like object with a brown head, deer's eye, bird feather, bird bill, bird, toad, fly, bug, small piece of skin, hair, fishing tackle, piece of briar pipe, chewing gum. Some are more difficult to extract than others. Hair, deemed one of the most powerful, almost always defied the shaman's skill. It lodges "right on the mouth of the lung," causing consumption.

After extracting the source of sickness, the practitioner continues shamanizing. There is no time limit but we may assume that the treatment will last for the customary four days. More than one disease-object may be drawn from the patient in the course of a session. A shaman does not always remove the object when he first sees it. He might wait until the fourth night.

Few examples of legerdemain are reported.[28] Feats demonstrating imperviousness to injury by fire when in a state of trance are not uncommon. When the sickness-object strikes, a shaman can fall into the fire and emerge unscathed. On two occasions Dick Bagley fell into the fire with all his clothes on—once he lay there for fully five minutes—and was not burned. In a state of trance, as a matter of fact, tricks of a miraculous character are altogether possible. Once, Joe Ryder, in a trance following disease-object extraction, jumped in between the relatives sitting close together without touching them. "His dream enabled him to do this."

Offerings of two kinds are made during the séance, the object of both being to persuade the disease to leave the patient. The first is a directional offering which may be made any time during the four nights. From a small pile of seeds placed on a miniature winnowing tray, the shaman takes a pinch, waves it clockwise once or twice about the patient's head, and throws it toward the four directions (in no particular order). Buffalo-grass seeds are preferred "by the sickness." They are used only for this purpose and never eaten. If this variety of seeds is not available, however, sunflower seeds, pine nut flour, acorn flour, crushed abalone shell, or small beads may be used. This offering is scattered while the shaman addresses the sickness; the native term means, "the one I talk with."

A second offering is made on the fourth night of the extended ceremony. It is prepared by the woman of the house prior to the beginning of the final night's proceedings. Four small piles of pine-nut or acorn meal and four small pieces of meat or fish (considered the equivalent of meat) are heaped on a winnowing tray and placed close to the wall near the patient. The belief is that the sickness will accept this offering and leave the patient alone. "It is just like paying the sickness to stop bothering the patient." (Henry Rupert added, "Maybe this is the same as the burnt offering in the Bible.) Usually the meal and meat are sampled only by the older folks, "because they know just what to do." Salt may not be used with them. The shaman does not eat of this food. What remains of the offering in the morning is thrown into the water. This offering is one of the indispensable elements in the four-night ceremony.

At midnight of the final night, a meal is eaten by all present including the shaman and the patient. The repast is characterized as a "small lunch," "not a regular meal." The aboriginal foods, pine-nut or acorn soup and, perhaps meat, predominate. Connected with this rite is the practice of providing pine nuts or acorns for the visitors who have come from other settlements. These are features which contribute to the social character of curing sessions. After the meal, a breathing spell intervenes before the shaman proceeds with the final rituals.

Before sunup the practitioner washes the patient from head to foot. Fine sage leaves are dropped in the water used for washing.

The actual washing follows carefully ordained procedure. From the head down all parts are bathed in prescribed sequence. All washing strokes are downward and outward, never the reverse. The reason given: "You've got nothing to worry about down there. Upward there's danger of forcing out what you're thinking."

Often the patient who has been seriously ill will be urged to lie abed after the séance is concluded. He will be told that "the sickness leaves him slowly." The shaman will advise caution in strenuous activities, probity in harmful habits—the counsel of common sense.

If the patient dies, certain purificatory rituals must be undergone by the shaman. He "fixes himself over"—refurbishes his power during a four-day period in which the usual taboos are maintained. Every morning he bathes. He washes (with spraying technique used at a séance) his paraphernalia. The outfit is viewed as unclean since death has come to one treated by it. At this time his dream might instruct him to throw away his rattle, which he must, of course, proceed to do.

One informant stated that a shaman must allow a four-day period to intervene between major cases. He may not proceed immediately from one four-day ceremony to another without waiting at least four days. There is no restriction with a succession of abbreviated ceremonies. However, whereas this may have been aboriginal practice, it is no longer binding. To my knowledge, Mike Dick officiated at two séances over an eight-day period with no interruption.

The house in which death has occurred must normally be abandoned. However, it could be made habitable if ritually fumigated. This ceremony, called *satu*, is performed by the shaman and is thought to drive away the sickness or the ghost of the dead. Sage or juniper is burned while the shaman utters appropriate words. Relatives will hire a shaman to perform the ritual, the regular fee being five dollars. A shaman may, however, refuse to officiate. The ceremony is also performed in the house of a sick person. Anyone may do the fumigating in this case except the shaman. As protection against thunder, Susie Rube once burned some sunflower seeds.

FEATS OF PROWESS

Shamans sometimes engage in demonstrations of supernatural prowess. These are informal occasions at which laymen are not as a rule present. Such encounters are regarded as "run, playing," although serious consequences sometimes result. They are designed to show the comparative power of the participants.

Thus one shaman might meet another by chance. Having exchanged greetings, they will sit down. One will ask the other for a smoke. While rolling the cigarette, the latter will add a little saliva. He will tender the cigarette to the first, who will take one puff, inhale, and fall over unconscious. This is done quite commonly. The effect of inhaling might be instantaneous flatulence, urination, or defecation. But it is all in fun. Charlie Rube said, "This is not to hurt them bad. It's just for fun. The one who asked the other to roll a cigarette wanted to see if he could do it."

Mike Dick's uncle, a powerful shaman from Sheridan, once rolled four cigarettes for Dick and told him to smoke them down, inhaling and without pause. After negotiating three, he fell over unconscious. He was not a full-fledged shaman at the time; that is, he was not master of sufficient power to withstand the force of his uncle's power.

A number of shamans will sometimes gather outdoors and test their respective powers. A row of about six willow or grass stalks will be set up. At right angles to them will stand the shamans in line. Having ritually fortified themselves beforehand through the four-day period of ceremonial cleansing in which the necessary taboos have been observed, they will concentrate on the business at hand. They are "working up the power," thinking, "I am a better man than you are." When ready, they take turns "shooting" at the stalks. (Dick Bagley said the shooting was done at fifty feet.) Each turns his back to the target, bends over, and with his fingers flicks the power between his legs. Sometimes all the stalks will be knocked over; sometimes they won't budge.

At these exhibitions of competitive power-testing, other feats reported include walking straight up a cliff, making oneself invisible and suddenly reentering the dance-house, and walking and dancing in fire. Henry Rupert noted the use of a mineral compound ("a scum, found on the surface of the water") which was rubbed on the legs before fire walking.

These occasions might also be used for mutual witching. Such affairs are "to see what the other fellow can do." In the summer they are held outdoors; in the winter they take place in the dance-house. The latent enmity which existed among the shamans would suddenly come to the surface. "They might bewitch each other right there and then. Sometimes they kill. They don't like each other very much.'' Each shaman will bring his outfit, although it is not displayed. They stand around, concentrate, and smoke. Smoking is apparently the most significant activity in this context. They then strive to "overpower" one another with the tobacco. They try to induce unconsciousness or unwitting flatulence, urination, or defecation. They attempt to shoot disease-objects into each other. If a participant falls over unconscious, the rest will observe whether he is strong enough to extract the pathogenic object unaided. If he is unsuccessful, the shaman responsible will remove it. The victim will then be restored. A shaman shown to be weak in these bouts might become an object of ridicule. His professional superiors will tell his relatives and friends, "After he saw what I could do, he found out [i.e., he found out what happened to him, how powerful I was]." However, contestants do not boast of their achievements afterwards and no "champion" emerges.

Another possible consequence containing serious implications is that of loss of power. One shaman might succeed in permanently taking away the power of another. Long Pete added, "And they call this playing."

A layman dreamer might participate in these rival demonstrations of prowess provided he had sufficient power. To enter the lists inadequately prepared, is, of course, to invite all manner of trouble ranging from contumely to death.

SPECIALIZATION

Almost unique is the lack of specialization in Washo shamanism. Enterprises like hunting antelope, deer, or bear; driving rabbits; gathering pine nuts; and other activities important in the tribal economy and bearing religious overtones were headed by leaders chosen for individual ability. They might dream, they might perform prescribed religious rituals, but they were not shamans. According to Lowie, "The antelope chief . . . was a shaman." My data do not confirm this observation. True, the leader of an antelope hunt dreamed, but such dreaming was not tantamount to shamanship. Evidently this distinction was not made to Lowie, for he writes, "He alone [the antelope chief] got his power by dreaming, that is, was a shaman."[29] It was repeatedly emphasized to me that while many dreamed, comparatively few were shamans.

In a word, they were possessed of some of the power generally diffused among many members of the tribe. For example, when hunting antelope, a number of men would sing. These songs would "hypnotize" the animals.

It did happen, however, that certain shamans became known as proficient in curing particular ailments. Thus, some were skilled in women's disorders, some in "mental" cases, some in eye trouble. The possession of special decoctions was often held responsible for such capabilities. No singular supernatural power was involved.

THE SOCIAL STATUS OF THE SHAMAN

The shaman's status in Washo society is unquestionably higher than that of any other functionary. There are two reasons for this: the lack of potential rivals and the supernaturally secured position of the shaman himself.

The structure of Washo society leaves no room for the development of any leader who might challenge the supremacy of the shaman. Until the coming of the whites, chiefship was a weakly defined and fluid affair. Men of known capability would assume the lead in important group enterprises such as war, hunting, pine nut gathering, communal get-togethers. If such an individual dreamed, it was an added qualification. Rarely, a shaman would lead in such activities. A similar randomness attached to political leadership. Persons of laudable personal traits were looked upon as heads of the various winter settlements. This was as far as political authority went. The Washo recognized three tribal divisions, largely along linguistic and geographic lines, but there was no implementing political organization. Hereditary succession was nonexistent, and even though a rabbit boss may have had a father who filled the same position, the former occupies the office on the strength of his merit alone. Again it sometimes happened that a shaman would be considered head of a local settlement.

A change came with white contact. The selection of a tribal spokesman and representative became a necessity for intergroup communication. As might have been expected, those members of the tribe who were prepossessing enough to carry the aura of authority and who could communicate intelligibly with whites became "captains." The choice, let it be remembered, was determined essentially not by the Indians but by the whites. In time, bitter rivalries grew up between captains, a condition made possible by the absence of any aboriginal sanctions for the assumption of high political office.

A second factor that squelches any possible challenge to shaman-istic status is the supernatural weapons at the disposal of the sha-man. The threat of sorcery is a paramount fear in the lives of the people, and the shamans, masters of witching techniques, exploit this fear to the limit. Sorcery is a means of social control, of status preservation, in the hands of those who manipulate supermundane power. Under these circumstances none can vie with the shamans. That the shamans are extremely vigilant in guarding their position is evidenced in the supernatural liquidation of temporal leaders who threaten to become too popular. The witching of Captain Jim, cited earlier, is a case in point.

The unassailable social position of the shaman, secured by such awesome means, is accompanied understandably by the corollaries of popular suspicion and fear. Some shamans are hated. Not a few are feared. All are suspect. The least serious indictment leveled at a shaman is that he is mercenary. Every layman's testimony bristled with a cynical and resentful awareness of the grasping character of shamanistic practice. Neither were the known jealousies and rivalries between shamans calculated to inspire confidence in the layman. Yet the brooding fear of sorcery conspired for the most part to keep resentment and animosity submerged.

Occasionally, as we have seen, the smoldering antagonisms would burst forth into violent aggressions. Victims of witching would then be avenged by relatives. The killing of shamans in such circumstances received tacit social approbation. A recent case of the employment of tribal sanctions against a witch, necessarily less drastic than those allowed in the original pattern, was the expulsion of Becky Jack from the Dresslerville Indian colony. These acts of requital, although furnishing an ultimate means of control over a sorcerer, are withal exceptional. Meanwhile the shaman enjoys his preeminent status unchallenged.

Within the limits imposed by these attitudes, the shaman lives a normal life. He joins his fellows in the usual pursuits and occu-pations, living as they live. The stranger notices no difference between shaman and layman. Indeed, there are no outward signs of distinction. (Mike Dick carried a staff on which he had notched a record of his cases. However, since he was blind, the staff probably served as much for a cane as for an insignia of office.) In a former time, workaday shaman's attire may have been better than that of the majority of the tribe for the shaman never lacked buckskins — classical payment for different ills. Informants remarked repeatedly that shamans always had more than laymen, but we must not be misled into thinking that they were therefore men of wealth who lived on surplus. Such a conception does not reckon with Washo economic realities, which, based on a seminomadic, gathering-hunting existence, precluded the accumulation of commodities. Payment for curing — baskets, buckskins, beads — was more often than not presented as gifts to relatives and friends or used as stakes in gambling. Nonetheless, it is probably true that in a tribe which suffered not infrequent shortage of food and in which a paucity of material goods is characteristic, the shaman knew no lack.[30]

3. THE AFFILIATIONS OF WASHO SHAMANISM

INTRODUCTION

Having discussed the nature of Washo shamanism, we turn now to a consideration of its relationship to the religious practices and beliefs of surrounding cultural provinces. We shall expect to find the traits that compose the shamanistic complex combined in different ways as they are distributed through the contiguous areas. There will be different emphases, variant phrasings of the same generalized pattern. The cultural position of the Washo will be clarified as we assess its religious forms in relationship with those of its neighbors. Without ignoring its distinctive characterisitics, we shall perhaps find that what Spier has said of Klamath shamanism applies equally to the Washo complex: namely, that it is best interpreted as a function of Washo geographic location.[1]

No detailed interareal study is contemplated. The ground has been admirably covered by both Spier and Park.[2] I shall merely assess in general terms the place of Washo shamanism in western North America. My chief reliance has been on the two studies just cited, although additional material on Great Basin shamanism since their publication has been utilized.[3]

SHAMANISM IN WESTERN NORTH AMERICA

Shamanism is the focal expression of religion over a large part of western North America. In the Great Basin, for all the unevenness of available information, we may conclude that it is the authentic aboriginal culture complex which comprehends all religious phenomena. Typical Plateau culture finds its religion rooted in shamanism. In northern California, shamanism is seen as a substratum to such religious manifestations as the Kuksu cult, and farther south as interweaved with the Chungichnich religion. Among central California tribes like the Nisenan and Yokuts the shaman achieves a noteworthy status. Southwestern non-Pueblo tribes like the Mescalero Apache accord shamanism an outstanding role in the culture. Concerning the Washo it may be said that shamanism is not only the focus of religion but a culturally predominating order of beliefs, practices, and practitioners. In an area where it everywhere occupies a prominent cultural position, shamanism achieves an unsurpassed eminence in this west-central Nevada tribe.[4]

SPIRITS

The derivation of supernatural power from a host of spirits is a conception widely diffused in the Great Basin and adjacent areas. Spirits of animals, birds, reptiles, and natural phenomena are sources of power for the Northern Paiute, Chemehuevi, Northern Ute, Southern Ute, Wind River and Lemhi Shoshoni, and White Knives—Great Basin tribes. Among Plateau and neighboring California tribes—like the Thompson, Lillooet, Sanpoil and Nespelem, Tenino, Wishram, Nez Percé, Takelma, Klamath, Modoc, Wintu, Achomawi, Atsugewi, Northern Maidu, and Nisenan—the belief is equally pronounced. Other areas where these spirits are recognized as sources of power are south-central California and southern California, in the latter region in connection with jimsonweed initiation rites. Among the Yumans of the Colorado and Gila rivers the spirits of animals and of natural phenomena confer power out of that mythologic dreamworld in which the local religions are rooted.[5]

Natural phenomena do not figure prominently as Washo spirits. We may regard this as a local specialization. Inconsequential and bizarre spirits like a sound and a gun, found occasionally with the Washo, are paralleled in the Plateau and northern California.[6]

The importance assigned to water babies in Washo supernaturalism merges nicely into the status accorded manikin spirits west of the Rockies and reaches a particularly high development in this area. In the Great Basin, the Northern Paiute, Northern Ute, Wind River Shoshoni, and White Knives recognize water babies as potent supernaturals. The same is true of the Plateau tribes Thompson,

Shuswap, and Klamath. To go further afield, dwarf-like creatures are not unknown in Plains visions.[7]

In northern California among the Shasta, Yuki, and Northern Maidu, where the conception of "pains" as a familiar is common, an undifferentiated class of dwarf-like spirits is an important source of power. Spier sees a connection between these and the ghosts of the dead, who are a source of power for other neighboring California groups like the Yurok, Sinkyone, Nisenan, and Yokuts. Park, however, sees no relationship. As for the Washo, both are found — water babies frequently and ghosts (in the form of a skeleton) rarely. So far as present information goes, the only Basin tribes which claim ghosts of the dead as supernaturals are the Washo and Northern Paiute in the west and the Shoshoni Seed Eaters in the east.[8]

Specialization among spirits is an attenuated belief with the Washo. The notion that certain spirits can best perform specific tasks is little developed. Beyond the recognition that eagle can bring back a departing soul, there is no hint of specialization of function. Tasks to be accomplished are difficult or easy, and whether a task will be successfully performed depends largely on the power resident in a spirit. The most powerful spirits are eagle and water baby. Shamans whose dream is rattlesnake or bear could not necessarily cure injuries inflicted by these creatures, although they themselves might be immune to them. Certain shamans occasionally gained reputations as effective practitioners for specific ailments, but the curative agency was not spiritual but herbal.

Elsewhere in the Basin the concept of specialization is less nebulous, although it is nowhere strongly developed. Northern Paiute, White Knives, and Chemehuevi shamans are known for special skills that derive from certain spirits. In the northern Plateau, Thompson, Lillooet, and Shuswap shamans are associated with a special class of spirits, while farther south among the Sanpoil and Nespelem, Southern Okanagon, Tenino, Wishram, and Klamath, locally phrased specialization also occurs. Among the California tribes the feeling for specialization is weak.[9]

The Washo spirit world, then, is of a piece with that of surrounding areas. There is the local difference that natural phenomena are not often encountered. Insofar as the array of supernaturals is highly diverse and predominantly animal, affiliations with the Plateau and the Plains are indicated. The prominence of water babies as potent spirits points clearly in the direction of northern California, although these beings are found both in the Plateau and in the Plains. The weak development of specialization in function is characteristic of Great Basin, Plateau, and California shamans and spirits, although with the Washo this concept is especially tenuous. Thus, in the sphere of power derivatives, the Washo are a typically Great Basin people with connections east, north, and west.

SHAMAN AND LAYMAN

That shamans are set off from nonshamans—not so much by distinctive revelations and potency as by the possession of a greater degree of the supernatural power that is generally diffused—is a notion shared by the Washo with many western North American peoples. Through the Great Basin, Plateau, northeastern California, and even western Plains this conception is general. An exception occurs with the Takelma where shaman is differentiated from layman in terms of kind rather than degree of power. A differentiation still more marked obtains for the northern and north-central California tribes Shasta, Yurok, Sinkyone, Tolawa, Pomo, and Northern Maidu. Central California is linked to the Great Basin with respect to shaman-nonshaman differentiation, as are the tribes of the lower Colorado and Gila rivers. However, among the latter the Maricopa distinguish sharply between shaman and layman, a distinction likewise found among the Havasupai, Walapai, and southeastern Yavapai.[10]

Park is of the opinion that among the Northern Paiute the shaman is further removed from the layman than is the case in contiguous areas, than in the Great Basin itself. He bases his conclusions principally on the Northern Paiute emphasis on the shaman's curative function, a development that set the shaman distinctly apart.[11] The fact remains, however, that anyone might become a shaman, that curing was merely a skill which came to those who accepted the call and devoted themselves diligently to the supernatural craft, that curing was, in a word, the tangible evidence of greater power possession. This is the case with the Washo and as such, renders them affiliate with the bulk of Basin, Plateau, northern and central California, and Yuman-speaking Southwest tribes.

THE SHAMAN'S SEX

Both men and women are shamans in relative numerical equality among the Washo, with the balance tipped in favor of the men. Throughout western North America we find both sexes eligible for shamanistic office. The situation among the Washo is duplicated throughout the Great Basin and Plateau. In northern California, however, women strikingly eclipse the men. "Pains" as a source of power, control dances, and the predominance of women shamans are suggested as historically connected by Park. Farther south in California men outnumber women, a tendency which increases as we proceed south. No homogeneous pattern exists among the non-Pueblo peoples of the Southwest.[12]

Berdaches do not become shamans in the Great Basin. In the Plateau the same condition holds, except with the Klamath. The Yurok in northern California constitute an unusual example of transvestite-shaman synonymity, the only case in this area — indeed, the most noteworthy example in western North America.

THE ACQUISITION OF POWER

Among the Washo supernatural power is acquired through the medium of involuntary dreams. There is no vision quest and only the vaguest feeling for the inheritance of power. The situation in surrounding regions is by no means uniform. In some tribes acquiring power is an involuntary affair, in others the quest is consciously undertaken, in still others power is inherited. In many, various combinations of these three methods will be found.

The Involuntary Dream

Unsolicited dreams constitute a primary source of power acquisition in all Great Basin tribes. In addition, voluntary quests are undertaken by Northern Paiute, Seed Eaters, White Knives, and Northern Ute. A flexible kind of inheritance is experienced by Northern Paiute. The voluntary quest accompanied by physical privation predominates in the Plateau. In the northern area, with the exception of the Thompson, Shuswap, and Southern Okanagon, involuntary dream visitation is wholly absent; and in these exceptional tribes, a random form of involuntary inheritance obtains. Among some southern Plateau and northern California groups, the quest is followed by dreams that bestow power. Among other northern California groups, power is bestowed by "pains," which either accompany or follow unsought dreams. In the Kuksu area, power comes either in dreams or by initiation. Central California groups acquire power either in ordinary dreams or in quested visions. As we proceed south, dreams dominate the picture. This is true of southern Californians, where they are often associated with jimson-weed ceremonialism, and lower Colorado Yumans. In the non-Pueblo southwest, both the quest and involuntary dreams appear, although in the great majority of cases the dream is fundamental.[13]

Spier has drawn a distinction between vision and dream, the former involving an auditory or visual experience with a spirit, the latter being an ordinary dream. Under this terminology, the Washo obtain power through visions and these are largely auditory. The literature provides only meager data concerning the nature of the dream elsewhere. Northern Paiute, White Knives, and Salmon Eaters visions are also predominantly auditory. A characteristic shared by both some Basin and Plateau visions is the appearance of an animal spirit in human form.[14]

The Vision Quest

The only mention of anything resembling a vision quest in Washo shamanism was Henry Rupert's testimony that in preparation for shamanistic office, "some used to wander around the mountains. They would get inspiration, seek advice." Presumably this took place after the initial call had come and may be a vestigial form of power quest. Among other Great Basin tribes the vision quest is found in diluted form. The Northern Paiute quest involves none of the physical hardships or turbulent psychological repercussions of the typical Plateau variety. It is not universally sought, as in the Plateau; neither do any but mature individuals undertake it, in contrast to the youthful age of Plateau aspirants; nor are there power renewal ceremonies. Would-be shamans in other Basin tribes seek power largely after the manner of the Northern Paiute. If the conscious search for power in the Basin is a weakened form of the Plateau prototype, it is also not to be confused with the Plains vision quest.[15]

The vision quest is found in northern and central California but is absent in the southern part of the state. Dreams now come to displace other forms of spirit visitation, a contingency which accounts for the negligible incidence of the quest in the non-Pueblo Southwest.[16]

THE INHERITANCE OF POWER

Inheritance of power among the Washo is a weak and elastic concept. Power may or may not be inherited. The potential inheritor must be adequately receptive; he must dream. The Basin inheritance pattern is mixed. Unreported in the eastern boundaries, it occurs with the Southern and Northern Paiute (although foreign to some Southern Paiute bands), Chemehuevi, and Las Vegas. For many tribes in the Plateau, inheritance is an auxiliary means for securing supernatural power. Fixity of inheritance characterizes much northern California shamanism. As is to be expected, inheritance is practically nonexistent in southern California and infrequently encountered among the non-Pueblo Southwest, where dreams tend to obliterate all other channels of power acquisition.[17]

EXHIBITIONS OF POWER CONTROL

Unreported thus far in the Great Basin are two shamanistic rites: the novice's inaugural performance, in which control of the supernatural is demonstrated, and public exhibitions of power by full-fledged shamans customarily held at midwinter. Insofar as they have both, the Washo stand unique in this area. By the same token, affiliation is indicated north and northwest, for both in the Plateau and in northern California there is a strong development of these elements.

THE NOVICE'S PERFORMANCE

Two types of inaugural dance have been differentiated by Spier: the demonstration type, whereby the neophyte proves his ability to cure, and the control type, in which he acquires control over his powers. The former centers in Oregon, the latter in northern California. Washo novice dances conform to the control pattern.

The ideology of northern California control dances, in the

course of which control over the "pains" must be demonstrated, bears close resemblance to that of the Washo. With the latter, mastery of the disease-object must be established. This conceptual equivalence lends additional justification to Spier's dissatisfaction with the broad inclusiveness which has been assigned to the phenomenon of "pains."[18]

The dance-house is the scene of inaugural dances among the Washo; occurrence of the dance corresponds exactly with the incidence of the dance-house. This may be significant for an understanding of the absence of the inaugural dance throughout the Basin, where beyond Washo terrain the dance-house is nowhere found.

Exhibitions of Power

Exhibitions of power by Washo shamans may be a loose analogue of the regimented performances found farther north in the Plateau, which are linked in turn with Northwest-coast secret-society rituals. There is no fixed time for them as among Plateau and northern California groups;[19] they appear to be private affairs between professionals, the whole ruled by a sharp competitive spirit.

The idea of power renewal implicit in these performances finds its echo in the rites of power refurbishing deemed necessary in many Washo shamanistic contexts. Informants invariably referred to this procedure as "fixing up," and it assumed a place of greatest prominence in the Washo complex.

PARAPHERNALIA

Outside the curing séance, Washo shamans wear no distinctive regalia. Feather headdresses, emblematic clothing, tattooing, and other constant tangible reminders of shamanistic office are common in the Plateau, less so in northern California. Analogous practice is encountered in the Plains, where supermundane contacts receive pictorial representation on some object significant to the visitant.

Paraphernalia may be elaborate or simple — the dream will decide. But no matter how simple, eagle feathers, rattle, pipe, headdress, and miniature baskets will always be found. Of these the first two are the most important.

Eagle feathers are everywhere used by western North American shamans. The manner of use varies, but Park suggests a linkage between the feather wands of the northeastern Maidu, Northern Paiute, White Knives, Salmon Eaters, and Kaibab, with the prayer plumes widely diffused in the Southwest.[20]

Two rattles are used by the Washo in curing: the cocoon rattle, the more common type, and the deer dewclaw rattle, of limited distribution in the tribe. The former is distinctly a California variety, used by the central California neighbors of the Washo. Its religious use in the Basin is unreported. In this region, the deer hooflet rattle seems to be the favored type. However, the Southern Paiute have the cocoon rattle of their Washo and California neighbors. Mention should be made of the nonshamanistic uses to which the deer hooflet rattle is put throughout California. Comparatively few Plateau tribes know this type. In the Southwest the gourd rattle everywhere predominates. The rattles used by the Washo shamans, then, affiliate both east (dewclaw) and west (cocoon).[21]

THE CAUSE OF DISEASE

Washo disease concepts are similar not only to Basin but also to general western North American beliefs. The function of the shaman as healer both of naturally and supernaturally caused sickness is common. His principal preoccupation is, of course, with the latter, and with that none but he can cope.

Sorcery, intrusion of disease-objects, soul-loss, and ghosts are the most frequently recorded cause of disease in this whole area— Great Basin, Plateau, and California. Anticipated local phrasings will be found to exist in the regions under consideration. Beyond this, Clements has discussed and mapped the worldwide distribution of these concepts.[22]

Most prominent as a source of disease with the Washo seems to be witchcraft. With other Basin peoples dreams appear to be the chief cause. It is the dreams themselves that bring sickness, whereas in the Plateau and California, dreams merely foretell the onset of sickness. Again as should be expected, the strongest belief in the disease-causing quality of dreams is to be found in the Yuman Southwest. Here again it is the dream as such which directly brings on sickness.[23]

THE CURING CEREMONY

The basic elements in Washo curing have already been cited. Available data for western North America are far from comprehensive, but as far as they go, they indicate that over a wide area, a broad similarity in procedure exists. Having been summoned by the family of the sick person for a fee, the shaman smokes, sings, dances, diagnoses the sickness, and extracts the disease-object. This is the pattern found in the Great Basin, Plateau, northern and central California, and non-Pueblo southwest.[24]

Disease-objects are extracted most often by sucking. However, different tribes and different shamans within tribes use variant methods: massage, incantations, spraying. And we have seen how the Washo themselves employ different nuances of the sucking technique.

Illness caused by soul-loss is treated by attempted soul-restoration by the shaman. He falls into a trance, and it is his spirit that takes flight after the errant soul of the sick person. This practice is general in the Basin, Plateau, California, and non-Pueblo Southwest.

Washo curing ceremonialism, like that of the Northern Paiute and other Basin tribes, constitutes the most important religious activity of the tribe. In the Plateau and northern California, the emphasis is upon the novice performance and the midwinter shamanistic exhibitions. Whereas both the control dance and the professional displays of power are found with the Washo, they do not eclipse in religious significance the shaman's individual curing ministrations. Thus in these traits the Washo affiliate both east, with their Basin congeners, and north and northeast, with Plateau and northern California groups.[25]

THE SHAMAN'S ASSISTANT

The practice of having functionaries assist the shaman during a curing is not found among the Washo, but it is found in a few Great Basin tribes, in the Plateau, and in a scattering of northern California tribes. The Northern Paiute assistant, possessed of no spiritual power, interprets the shaman's incoherent speech, leads the communal singing, and aids in other minor ways. Unique in the Basin is a woman dancer as assistant who follows the shaman as he dances about the fire. Some Plateau shamans use a small corps of assistants. Northern California assistants are largely interpreters, but the assistant among the Northern Maidu is, aberrantly, a clown.[26]

THE SHAMAN AS SPECIALIST

The lack of specialization which marks the Washo spirit world, already discussed in its distributional aspects, also characterizes the shamans. A perusal of surrounding religious cultures is clear evidence that nowhere is this aspect of shamanism so weakly developed as among the Washo. Shaman specialists in weather control, clairvoyance, antelope charming, war, are unknown to them. Only in the acknowledgment of certain successful therapies for which individual practitioners are known and in the gradation of shamans in accordance with general reputation and experience, do we perceive a vague kind of specialization.

The distributional picture is not without its complexity due to the varied kinds of specialization encountered. In the Great Basin, minor specialization is found, including, as a rule, antelope charming. In the Plateau, both sharp differentiation of function and its lack exist. Specialization is the norm in California with frequent occurrence of weather, bear, and rattlesnake shamans. Functional distinctions are recognized in non-Pueblo Southwest shamanism but not so sharply as in California. An enclave of complexity is found with the "Pai" tribes: no specialization among the Walapai, some among the Southeastern Yavapai, more among the Havasupai.[27]

The dualism of the shaman's power, which may work either weal or woe, is found throughout western North America. The Pomo and other central California peoples, whose religion is overlaid with the Kuksu cult, are an exception. They distinguish sharply between benevolent and malevolent shamans.

An additional word should be said about antelope shamans. They are prominent in some Great Basin tribes, like Northern Paiute, White Knives, and Salmon Eaters, while in others they are absent. Among the latter, and the Washo are included here, antelope drives are highly ritualized and formalized affairs shot through with religious overtones, but presided over not by a shaman but by a person possessed of limited supernatural power. Taking game is informed with a similar ritualistic motif in the Plateau and California, and charming by shamans is not commonly found. The non-Pueblo Southwest witnesses the execution of analagous magical and ceremonial practices in connection with hunting larger game without benefit of shaman. Park notes significant similarities between Basin and Plains communal game drives in association with shamanistic beliefs and practices.[28]

THE SOCIAL STATUS OF THE SHAMAN

The unrivalled position of the shaman in Washo society finds no parallels in the existing literature. As has been indicated, the reasons for his influence are twofold: lack of a strong chiefship and social control wielded through sorcery. Perhaps it is the absence elsewhere of these powerful factors — irresistible in combination — that renders the Washo picture unique. Perhaps the reason lies in our limited information. It is significant that the only extended study made of the social status of the shaman in this general region, namely, Gayton's *Yokuts-Mono Chiefs and Shamans*, reveals the shaman as the functionary of crucial influence in the tribe.[29]

When the gaps in our present knowledge are filled, the Great Basin tribes may suggest greater resemblances to the Washo. From the scant data now available, it can be said that in the Great Basin, shamans are important figures commanding respect commensurate with personal achievement. They are not commonly chiefs. In the Plateau, shamans attain high position, often eclipsing chiefs. This is especially true of the Klamath, although farther north the chief comes more into his own. Data concerning the shaman's status are almost wholly lacking for northern California, where women predominate as shamans, and the north-central province, where the Kuksu cult centers. Northern Maidu and Wintu shamans are the most important individuals in social as well as religious matters. Yokuts and Western Mono shamans ally themselves politically with chiefs, maintaining for themselves an impregnable economic and social status. The shaman continues as a significant influence in southern California, along the lower Colorado and Gila rivers, and in the non-Pueblo Southwest, more often than not enjoying equal rank with chiefs.[30]

SUMMARY

The principal beliefs and practices of Washo shamanism take their character from the generalized shamanistic complex widespread in western North America. Great Basin, Plateau, and northern California patterns share in common fundamental elements — spirits drawn from the animal and natural world; importance of shamanism and the shaman in the religious, social, and political fabric; basic concepts of cause, diagnosis, and cure of disease; the moral duality of the shaman's function. Elaborations on this undifferentiated base occur, of course, everywhere, and these developments cluster in accordance with relative geographic and cultural propinquity. Thus Washo shamanism represents a crystallization of traits that relate with geographic logic to elements encountered in the complex of surrounding peoples.

In some respects the Washo pattern suggests noteworthy features. To the extent that it includes the novice's performance and the shamans' exhibitions of power, it links firmly with the Plateau. It is thus differentiated from the other Great Basin patterns. The appearance of the dance-house, especially prominent with the Southern Washo, as well as the use of the cocoon rattle, prove close contact with east-central California, again a mark of differentiation. Other characteristics point to a strong association northward and westward. Yet it would be incorrect to infer that the Washo complex is wholly, or even largely, aberrant from Basin norms. Profoundly it is Great Basin shamanism. Its marginal physical position on the California and Plateau borders ultimately explains its extra-Basin resemblances.

Mention might be made of certain items that set off Washo shamanism from the surrounding forms. The following are suggested as local specializations: a striking paucity of natural phenomena and the infrequent occurrence of ghosts as supernaturals; the weak development of specialized function among both spirits and shamans; the emphasis on the pattern-number four in all contexts; the lack of any religious assistant; the random power-refurbishing and renewal rites; the ascription of sickness chiefly to witchcraft. The pervasive quality of witchcraft phenomena may, in fact, be said to mark Washo shamanism, and through this religious channel, the whole culture. From this conceptual and emotional background the shaman naturally rises as the most powerful figure in the tribe. With the Washo he achieves a status unique in the area.

4. WASHO PEYOTISM

THE PEYOTE CULT

The peyote cult, which began to make serious inroads into traditional Washo life in 1936, was diffused initially from a southeastern source. Peyote (*Lophophora williamsii* Lemaire) grows in the valley of the Rio Grande and in the northeastern desert plateau of Mexico, and it is this region which is undoubtedly the center from whence the cult spread both north and south.

La Barre has given a comprehensive picture of the history and diffusion of peyote, based upon the extensive literature which has been devoted to the subject.[1] The antiquity of peyote-eating in Mexico is attested by the evidence of Sahagún, recorded in 1560. Indeed, peyote's peculiar properties and associated ritualism have come in for some attention by not a few early Spanish explorers and other writers through subsequent centuries. In more recent times Lumholtz has described the cult for the Huichol and Tarahumara.[2] Peyotism was established in the United States about 1870, although the Tonkawa are said to have used the cactus as early as 1716. M.E. Opler has suggested that the source for the northward spread of the cult is with the Lipan, who got it from the Carrizo.[3] From the Lipan, Mescalero, and Kiowa, the first tribes north of the Rio Grande to adopt the cult, it has spread as far north as the Canadian Cree and Chippewa, the diffusion covering a span of more than sixty years. As it diffused it took on different mutations, largely in terms of local aboriginal patterns. One of the most noteworthy developments is embodied in the Native American Church, which represents a merging with Christian elements and which served to unite peyote-using tribes into a confederation. Studies of North American Indian peyotism, to which the work of Mooney and Radin provided chief impetus, indicate that there are basic similarities in the cult as practiced by all peoples north of the Rio Grande.

More than ten years ago the cult crossed the barrier of the Rockies, despite Shonle's prediction that Basin and California peoples would not find peyote culturally congenial.[4] Since that time it has been incorporated into the life of several tribes—Ute, Gosiute, Shoshoni. When the new religion was brought to the Washo and their eastern and southern Shoshonean neighbors by Ben Lancaster, it had reached its farthest boundary of westward penetration. According to present information, it has not crossed the Sierra Nevadas.[5]

A few words should be said about the botanical and physiological properties of peyote.[6] Peyote is a small cactus, spineless, and carrot-shaped. Only a small portion of the root-like growth shows above the soil, and it is this top surface which when sliced off and dried becomes the peyote "button." In its dried state it is very hard, its center bearing a small circular tuft of fine fuzzy hair.

Chemical analysis reveals that mature plants contain as many as nine alkaloids.[7] These are of two kinds, distinguished in terms of their physiological effects, strychnine-like and morphine-like. The characteristic progress of peyote intoxication may be charted in relation to the workings of these contrasting chemical constituents. A general euphoria is followed by depression accompanied by nausea. This is succeeded by a period in which visual hallucinations are experienced. No loss of consciousness comes with intoxication, and it is generally agreed that neither harm nor habit formation results from peyote's use.

The eating of peyote is the central feature of the religious cult named after the sacred cactus. Its ingestion is set in a ceremonial and theological matrix. A brief description of generalized peyote ritualism and theology follows.

Meetings are held for a single night, usually on Saturday, and last all night. The locus for these gatherings is a tipi or house. Before the ceremony begins, all assemble at the entrance and stand silent while the peyote chief prays; then they enter and walk to assigned places in a clockwise circuit. Clockwise movements govern all procedures throughout the night.

Ceremonial focus of the meeting is the half-moon earth altar bearing a large peyote button, which becomes the channel for prayers offered by the leader and members through the night. A staff, feather fan, rattle, drum, and whistle compose the paraphernalia. Everyone smokes ritually prepared cigarettes, sings, prays, drums, and eats peyote. The singing, done to rattling accompaniment, is in clockwise order with one's right-hand neighbor drumming. At midnight water is brought in and drunk, and at dawn water and special foods are carried in, imbibed, and eaten with ceremonial propriety. Functionaries at a meeting are the peyote chief, chief drummer, cedarman, and fire chief (see Figure 4.)

Peyote beliefs also have a fairly uniform base. Primarily, peyote heals through a union of intrinsic therapeutic agents and faith. Healing is effectuated by the purging action of peyote on both a physical and spiritual level, as well as by attendant ceremonies — incensing the body with cedar smoke, rubbing the body with sage leaves, smoking special cigarettes, baptism with "holy" water. A supreme being is invoked through peyote, which thus serves as intermediary between supplicant and deity. The attributes with which peyote is endowed are legion, the refinements of theological doctrine highly personalized. That peyote unites men in a brotherhood espousing the virtues of honesty, kindness, ambition, and love and that it sternly opposes liquor are unanimously avowed tenets. Portentous revelations come in visions induced by the sacred cactus, and these are interpreted variously as prognostications, warnings, retributions for past deeds, guidance for the future.

Such in outline are the background and nature of peyotism. From this point we proceed to a discussion of Washo peyotism, beginning with a description of a Washo peyote meeting. This will be followed by a comparison of the Washo rite with the prototype Kiowa-Comanche ceremony, the significant variations noted. The circumstances under which peyote was introduced and its subsequent career among the tribe will then be related, to be succeeded by a section depicting the social consequences of the newly introduced cult on tribal life. Finally, the reasons openly expressed for accepting or rejecting peyote will be delineated. This approach to the history and diffusion of peyotism among the Washo is, for the time being, historical; the orientation, from the point of view of an observer, from without. Discussion of the deeper implications, culturally and psychologically, is reserved for the final chapter.

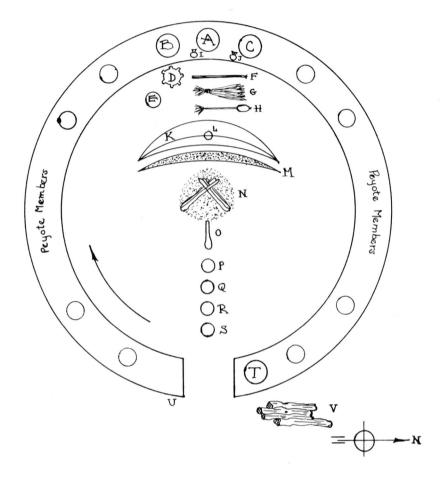

LEGEND

O Men	G. Fan	O. Fire Stick
◗ Women	♯. Rattle	P. Water
A. Peyote Chief	I. Bag of Peyote	Q. Corn
B. Chief Drummer	J. Bag of Cedar	R. Rice
C. Cedarman	K. Moon Altar	S. Meat
D. Drum	L. Father Peyote	T. Fire Chief
E. Peyote Bucket	M. Ash Moon	U. Enclosure Wall
F. Staff	N. Fire	V. Wood Supply

Figure 4. Diagram of Washo peyote meeting. (After Stewart 1944:65.)

WASHO PEYOTE RITUAL

The season of the year will largely determine where meetings will be held.[8] In winter a large room in a house is customarily used, although during the height of peyote's popularity (late 1936 and early 1937) meetings were held outdoors because no room in Dresslerville was large enough to accommodate the devotees. In summer meetings are held outdoors within a circular canvas or willow enclosure about seven to ten feet tall.

Several hours before the meeting begins the crescent moon altar, center of the cultus, will be prepared by the leader. It is fashioned out of earth, about two feet long and six inches high. A slight depression is scooped out of the top and a fifty-cent piece temporarily lodged in it, marking the place where the chief or father peyote will be ensconced. The moon is oriented toward the east, "because light is received from the east by every human being." The entrance to the corral (or house) also faces east.

A half-hour or so before the session is scheduled to start, the drum will be tied. An iron kettle with three or four legs and two handles is partially filled with water, into which seven pieces of red-hot charcoal are dropped. The glowing coals represent lightning; the water, rain; the drumming, thunder. A wet buckskin is stretched over the kettle and seven pebbles placed peripherally around its mouth. A rope is passed tightly around each pebble, creating seven skin-covered bosses, and then drawn and tied under the drum. The seven "marbles" stand for the seven days of the week. They were also said to represent the "seven" stars that travel together at night—"the seven sisters," the Pleiades. It was a concept taken from the aboriginal culture. The rope is tied so as to form the pattern of a star on the bottom of the kettle. It is the chief drummer's function to tie the drum, but when a woman filled this office, as was the case in many of Lancaster's and Dick's meetings[9]—a bold departure from peyote tradition—the leader would execute this somewhat strenuous task. It requires brawn to tie a drum proficiently.

While the drum is being tied, the fire chief prepares and kindles the fire. The fire, which will burn all night, consists of four pieces of wood placed in the shape of a V, its base immediately in front (i.e., east) of the moon. The fire chief will tend the fire diligently, preserving throughout its original V shape. Indeed, this functionary will be constantly busy through the night; besides tending the fire, he must carefully shape the ashes into a crescent between the fire proper and the moon, sweep the altar and the floor periodically to keep them clean, pass the stick used for lighting cigarettes and kept aglow in front of the fire, assist in distributing water and food at the midnight and dawn ceremonies, and upon the peyote chief's instructions, lead participants to and from their appointed places in the course of the evening. In a word, the fire chief is the general custodian assigned to menial tasks. Directing all procedure is, of course, the peyote chief.

Meetings begin between eight and nine o'clock in the evening. All assemble outside the meeting place. At the door, the peyote chief prays, asking "God for help in tipi way meeting so that we may be well and happy." Participants sit in a number of concentric circles around the altar and fire. There is no fixed seating arrangement save the places of honor reserved for the principal functionaries. The peyote chief sits at the head of the altar with the chief drummer on his right. At his left sits the cedarman, whose duties consist of throwing cedar on the fire at various intervals at the behest of the peyote chief, causing it to give off a fragrant aroma. Actually, juniper berries are used. However, as one informant put it, "We call it cedar all the time." Cedar is an agent of purification. "We put smoke on everything. When we go out and come back into meeting we have to put smoke on. It makes it right." The fire chief is stationed at the entrance. Seats in the front row are assigned to the privileged. In traditional peyote ritual these are reserved for men; but Lancaster and Dick not only place women in the front row, they make something of a point of so doing. Individuals are personally conducted to their places by the peyote chief, who deliberates briefly before each seating decision. Walking direction in this and all future contexts is clockwise.

All come dressed in their best clothes. The men will wear silk shirts, the right sleeve bearing the sacred altar design and the left a Plains warrior Indian-head design. Abalone or silver water-bird brooches are worn by those fortunate enough to own them. The peyote chief's attire will carry the expected distinction and include, usually, beaded moccasins. Colorful blankets, cushions, and robes will be borne into the meeting by practically everyone as protection against the rigors of the all-night session, which work particular hardship on the children, the aged, the sick, and those sitting on the outer circles shut off from the warmth of the fire. However, tules spread beforehand afford some protection from the cold, damp ground.

The drummer ties four sprigs of sagebrush to the head of the peyote chief's staff, an important ritual object that is held by everyone who sings. A bunch of sagebrush is also bound around the middle of the staff. Lancaster said that the sprigs are "spurs" for the songs. The staff is propped against the wall for the time being since it will not be used until the first eating of peyote when the songs begin. While the staff is being prepared, the chief places the father peyote in the hollow that had been scooped out on the altar. The father peyote is a strikingly large and well-formed button, much prized and carried on the person in a special receptable. For example, Sam Dick used a silver watchcase, his most valued possession. The belief is that "everything goes through the father peyote—all that is said. Therefore he must be there when things start."

The cedarman now takes a handful of cedar, rises, approaches and bends over the moon, waves his hand in a sweeping motion twice from the father peyote toward the right tip of the moon and twice from the left tip of the moon toward the father peyote, and throws the cedar on the fire. This is regular incensing procedure. The peyote chief next passes two unopened sacks of Bull Durham simultaneously to the right and left, and all who wish to smoke roll cigarettes. When the sacks have completed half their circuit, the fire chief begins lighting the cigarettes clockwise with the fire stick, rekindling it from the fire as occasion demands.

When everyone is smoking, the chief offers his first prayer of the evening. The prayers that Lancaster and Dick declaim are of a more or less fixed pattern, differing in length but always revolving around stereotyped phrases that quickly become familiar. The petition for "health, strength, energy, and ambition" is a recurrent formula. Prayers are addressed to God. Christological reference is minimal. Dick said, "We pray to Jesus and Mary the last time around." Lancaster said, "Some peyote doctors use Jesus in the meetings. I use God. God is the key to the car when you want to get in." Peyote is exhorted to work its physical and spiritual healing, to unite all the faithful in a happy and benign brotherhood. Blessings are invoked for all and sundry, including the president of the United

States, the commissioner of Indian Affairs, and the officials of the Native American Church. Except for the allusions to peyote, the prayers could pass muster in any Protestant evangelical religious assembly.

Here is a typical prayer offered by Sam Dick:

> Our Father, God, bless us all. Give us all health, strength, energy, and ambition. Put powers into this peyote so that it can work through our body and mind and remove all our weakness, sickness, troubles in body and mind. Give us a clear mind by the use of it. Give us—brothers, sisters, and children—give us clear minds. Give us good thoughts, give us good ideas by using this peyote which you have created for each and everyone. Let us be friends, brotherly, sisterly, and help one another by using this peyote. Forgive us for our mistakes, remove evil thoughts away from our heads so that we can enjoy this great life which you have given each and everyone so that we be happy. Guide us in the right path and guide on us the light side of this world. Get us away from darkness so that we can come into this tipi way meeting, this American Native Church.
>
> Let the children grow up to be men and women so that they continue the use of peyote and serve you. Our brothers and sisters, the white people, are building a great, fine road so that we can all travel back and forth—(protect us in the right road) so that we be happy. We realize we are your children. I sure am thankful for what you have done so far. Give us life to live—you are the master of all things in this world. All live things have connection in your power. I beg you for all brothers and sisters and children in the United States. Remove their weakness. Give all the peyote-users back east power so that they be happy. Let our prayer reach them so that they can think about peyote-users this far [west] and pray for us. We need their help. I sure am thankful for what you have done in this great life which you have given each and everyone. God. Father. Amen.

Prayers vary in length. It may take twenty or thirty minutes to include everyone who is singled out for special blessing. (At all meetings that I attended the leader included me in his prayers, calling down the usual blessings. Sam Dick once prayed: "O God, bless our brother who has come to us to study our works, so that he be happy. Guide him in the right path. Bless him every place he goes. Clear the road for him. Let him see the good things so that he be happy in this great life which you have given each and everyone.") As a rule the prayers get longer as the meeting wears on. "Each prayer goes a little farther all the time." Perhaps this was due to the general nature of the meeting as it developed under the influence of peyote's chemical properties in the course of the night. Also, the euphoria that characterizes the initial stage of peyote ingestion later gives way to a calm lassitude conducive to contemplation and prayer. Inspiration and direction for praying are drawn from the altar. Declared Sam Dick: "I ask in the moon how to pray. I study every corner for what I say. The prayers look good; they have a good design like flowers. In a meeting you will not be shown all the time. Sometimes it will show you just once."

The prayer finished, the peyote chief places his cigarette butt on the sloping base of the moon immediately behind the father peyote. The drummer puts his butt next to the chief's on the right, the cedarman at the left end of the moon, and all who smoked deposit their butts according to the seating order.

The chief then takes a sprig of sagebrush, eats a little, spits in a fine spray on his hands, and rubs his head, face, body, arms, and legs with a washing gesture. The drummer does likewise. Then the bundle of sagebrush is passed clockwise from the drummer until all have followed suit. The purpose of this rite is to "clear the throat." As Sam Dick said:

> That clears the throat. Just makes you feel good. A year ago when Ida McBride was pretty sick, a meeting was called for her at the wood camp. We were in a hurry and we forgot to perform the sagebrush ceremony. We were weak that night. The songs went down the throat dry. We learned we got to have sagebrush in there. We learned that much that night.

Cedar is thrown on the fire by the cedarman and, as the pungent smoke rises, the peyote chief waves a bucket of peyote tea through it four times. The tea is brewed beforehand by boiling anywhere from thirty-five to fifty peyote buttons, the amount depending upon the number of people expected. The bucket is passed clockwise and anyone may drink from the communal cup that is provided. A sack of peyote is next passed through the incensed fire four times and, after the chief has eaten four buttons, sent around the meeting clockwise. All are enjoined to take no less than four, to eat them in a mood of supplication, and under threat of divine punishment not to spirit any of the sacred discs out of the meeting. Usually the aged and very young children content themselves with just the tea, the tough peyote buttons presenting too great a chewing problem.

From this point one may eat any number of peyote buttons. The average, according to Sam Dick, is seven to twelve for the night. One stopped when one had "had enough." "You can feel when." The chief is expected to eat more than anyone else, and Dick's capacity increased from meeting to meeting. A small sack of buttons rests at the chief's side for the private use of the principal functionaries — the chief and the drummer, and, if he wishes, the cedarman. This auxiliary store is utilized whenever the main sack has stopped in its circuit.

The actual eating of the buttons follows a conventional pattern. They are placed in the hand and regarded fixedly, a silent prayer being offered while the upper body sways slightly back and forth. There follows a series of alternate chewings and spittings into the hand until the softened peyote assumes the shape of a ball. Finally, after more gazing at the bolus, it is swallowed with the accompanying gestures of stroking back the hair, rubbing and patting the chest, and spitting into the hands and rubbing the head. For those who cannot do so themselves, the tough buttons are chewed into a soft pellet by the chief and put into the mouth of the waiting recipient. When this is is done for a sick person, it is accompanied by prayer and inhalations of fanned incense smoke.

The singing is now about to begin, but not before more necessary paraphernalia has been passed through incense smoke the customary four times. First, the chief drummer incenses the drum and three drumsticks — one blackened with charcoal, one with a knob ("marble") on the end, and one a simple drumstick. Then the peyote chief goes through the same motions with his feather fan, staff, and gourd rattle. Twelve eagle feathers, the quills joined by a buckskin thong and tied together with a beaded band, forming a handle, compose the fan. It is used to fan incense smoke upon participants or ritual objects whenever the occasion requires. The rattle consists of a gourd cleaned, filled with "Indian seed beads," and attached to a stick, which runs through it. Sometimes the top of the rattle shaft is decorated with beads, feathers, or horse hair, and the handle is often beaded and trailing a buckskin fringe. Rattles are an indispensable accompaniment to singing. The staff, taken from its obscurity in the rear of the enclosure, is newly decorated with sagebrush and, occasionally, with feathers. Many who attend will have their own feather fans and rattles, which are usually simpler than those of the leaders. A newcomer will receive an eagle feather from the peyote chief at the time of the Midnight Water ceremony. Each individual carries his paraphernalia in a suitcase.

The peyote chief sings first. He kneels while singing, in his left hand the staff and feather fan, in his right the rattle, which he shakes rhythmically. At his right the chief drummer beats the drum. Four songs are sung, and they are of no prescribed nature or order. Next the drummer sings four songs, then it is the cedarman's turn.

The peyote chief drums for both. Clockwise in turn the individuals in the front circle sing four songs, each holding the staff and rattling, each accompanied on the drum by the immediate right-hand neighbor. Sometimes a singer will call for the chief to drum or for someone who is known as a good drummer. Only slight variations differentiate the songs from each other. "All sing a little bit different but the same songs."

By the time the Midnight Water ceremony takes place, one and a half or two circuits have usually been completed. The number of rounds will, of course, depend upon the size of the circle, which in turn is regulated by the number of people present. If the meeting has drawn a large crowd, the drum will not complete more than two rounds during the entire night. Peyote-eating also depends on the drum, or song, circuits. One may eat peyote only after the drum has passed him. At Sam Dick's meetings, which were not too well patronized, peyote was usually eaten four times—because the drum completed four rounds in the course of the night.

Two songs are rendered by the peyote chief just before the Midnight Water ceremony. Again these are of no specifically ordained character; any song will do. The staff and drum, indispensable supports for singing, are brought, the fire chief meanwhile placing four fresh logs on the fire, sweeping the exposed floor within the circle, and heaping the ashes into a crescent parallel to the altar. All lay aside fans and rattles, placing them on silk handkerchiefs, which have been individually brought. The first two songs having been sung, the fire chief brings in the water and places it on the ground between the altar and the entrance. While he kneels next to the bucket, the chief sings two more songs. The songs finished, the fire chief "purifies" the water by wafting (with cupped hands) smoke emanating from the fire freshly incensed by the cedarman. The latter carries a cigarette of Bull Durham and sage rolled by the chief to the fire chief. Whereupon the fire chief, smoking the while, prays over the water, invoking blessings as best he can for all concerned.

The water is sent on its clockwise circuit around the assembly beginning with the person immediately south of the door, a little having first been poured on the ground. After drinking, each individual goes through the familiar procedure of rubbing moistened hands over head, limbs, and body, and then of spraying the paraphernalia arrayed before him. Water is poured on the drumhead by the chief drummer—"he gives the drum a drink."

The altar and the father peyote are watered by the chief. Last to partake of the water is the fire chief.

The peyote chief goes outside and prays to the cardinal directions. While he is gone, the bucket is taken out — clockwise around the altar — and the staff and drum made ready for their use when the chief returns. A period of relaxation ensues when the chief re-enters the meeting place. Many who have taken peyote will go out and attend to their physical needs. However, one must not pass the drum in leaving. Outside there is much retching and vomiting, especially by those who have partaken generously of the peyote. Inside as well during the session there has been a good deal of nausea and regurgitation, and practically all present have come provided with "spit cans." Upon re-entering, everyone is fanned with the purifying incense smoke which the cedarman produces by throwing cedar on the fire.

Visions come around midnight and continue until morning. As Sam Dick says: "You close your eyes and see. You see in the drum. It is like moving pictures. Or if you can read, you look into the fire. You study about yourself, then about others who interest you." Peyote determines the order and content of the revelations.

Singing and peyote-eating continue until dawn. The number of rounds made is, as mentioned, indeterminate, depending upon the number of people present. Two or three is the average. Praying and confessing, which do not interrupt the regular song circuits, constitute an important feature as the early morning hours are passed. Before praying, one requests a cigarette which, in keeping with the ritual, is made of Bull Durham mixed with sage, rolled by the peyote chief and lighted by the fire chief. The deepest emotions are exhibited by the individual engaged in such prayer. Men will weep without restraint. As daylight approaches, singers will be skipped so as to finish at dawn. When the chief, cedarman, fire chief and chief drummer have in turn each sung four songs, the circuits are completed.

The sacred paraphernalia are now assembled, spread out neatly on handkerchiefs. All the feathers the chief had given to those who came empty-handed are returned to the donor. On an altar cloth before the chief are arrayed feathers, staff, rattle, cedar, drum, and drumstick. The fire chief replenishes the fire, shapes the ashes again into a crescent, gathers up all the cigarette butts, and burns them in the fire. Then with a small brush he smooths the floor around the altar, sweeping clockwise from the peyote chief's seat to the door and back again.

With the advent of morning the time for eating the peyote breakfast has come. A woman is sent to fetch the water and food which have been prepared beforehand by the host. She is usually related to the person who has called the meeting, commonly his wife. ("Someone who can pray good," Sam remarked as an added qualification.) She leaves the meeting after making two clockwise circuits, joined by the fire chief as she passes his station and walking out with him. Upon returning, the woman carries the water, the man the three kinds of food—corn, rice, and meat. These are aligned east of the fire—the order is water, corn, rice, meat—between the chief and the woman. While the water and food are being brought, the chief sings four songs. He next rolls a cigarette which is taken to the woman by the fire chief, who lights it with the fire stick. She prays at length for the water and food. Then the drummer rises, goes over to the woman, takes her cigarette, returns to his place, takes four puffs, and then passes it to the chief, who continues smoking it while he prays for the water and food. This is the last prayer but one; the last will be offered at noon.

The cedarman incenses the fire and the woman kneels, stretches out her hands toward the fire four times, drawing smoke to her body and to the food. She spills a little water on the ground at her left and drinks. The water is then passed clockwise from person to person. Corn, rice, and meat are passed in that order.

While drinking and eating are going on, the chief passes staff, rattle, and dismantled drum to his left, and with these are performed gestures that carry a strong suggestion of magic. A man will point with the rattle, draw an imaginary bead, and say: "I'm going to shoot straight. I'm going to shoot rabbit, sage hen, deer." A woman will hold the staff horizontally between her hands, and moving it back and forth as though rubbing a washboard, will say, "I'm going to be a good washerwoman." The drum is sent on its clockwise round, and many, especially the sick, drink from it. While drinking, a man will tap his head with the drumstick and say: "I didn't think good thoughts. Put good ideas into it so I be happy. I feel sick. I worry all the time. Knock it out of my head so that I have good thoughts, feel friendly with people, so I be happy." When staff, rattle, and drum have made the circuit, the chief wraps up his paraphernalia—staff, rattle, feathers, father peyote—and replaces them in the special suitcase. Cigarette butts resting on the crescent altar are gathered and burned by the fire chief.

When all have partaken of food and water, the water woman, who has been the last to eat, and the fire chief walk around the meeting place, pick up the water and food receptacles, circle again and go out. All await their return, and when they appear the meeting is over. The peyote chief says: "Brothers and sisters, you can go out, get fresh air, look around, and after a while come back in."

After the recess, at about nine or ten o'clock, the people file back into the meeting place. A beaded basket has been placed on a silk handkerchief behind the altar and, into this, individual voluntary offerings are dropped. The peyote chief (Sam Dick in this case) exhorts: "Brothers and sisters, if you have a donation, put it here. If not, we appreciate it just the same. If you had no money when you came in, don't be afraid to come in if you need help." An atmosphere of informality prevails. There is much handshaking—with the chief and his assisting functionaries and with anyone else at hand. "Everyone feels good." They laugh. This is the time for reconciliation between personal enemies. "If a man growl at someone a long time ago, he feels sorry about it and makes up. They shake hands before they go out." As the people sit around, lounging and reclining, visionary experiences of the night before are recounted. Sometimes a circle dance will be held around the altar ashes, which have been newly fashioned into the shape of a bird.

Dinner is served at noon. Expense is not spared to make the meal good, even lavish. Before eating, while everyone stands with reverential mien, the peyote chief offers a long prayer. Most of the company leave for home about five o'clock.

WASHO PEYOTISM AND THE PLAINS RITE

Washo peyote ritual conforms closely to the Kiowa-Comanche Plains type.[10] Differences exist but these are not of major significance. And whereas some are traceable to the influence of aboriginal forms, most are in the nature of variations adopted for a variety of reasons by the leaders. Changes in the ritual as it has moved from tribe to tribe are common, the cause usually inhering in the personality of the leader. Under the influence of a bold and resourceful personality like Ben Lancaster, one might reasonably expect a considerable number of changes.

In contrast to widespread practice, women play a prominent role in Washo peyotism. Restrictions against women in other tribes vary from a one-time prohibition against their attendance at meetings, as among the Kiowa, Comanche, Tonkawa, Sauk, and Oto, to a universal ban against their use of eagle feather fans.[11] Only among the Cheyenne and at Taos are women full participants. With the Washo, women are accorded places of honor. They sit in the front row, are provided with feather fans, take their turn singing and rattling, beat the drum, and even become chief drummer. In all other tribes a menstruating women is in no instance allowed to enter a meeting; the Washo permit such a woman to participate provided she ties feathers on her wrists.

Both Ben Lancaster and Sam Dick attempted a rational explanation in justification of this departure from normal practice. Women should enjoy equal rights, they asserted. "Women feed us, they take care of us, they bring water." Probably the reason is to be found in the easy availability of women as converts and the further advantage of having one's wife act as a principal in the rite, a practice followed by both men. The prominence that women achieve under shamanism—in which, as shamans, they occupy equal status with men—should not be overlooked as a possible explanation.

Children, too, are unusually conspicuous as participants in Washo meetings, drinking peyote tea, and on occasion even singing and drumming.

The absence of a fixed order of songs is also a distinguishing feature of Washo peyotism. The four songs used by the Plains peoples—Opening, Midnight, Morning, and Closing—are not established in the Washo ritual. There are two probable reasons for this. For one thing, aboriginal Washo songs are largely amorphous both as to content and occasion. Word texts are unknown and the same song may serve any occasion—hand game, girl's puberty dance, social dance. There is no feeling for specificity in song. That this feeling should be carried over into a new cultural form during its introductory stage is only natural. Devotees were allowed to sing any song they knew, a breach of traditional peyote form. However, this unorthodox approach was felt to be temporary, a necessary expedient until time would permit the learning of established cult songs. Thus a second reason for the absence of fixed song is to be found in the newness of the cult, which had not yet had time to absorb an alien musical tradition.

In this connection there was constant reiteration of the need to learn more about peyote. Both Lancaster and Dick, the latter particularly, disclosed feelings of insecurity concerning their knowledge of the cult. Lancaster was fond of expatiating upon the infinite scope of peyote lore. "No person could say he knows *all* about peyote. The more you go to meetings the deeper the subjects are. There are big empty spaces in the knowledge of every human being. Peyote is endless. You never know all about it. The more you know the more there is to know." Dick's insecurity was revealed in his frank yearnings to revisit Utah, where he had been taken by Lancaster during the apprenticeship period in order to learn more about peyote.[12]

Both men attempted to teach their adherents the peyote songs. Lancaster would hold frequent song sessions during his first year in Nevada, and some did acquire a facility with the new songs. Dick, ambitious for a ritual that would more closely approximate what he had seen in the east, went even further and was in the process of establishing a fixed order of song. Based in large part on what he remembered from brief contact with eastern peyotists, the songs were understandably of indeterminate form. But that he was progressing toward some fixity in song order and content was evident in the firmer crystallization of musical form in the 1939 meetings as compared with those of 1938. By the summer of 1939 a "Water Bird Song" and a "Morning Song" had become stabilized in the repertoire of Dick's sessions. There was every likelihood that as he continued to lead the cult, he would develop the full four-song fixed cycle, which, though different from the orthodox eastern variety, would yet bear interesting resemblances to it and would constitute an arresting example of cultural mutation.

Sam Dick's intense desire to fashion a ritual based on eastern models and his progressive realization of this ideal are manifest in still another rite. The blowing of an eagle-humerus whistle is a conventional part of the Midnight and Morning Water calls and of the peyote chief's midnight prayers to the cardinal directions. Naturally the whistle becomes an important item in the sacred paraphernalia, and it is ritually displayed near the altar. Hitherto the whistle and the ceremonialism associated with it have played no part in Washo peyotism. But Dick knew of them, and in August 1939 spoke of their use with warm approval. There can be little doubt that in time he will introduce it into his gatherings. Moreover, there is an ancient precedent for whistle-blowing in shamanistic practice;

whether this will serve as a deterrent rather than as a sanction to a renegade shaman like Sam Dick one cannot know.

There are other deviations from the Plains ritual. Holding meetings in circular canvas enclosures is mentioned only for early Kiowa gatherings.[13] The tipi is known to the Washo only by hearsay, and the erection of one would have been no easy task. Conversely, to rig a canvas enclosure is a simple matter. However, Lancaster and Dick sometimes called their gatherings "Tipi Way meetings."

The use of sage is a local specialization. Ground sage is mixed with tobacco in rolling the cigarettes smoked at the meeting, a unique phenomenon not found in the literature for any other tribe.[14] Cornhusks are used in the Plains for cigarette wrappings; the Washo use wheat-straw papers. Sage is not spread for members to sit on during the meeting. The sage used for cigarettes, chewing, and body rubbing at the beginning of the session is not the *Artemisia tridentata* found locally but a sage imported from Texas.

Uncommon if not unique elements occur in the peyote paraphernalia of the Washo. Except for newcomers, each individual possesses a gourd rattle which he brings to the meetings and which he may use during the entire performance. Elsewhere, as among the Delaware, rattles individually owned may not be used until after midnight.[15] In some cases, rattles are decorated with small features bound to the top of the shaft; customarily in the Plains, horsehair is used. Not mentioned elsewhere is the rite of "magical" gesturing with the peyote chief's staff and rattle when they are passed from hand to hand at the termination of the meeting—the men sighting as with a rifle, the women imitating the movements of domestic tasks, and accompanying their actions with appropriate words. A rare feature is that of drinking the water out of the dismantled drum.

Tin cans used for vomiting and spitting into are brought by practically every individual, a practice not reported for other tribes. The belief is that peyote is a spiritual purgative, that the nausea expels all meanness from the individual. "A mean man or woman will talk out or cry out meanness. They will growl, confess to everybody where they have been mean. They will spill it right there. Drunkenness the same way. They will spill the load in the can any time during the meeting."

Although a part of the Mexican peyote ritual,[16] dancing is not found in the classical Plains rite. It was not a regular feature of Washo meetings, taking place only in answer to a spontaneous impulse after the formal rituals were concluded. Its roots may be found perhaps in the old tribal pattern, which calls for a dance at any "big time." In the serenity and well-being of the morning after, when all are feeling "happy" and "brotherly," the general mood is one that might quickly lead to dancing.

Ben Lancaster's personality is the likely explanation for some further departures from the Plains norm. The pressure, tacit and overt, upon members to make a contribution at every meeting through the morning ceremony of filing past the beaded basket and depositing as much as one could afford, is a violation of the freewill principle of peyotism and attributable to his mercenary appetite. Moreover, for peyote consumed outside regular meetings he exacted the stiff charge of ten cents a button. (According to La Barre, "The price of peyote from dealers in Laredo, who supply most of the Northern Plains and Great Basin users, is from $2.50 to $5.00 a thousand buttons.") Whereas the motivation of personal gain is by no means unique among peyote leaders, it nowhere achieves the exaggerated emphasis found with Lancaster. (La Barre and Petrullo report that Jack Wilson and his Quapaw and Delaware followers made money from peyote. Leo Okio and Lone Bear, among the Northern Paiute and Washo, respectively, were also mercenary. However, of all the tribes only the Oto pass around a vessel in the morning for a "free-will offering.") As Stewart suggests, Lancaster's arbitrary edicts as to who might attend his gatherings are best understood in terms of personal gain.[17] Lone Bear and certain Gosiute Indians were not allowed to come. When Carnegie Smokey visited Lancaster in Oklahoma, he was forbidden to go to meetings. Lancaster did not want his converts to come into contact with anyone who might acquaint them with the freewill character of other meetings. And in order to carry out his pecuniary ends, he did not hesitate to break some of peyote's strongest traditions.

However, in seeking an explanation for the materialism of Washo peyote leaders, one is at once reminded of the powerful emphasis on monetary gain found in the shamanistic complex. To be mulcted by a religious leader was no novelty for the Washo. In shamanism one undeviatingly paid before curing—and heavily. In peyote, at least, there was a nominal voluntarism with respect to payment, which to many a Washo accustomed to rigid obligation in such matters must have appeared a lenient dispensation.

The Washo structure of belief differs only in minor details from prevailing Plains peyote theology. Conceiving of a meeting with its unvarying clockwise procedures as a machine whose inexorable movements one dare not interrupt, seems to be a unique theological excrescence. Equally singular are the concepts of the fan as God's intermediary during creation and as an agent winging prayers Godward, and of the moon altar as a representation of the creating deity. The lessened emphasis upon Christological elements is also a distinguishing characteristic, although Mescalero peyotism also lacked evidence of Christian influence.[18]

Beliefs about witchcraft, so potent a force in Washo culture, have intruded into the peyote complex. This strikes one as somewhat strange since, according to orthodox doctrine, peyote abolishes sorcery. Significantly, it is Sam Dick who clings to the old outlook. A former shaman, he evidently finds it no easy matter to adjust to a world that is not swarming with potential malevolence. This same difficulty colors the devotion of a considerable proportion of the people. But Ben Lancaster and his devotees in open assembly strenuously deny that songs have power, that there are good songs and bad songs—a dualism that stems from the old ideology. Some Washo hold that bad songs cause one to see blood and exrements in peyote visions and that these represent sickness sent by people practicing witchcraft at the meeting. (The Mescalero Apache are the classical case of a tribe that practices witchcraft at peyote meetings.)[19] That "bad" visions are associated with witchcraft happens to be the belief of Sam Dick and his coterie of followers, although since strife has arisen because of suspected practice, no believer will admit to it.

Two forces, then, made for the differences that exist between Washo and Kiowa-Comanche theology and ritual. One was the character of the indigenous culture that intruded itself subtly in a variety of forms. The second was the personality of the leaders, especially Ben Lancaster, who out of predilection and opportunism shaped the cult in accordance with personal desires.

INTRODUCTION OF PEYOTE TO THE WASHO

Peyote was not unknown to the Washo at the time of its successful introduction by Ben Lancaster in the fall of 1936. From their Northern Paiute neighbors they had heard of the activities of Leo Okio, who had won a considerable number of adherents to peyote in the course of a series of meetings held at Nixon, Fallon, and Schurz (Nevada) during the latter part of 1929 and the early months of 1930. Others had come in contact with peyote in more distant parts. Thus Ray Fillmore, young leader among the Washo, had seen "the boys boil peyote and drink it like beer" while a student at Bacone College, Oklahoma, from 1930 to 1933.

Lone Bear,[20] a Uintah Ute who had learned the practice of the cult many years before by attending numerous meetings in the Plains and eastern Great Basin, had appeared among the people in 1932 and had conducted peyote meetings that were well attended. He lived with Sam Dick, and it was at this time that the latter first became attracted to peyote, learning its songs and the technique of tying and beating a drum. However, due to a penchant for liquor, which frequently put him in jail for drunkenness, Lone Bear suffered a swift decline in public esteem. He played no part in the renaissance of the cult which was soon to follow. In fact, he was forbidden by Lancaster to attend meetings. His success, brief as it was, does suggest that circumstances favored the introduction of peyote. Had Lone Bear been more prudent, resourceful, vigorous, the flowering of the new religion might have begun in 1932.

It was in the fall of 1936 that Ben Lancaster appeared on the scene, and in him were to be found those personal qualities which, when joined to the prevailing social conditions, resulted in a wide acceptance of peyote. Lancaster[21] was a native Washo who had been away from the tribe for twenty years. During that time he had knocked about in many parts of the country, had worked at numerous savory and unsavory jobs, brushing shoulders with Indians and whites of all kinds and in all circumstances. Lancaster was keen witted to begin with, and his experiences had served to widen his cultural horizon, enhance his capacity for getting along with people, and sharpen his sense of opportunism.

Since he looms so large in the growth and spread of peyote among the Washo, Lancaster's life story has a special pertinence. He was born about 1880 near Mountain House, an old stagecoach station in west-central Nevada near the California border and the location of a Washo settlement. His early years were spent in the familiar pattern—playing and idling in various Carson Valley Indian settlements, a minimum of schooling at the Agency school, working seasonally as a ranch hand, haying, herding. There was also the customary addiction to liquor.

Lancaster, like any Washo, had the opportunity of coming into frequent contact with whites. The Washo are not reservation Indians, and living on the fringes of white settlements, working as domestics and ranch hands in white establishments, as well as acting as guides and museum specimens at Lake Tahoe—traditional Washo summering territory—frequent association with whites is not uncommon. Lancaster, moreover, could pass for a white—his father, whose identity is not known, is said to have been a white man. It was not surprising, then, that after a time he left his own people and "crossed" into the world of the whites. He became a bartender and professional gambler. Along the waterfront in San Francisco, where he was known as "Blackie," he learned to cook opium. Whether from a restless disposition or from occupational hazards, he traveled about extensively, working at a variety of jobs. During the years 1907 to 1919 we find him prospecting in Nevada, doing odd jobs in Utah and South Dakota, "busting bronchos" in Omaha, bootlegging in Hot Springs, Arkansas.

It was while employed as a farmhand near Clinton, Oklahoma, in 1921 that Lancaster had his first experience with peyote. He attended a Cheyenne peyote meeting, and for the next ten years spent Christmas with his Cheyenne friends. He now became a vendor of "Indian" medicine. He let his hair grow long, wore the Plains feather headdress and beaded buckskin clothes, traveled "all over the United States" selling "Chief Grey Horse's Indian Herbs—a Natural Laxative." (When he came back to the Washo, he still had a few bottles left. These he sold to his followers at one dollar per bottle.) With his ability to speak and to harangue, developed through the years of multifarious fortune, combined with an arresting presence, he must have been a persuasive salesman indeed. With the depression, however, the bottom dropped out of the medicine market, and he was again forced to drift from one precarious job to another.

Apparently it was during these lean days that Lancaster resolved to bring peyote to the Washo. After an initial period of skepticism, during which he attended a number of meetings in different tribes, he became a firm peyotist. "I thought peyote a lot of foolishness at first," he declared. "I didn't know how much it could mean to people. I had a tough time for two years—I was an outcast—and then I saw the light."

The conversion experience itself is of interest.

I was no good. I had done a lot of wrong things because I was traveling alone. I got away from here alone. I learned lots of things. I was a gambler, miner, bootlegger, hijacker. I went through everything—that low stuff. A man can't help it—I starved once in a while. I got into mischief and did things I shouldn't do—all the bad things in this world. I couldn't make headway anywhere. I was running down all the time. I couldn't make money anywhere. I was looking for something good in my travels.

I was walking down the road in a reservation somewhere in Oklahoma. Someone invited me for dinner. There was a meeting going on. The boys asked me to sing a song. But I had no songs. I knew one old Indian doctor song that I learned in Smith Valley [Northern Paiute territory]. It sounded funny. I had a tough time all night. I threw up.

Next morning at quitting time, everything came out on me. I had to face the music. But I couldn't face it then. I left the meeting and walked a little way to the feed corral where a cow, a horse, and a rooster were. It was a white rooster. The horse and cow were eating hay, and while eating, the horse whispered, "There's Ben." I looked back every once in a while to see if anyone noticed me. Pretty soon the rooster jumped on the fence and flapped his wings. He crowed, "A-ha, now you've got it." My hair stood up. I was ashamed and ran back to the peyote corral. I said to myself: Why does that rooster know me? When I got back, it sounded as though the boys were laughing at me, but it was only the sound of my own voice in my head. After a while I felt better.

Although Lancaster had determined to return to his people with peyote as early as 1930, it was not until October 1936 that he appeared in western Nevada. The intervening period may have been one of preparation. He began to conduct meetings himself—at Randlett, Utah, for the Utes, at Ibapah for the Gosiutes. It may have been that he wanted to perfect his technique as ritual leader before undertaking his missionary task.[22] Perhaps he was detained in the east by his wife, a white woman who ran a restaurant in Lawton, Oklahoma. (Carnegie Smokey, who subsequently traveled east to visit Lancaster, told me of this woman—Sylvia Grey Horse. Lancaster never mentioned her. Being married to another woman at the time, he had good reason not to.) In any case, in the fall of 1936 he arrived in Minden. He stayed at the house of Susie and Sam Dick, mother and son ("aunt" and "cousin" to Lancaster), and spent a brief period in Gardnerville, geographic center of Washo territory, putting himself on display and renewing old friendships with white townsfolk and Indians.

Soon he embarked upon his self-appointed mission. His first convert was Sam Dick, who must have struck him as an especially valuable ally. For one thing, because of past association with Lone Bear, Sam Dick was familiar with peyote practice; he knew songs, he could tie and beat the drum. Then family kinship provided a bond, which a strong character like Lancaster could be depended upon to exploit to the hilt. Dick would become his subservient tool. But most important Dick was a practicing shaman, and to win a practitioner of the old religion to peyote would be a victory of the utmost importance for the new cult. Such a victory would boldly challenge the power of the shaman, so pervasive in traditional Washo culture. It might even undermine confidence in the efficacy of shamanism itself. In a word, it would endow the new cult with enormous prestige.

Sam Dick's conversion was a dramatic and, for him, emotionally overwhelming experience. Because it reveals the interplay of characters—one worldly and acculturated, the other unsophisticated and still immersed in traditional lore—because we are afforded an insight into peyote theology, and because of the vivid illustration of the nexus between the old and the new, shamanism and peyote, the conversion experience as narrated by Dick bears retelling.

> Ben came and lived with my mother, who was a cousin-sister to his mother. He said nothing about peyote. I asked him about it. I wasn't feeling too well. Dust from the hayfield made me short-winded all the time. I quit my job and worked around Minden doing handy work—gardening, painting, doing odd jobs. I told him about Lone Bear's peyote medicine. I had also heard about peyote from Harry Jim. Lone Bear had brought in some and I had eaten one or two once in a while and had felt better. After I mentioned it a lot, Ben finally let on that he knew about peyote.
>
> That night I saw that Ben had six sacks of peyote. Ben asked me if I knew anything about songs. Lone Bear had brought in songs from Oklahoma and we used to sing together. That night Ben and I sat and ate peyote. Ben prayed for the peyote and I prayed a little while. I ate twenty-four—small ones. I made six rounds, eating four each round. We stayed up till twelve. I felt dizzy the next morning. I felt drunk. But it wasn't the peyote, although I thought it was. It was just stirring up what I'd been drinking. I threw up a great deal. After that I didn't even like the looks of liquor. When I would see it in a saloon or a store, it would make me sick, give me a headache. Then I decided to drink no more. I haven't touched it since.
>
> A week later, I was working near Mountain House cutting wood in Pine Nut Range. Ben came out to visit me. In the afternoon we walked a little way from the wood camp. Looking over a hill, Ben said he saw two coyotes, heard them howling. I didn't see them. But coming over the ridge, I heard lots of coyotes howling all around, humming close. One of them sounded like a man. Grey Horse said, "You see those coyotes, as big as horses?" "No," I said, "I don't see them." But I heard them. [This is the familiar Great Basin visionary experience in which the vision is heard, not seen.] They were running [across] behind the pine nut trees making a big noise. He told me, "Brother, if I hadn't come here, perhaps the coyotes would have eaten you up." Coyotes were a disease of Indian doctoring coming close to me. I could see the design of coyotes. The disease came crowding in on me like hard feelings. [Here, Dick

clutched his chest with both hands.] I was left weak, down. My eyes were dim. Ben said, "Brother, I'm going to fix you up tonight so that you'll be happy."

That night he tied the drum and cooked the medicine. We sang all night. I drank some and chewed some. I ate lots of it. Next morning Grey Horse told me, "You've got your doctor outfit there. It's no good. It hunts disease for you and loads you up. If you make up your mind to throw it away, I give you my life, peyote. I know what peyote has done for me. You're going to feel better. You're going to feel happy. Now when you go out to hunt deer, you don't even see them—even if they stand in an open place. This peyote is going to clean your body. Whenever you will go out to hunt, you will see. Your eyes are going to be clear. You will see any place."

In the morning he said to me, "Throw away your Indian doctor outfit. It does you no good. I'm going to give you something better than that." That day about ten o'clock, I brought everything out in a small suitcase. I made up my mind to get rid of it. It was just as though my whole life was going to be destroyed. I started to cry. Grey Horse said, "Brother, don't cry for a bad thing; cry for a good thing!" So we went up the hill a little way, dug a large rock out of the ground, put the suitcase in the hole, mashed it down, and covered it with dust. [Dick knows where the paraphernalia are buried.] Then I prayed, "Forget about me. I forget about you. Go to dust. I'm going to use peyote—the right way." Grey Horse said, "Remember, brother, pray. You will never get into trouble so long as you are right. Indian doctor way is no good. The Indian doctor gets into a fight, is bumped off, killed once in a while. But this is the right thing. Stay on the right road. You will always feel happy, have lots of friends. Now your life is changed to the good way. You change your mind to the good way not to drink any more." He gave me a father peyote. It is what the machine runs with. That is our life—what the Creator made in our body.

The "machine" is the peyote meeting as a whole—the conception that the whole ceremony is a powerful machine running with inexorable drive and that nothing may be allowed to interfere with its course save those fixed prescribed periods during which the machine is stopped.

From then on Sam Dick was a passionate devotee of peyote. He became Lancaster's close companion and chief assistant and, in time, under Lancaster's tutelage learned to conduct meetings himself.

Then I attended Grey Horse's meetings all the time. I was learning to run meetings then. Grey Horse knew it. He wanted me to. He said, "Brother, let us go back east, get in meeting, get in tipi over there, learn some more." So we went back east. We were there [White Rocks, Utah] about a week. When we came back, I ran a meeting every once in a while. Twice Ben was present at these meetings. He said I was all right.

The diffusion of peyote through Washo and neighboring territory now begins. It was by no means confined to the Washo. Lancaster carried the doctrine to the Northern Paiute at Pyramid Lake and to the Southern Paiute. In time, meetings were held at Schurz, Wellington, Yerington, Fallon, Mono Lake, Bridgeport, and Nixon—all outside Washo territory. The distribution of these cult foci was random, Lancaster undertaking their establishment and organization as the demand arose. And the demand during the early months of his proselytizing was heavy: Fourteen communities in all witnessed the introduction of peyote. Neither was there any necessary logic in the places where meetings were held. One week a meeting might take place in Schurz, the next week in Coleville, the next in Fallon. Sometimes Lancaster would remain in a community for as long a period as the establishment of a strong peyote nucleus required. But for the most part he roamed extensively throughout the western Nevada territory occupied by the Washo and their Shoshonean-speaking neighbors without stopping too long in any one place.

There was also a good deal of traveling by lay peyotists to meetings held in other communities. The most zealous would sometimes travel hundreds of miles. The attraction may have been Lancaster, who, besides exerting a fanatical hold on his followers, always conducted the best meetings. In time, his disciples became leaders qualified to preside at meetings, but none approximated the master's proficiency or influence.

Washo, Northern Paiute, and Southern Paiute came together freely and amicably at the meetings. Naturally a gathering held at Fallon, in the geographic center of Northern Paiute territory, would be attended by a predominantly Northern Paiute group. But the meetings at Coleville, on the Washo–Southern Paiute boundary, would draw an equal number of individuals from the physically contiguous peoples. That such easy intertribal mingling should have taken place is not surprising in view of the increased intercourse which has attended the acculturation process. Although aboriginally the Washo and their Paiute neighbors were mutually suspicious and hostile, in more recent times they have come together through such means as intermarriage, attendance at the Agency School, and living in contact outside the white communities where they found employment.

Meetings were always conducted in English, the lingua franca which all would understand. Lancaster's command of English was, to say the least, fluent, although his malapropisms were classics. It was obvious that he exhibited this fluency as an additional symbol of prestige with which to impress his adherents. Sam Dick's English improved rapidly when he began to study peyote. Laymen, however, would pray and confess in their native tongue.

Peyote's career among the Washo was fitful. It spread rapidly from the outset, winning many converts from November 1936 through the whole of the following year. The peak of success was reached in 1938. But in the fall of that year a decline set in which saw the great majority of Washo leave the cult. In the summer of 1939 peyote could claim very few members of the tribe, and since that time, according to reports received,[23] there has been no recovery. For the present, the status of peyote seems to be stabilized on a weak and uncertain level.[24]

The history of peyote in Dresslerville will serve to illustrate the progress of the cult among the Washo. Dresslerville is a village occupied solely by Washo located about five miles from Gardner-ville. Unique in its homogeneity and in its relative isolation from white and non–Washo Indian contact, it constitutes a tribal enclave, where the residual aboriginal forms are still fulfilled in comparative freedom and where the intratribal tensions implicit in the process of culture change can be clearly observed.

Meetings were held in Dresslerville very soon after Lancaster's arrival—late in November 1936—and were initially greeted with an enthusiastic response. The first gatherings were held in the home of Willie Smokey, Tribal Council representative and a noteworthy leader of the people, who was sick at the time.[25] Lancaster would pack as many as fifty people into the house; and soon, because of constricted quarters, was forced to move the meetings outdoors, where a canvas enclosure was erected capable of accommodating all who wished to attend. Sessions now attracted in the neighborhood of one hundred individuals.

The people came for a variety of reasons—the customary traditional reasons for taking peyote. (An extended discussion of the manifest appeal of peyote appears later.) Sickness constituted a primary cause for calling a meeting, normally held in the home of the patient. Protection from sickness, liberation from liquor, and moral guidance are other important benefits which peyote was said to confer. One also often heard that peyote will take away the power of the shamans. Whatever the attractions and motivations, the people paid generously for the privilege of partaking ritually of the cherished cactus. And although donations were received as voluntary offerings, Lancaster, doubtless with skillful suasion, managed to net a handsome return. It was not unusual for him to collect seventy-five dollars at a meeting.

Not surprisingly the Smokey family became first prominent and later dominant among Dresslerville peyotists. Willie Smokey's illness had provided the reason for the first meeting. He was looked upon as a leader in the tribe. The family was well established financially and was highly esteemed by both Indians and whites. They showered attention upon Lancaster, not sparing their material substance at all. Moreover, they attended every meeting which the pampered cult leader conducted, not only in Dresslerville but in other settlements no matter how distant. Other families related to the Smokeys were moved to join—a clearly discernible phenomenon of affiliation with the cult through kinship. Their devotion was profound and their belief in the blessed efficacy of peyote so unwavering that even after their estrangement from the cult they had nothing but good to say in its behalf.

Nearly every Indian in Dresslerville and the immediate vicinity tried peyote. Even the shamans came to the meetings, although Mike Dick refused to eat peyote because "my dream told me not to." Fewer however was the number of actual converts to the cult, and it is a mistake to assume that the acceptance of peyote was anything in the nature of a mass-conversion phenomenon. Stewart has estimated that of the 281 Indians living in Douglas County, of which Dresslerville is the native center, 81 could be counted as members. Whereas this constitutes a greater ratio of affiliates to nonaffiliates than that found in any other western Nevada community, the preponderant majority remained outside the fold.[26]

If Dresslerville is an example of the progress of peyote among the Washo, no less are the Smokeys the bellwether of the cult in Dresslerville. This family became disaffected a little more than a year after Lancaster's arrival. By the beginning of 1938 the tide was in full ebb. There was a rapid falling away of members. At the year's end only one family in the community was attending meetings, and it had been several months since any meeting had been conducted in the village itself. Indeed, Lancaster had refused to officiate in Dresslerville because of the bitter factionalism engendered by the cult.

A powerful, aggressive opposition was unquestionably the most potent factor in the disintegration of the Dresslerville peyote

stronghold. The antagonists had united under a banner that
represented a number of formidable interests. There were the
shamans, who saw their authority, to say nothing of their livelihood,
threatened. There were the rivals of Willie Smokey, temporal antagonists of long-standing. There were those who were jealous of Lancaster and those who were *con* because others were *pro*—all the shabby
aggressions of inbred community relationships that the introduction
of peyote had whipped to the surface. Leaders of the opposition had
never been willing to tolerate peyote. True, they had sat in at early
meetings, but they had remained unconverted. They had come to
scoff and they remained to scoff—and condemn. Neither had there
been much chance of their conversion, for their antagonism was
rooted in psychological and political factors whose springs were to
be found deep in antecedent frustrations and conflicts.

The immediate cause of the decline, however, was a series of
conflicts among the peyotists themselves. These conflicts had as
their chief characters Sam Dick, the Smokey family, and Ben Lancaster. Late in 1938 Lancaster left Nevada for Texas, where he was
to gather peyote and join his white wife, who apparently made
periodic demands for husbandly attention. Trouble broke out soon
enough. Willie Smokey's sickness provided the spark that set off
what must have been long-smoldering intracult jealousies and
hatreds.[27] A meeting was called by Smokey's daughter, Frieda. It
was held in Coleville with Sam Dick and Mary Creek, Lancaster's
Northern Paiute wife from Schurz, the chief officiants.[28] But Frieda
Smokey Wyatt disapproved of Sam Dick's methods. There were
accusations and counteraccusations. She, and with her the whole
Smokey clan, complained that Dick had failed to pray for Willie
Smokey, that he had insulted the family, that his presiding was
unorthodox, that the meeting was "not held the way Ben runs it."
Dick charged that she was jealous because she wanted to officiate.
From this quarrel, a factional split resulted. The Smokeys assumed
leadership of the stronger faction—most of the Dresslerville
peyotists—which resolved to attend no more meetings over which
Dick might preside. A strong hand at this point might have settled
the differences. Both sides to the dispute eagerly awaited
Lancaster's return expecting vindication. But he was not to be back
until the spring, and by then the rift was wider than ever.

Ultimately, neither faction obtained the comfort confidently
anticipated from Lancaster's return. At a meeting called shortly

after the chief's arrival, the Smokeys again had occasion to feel humiliated. Thoroughly dissatisfied, they stopped attending public meetings altogether. Henceforth their peyote activities were confined to the immediate family—occasional gatherings with the members eating peyote, singing, and praying. Neither did Sam Dick win Lancaster's favor. Veiled accusations that Dick was employing sorcery in his peyote meetings began to be heard, charges that seem to have originated with Lancaster. Deeply disturbed, Dick shifted his residence to Coleville, thirty miles south of Minden, where a mixed community of Washo and Southern Paiutes live. Henceforth he conducted meetings in Coleville and, farther south, in the Southern Paiute settlement at Mono Lake. In Dresslerville and among a majority of Washo, peyotists and nonpeyotists alike, he was discredited and increasingly referred to as a trouble maker.

In time, Lancaster too found it expedient to shift the main scene of his endeavors. Dresslerville had become a battleground for contending peyote factions. Moreover, during his absence in Texas, the antipeyote opposition had become consolidated and threatened to make serious trouble. Lancaster's personal behavior did nothing to conciliate his antagonists. They pointed to the cavalier dismissal of his wife, Mary Creek, as evidence of his rascality. Soon Dresslerville ceased to be the cult center in Nevada, the Fallon Town colony taking its place. Lancaster was seen less and less in Washo country. In due time he had a new wife, Louise Byers, a Shoshoni living in Fallon related to Jim Street. The latter became Sam Dick's successor as Lancaster's chief assistant.

It is significant that Lancaster's removal from the Washo was accompanied by no bitterness or rancor on the part of his peyote converts. Even from those who received inconsiderate treatment at his hands no harsh judgments were heard, and both the Sam Dick and the Smokey factions united in speaking appreciatively, even reverently, of their erstwhile leader. There was plenty of feeling between the disputing groups but none was directed toward Lancaster. If one heard criticism and condemnation, it was always from one of the militant antipeyotists.

We have traced the history of peyote in Dresslerville, illustrating as it does the forces which shaped the career of the cult among the Washo. There were other meeting places. Coleville has already been mentioned. The home of Sam Dick and his most faithful followers, it became the principal focus of the cult after the collapse at Dresslerville. Woodfords and Carson City were also the scenes of ritual gatherings. During the summer, occasional meetings were held at Lake Tahoe, where a goodly number of Washo still repair in keeping with aboriginal custom. Four Washo communities—Dresslerville, Carson City, Woodfords, Coleville—yielded 131 peyotists out of a total population of 563.[29] Coleville, as mentioned earlier, is not a wholly Washo community. There is probably an equal number of Washo and Northern Paiute. Lake Tahoe is not counted a community since it holds a summer transient population drawn from other permanent settlements.

Correspondence, dated 1 April 1941, with the Carson Indian Agency yields the information that there have been few changes since the summer of 1939. No meetings have been held in Dresslerville or in any other Washo settlement. Coleville, with its marginal Washo-Southern Paiute community, is, however, the scene of a strong peyote colony. Sam Dick is still leader there. It is interesting that among some of the former Dresslerville devotees, like the Smokeys, belief in peyote remains strong.

Most arresting, however, is the reported fading of Lancaster's star among the tribesmen. "Faith in Ben Lancaster is completely gone." He is located in the Fallon area, is still married to Louise Byers, still undertakes his annual excursion to Oklahoma and Texas. In western Nevada beyond Washo boundaries, his influence has apparently suffered no diminution. The correspondence cites this dramatic evidence of his sway over the people.

> Our visit was made to the home of a boy of 20 who has a very far advanced case of tuberculosis. He refused any discussion of going to a sanatorium for care because Grey Horse was responsible for his well-being and would not fail. During the conversation he told us to see Ben and find out what he said about the suggested plan of hospitalization. At one time in reference to Ben he said, "You ask God what to do" (correspondence 1 April 1941, Carson Indian Agency, Stewart, Nevada).

Through his compelling personality Lancaster obviously remains "the outstanding leader for the whole area." Where he has unhindered access, the cult flourishes. The number of followers among the Paiutes in the Yerington, Stillwater, and Bridgeport areas has increased. But among the Washo, where Lancaster cannot freely come and go, the cult languishes.

SOCIAL CONSEQUENCES OF THE INTRODUCTION OF PEYOTISM

By the summer of 1939 the divisive influence of peyote had manifested itself in a series of domestic crises. Between members of the tribe violent hatreds were given free expression and bitter conflicts erupted. From a knowledge of these rather than from any statistical charts we can see how profound a disturbance in tribal life had been created by the introduction of peyote. Ray Fillmore, in speaking of this aspect of the cult remarked, "They're afraid of each other all around." This statement epitomizes an attitude that had bitten deeply into the tribe since the advent of peyote.

Peyote caused Frieda Wyatt to leave her husband, Evan. The daughter of Willie Smokey and, like him, an enthusiastic convert, she even had aspirations to become a leader. For weeks at a time she would leave her husband and children in order to attend meetings—in Fallon, in Coleville. Evan Wyatt, no peyotist himself, would cook for the children and take care of the house. His wife was suspected of having sexual relations with cult members in Coleville. Ray Fillmore explained that this was the direct result of peyote meeting ritual.

> You see your own mate at meetings in a vision. Peyote shows you if your mate is not the right one for you. Also it shows you who your proper mate is. That's the one you take. Peyote broke up families like this the first year. That's why Frieda left Evan.

To make matters worse, Willie Smokey sided with his daughter. "He told Evan that he was the head man in the family and that no one but he should tell his daughter what to do." When Frieda Wyatt quarreled with Sam Dick, she returned to her family in Dresslerville. But her relations with her husband did not improve. Even after the entire family had repudiated Lancaster and withdrawn formally from the cult, peyote continued to be a source of contention. Evan Wyatt, irreconcilable still, did not join the family in its private peyote devotions. In fact, he was "gathering evidence against peyote." This so infuriated his wife that one day she seized the papers and threw them into the fire.

The James family, which was reputed to be the most prosperous in the tribe, was riven with conflicts over peyote. Ben James ran a stable of horses at Lake Tahoe, owned the largest house in Dresslerville, and had money. His sons Earl and Roma were also well off financially. Extreme hostility characterized the relationships between members of this privileged family. In the fall of 1938 Ben James, family head and about seventy years old, had fallen seriously ill. He lay abed in his house at Dresslerville until December, and although his wife, Maggie, was living in the neighborhood, she did not once visit him. A staunch peyotist herself, she would have nothing to do with her nonpeyotist husband. Neither would three of her children, Enie, Don, and Roy, all devotees of the cult, have any contact with their father. But one day when the old man was desperately sick, Maggie James and the three children were prevailed upon by Enie's daughter, Mabel, and her husband, Ray Fillmore, to pay a visit. They immediately wanted to call a peyote meeting for the sick man, and were only prevented from doing so by the arrival of two more sons, Earl, who came from Bridgeport, California, and Roma. "Earl is the smartest of the lot. Roma was sore. They all cried and everything. They decided to try the white doctor." Ben James was taken to San Francisco, was operated on successfully, and recovered. Even after this crisis, family relations were not improved. Maggie, Enie, Don, and Ray firmly believed it was their prayers at the meetings that saved Ben James's life, and the case is publicly cited as a testimonial proving the healing power of peyote. Ray Fillmore said, "No matter what happens, if a person comes out alive they claim they did it."

Enie Cornbread, Ben James's daughter, is a fanatical peyotist. After her daughter, Mabel Fillmore, had undergone an operation, she refused to see her because she had been unwilling to eat peyote. "She didn't care if her daughter died. She didn't come to her for a whole year." Enie Cornbread and her husband, also a user, neglect and punish their two sons, Donald and Gillis, aged sixteen and fourteen, for not taking peyote. "Their father never takes them to town because they don't eat peyote. Donald has gone bad because of neglect. He was forced to go live with his grandfather, Bill Cornbread."[30] Bill Cornbread is the oldest living Washo. He is reputed to be a hundred years old, completely deaf and almost blind, hardly capable of taking care of a sixteen-year-old boy.

Bad blood arose among the James brothers. Don and Roy James, the peyotists, would have nothing to do with Earl and Roma James, nonpeyotists. Even between Don and Roy there was ill feeling after the latter got drunk and thus violated the antiliquor injunction of the cult. One informant said, "Don has hated Roy ever since."

The split caused by peyote was, of course, felt throughout the tribe. Dresslerville was the hub of the struggle between the champions and the enemies of the movement. The antagonists organized themselves into a militant opposition determined to expel peyote from the community. Under the leadership of Steve Earl, Joe Ryder, John Mack, and Martinez Kyser,[31] they circulated a petition stating their grievances and demands. Seventy-five people signed it (the petition, on record at the Agency, bears the date 20 April 1937). When by their silence the authorities indicated that they desired to remain aloof from the conflict, meetings were invaded and broken up by mobs of antipeyotists liberally fortified with liquor. Gradually this technique came to be adopted throughout Carson Valley. Little wonder that both Ben Lancaster and Sam Dick were compelled to hold meetings far beyond the reach of the irate Washo opposition.

The scars left by the conflict were deep. Whereas according to an abundance of testimony there had been, as one informant put it, "no splits until peyote," sullen hatreds and deep-seated suspicions were left in the cult's wake (see "Antecedent Conflicts," next chapter. Sam Dick seemed to become a special object of reproach. Even when there was an inclination to be lenient with Lancaster, condemnation of Dick was unsparing. The chief accusation against him was that he was splitting the tribe into contending factions. It was also said that he was so uncompromising in his devotion to the new religion that he would have nothing to do with nonpeyotists. One tolerant informant said, "He's all right, but he hates people who don't use it." This seemed to many intolerably high-handed. Ray Fillmore and Willie Jim both asserted that Sam Dick snubbed them.

Sam Dick for his part had his own explanation. One morning he complained that he felt depressed. In order to ease his sadness, he had built a moon altar near his house where he and his wife had prayed. He had been "stirred up," he said, by Willie Jim when they had met by chance at the carnival in Gardnerville. Willie Jim had demanded, "Why do you [create] class[es] among your people? You pray all the time for friendship and [yet] you class your people." Sam Dick took up the argument, although in a conciliatory tone, addressing Willie Jim as "brother." He maintained that he never coerced people to come to his meetings. He countered with the charge that the Dresslerville Indians had circulated the petition against peyote because they wanted to continue drinking and "staying rough." Willie Jim then demanded verifiable evidence for the supernatural things allegedly seen and heard at meetings. Whereupon Dick rejoined with a biblical analogy: "No one was there when it happened thousands of years ago, yet white man believes it." Anyway, religion is revealed in many ways. "Some listen to the Salvation Army in Reno. Some pass by. Our way the best we know how. It's the best we can do. That's our life."

Willie Smokey, long a recognized leader, also became unpopular through his espousal of peyote. It was clear that at one time he actually feared that in spite of his status, he might be driven out of Dresslerville. No doubt this prompted in some measure his official withdrawal from the cult. Ben Lancaster too became a particular target for abuse, as the many accusations against him, elsewhere described, demonstrate. Other manifestations of intratribal ill feeling are seen in the reported refusal of peyotists to give nonpeyotists a lift in their cars. On the other hand, the latter are accused of abusing the former "something unbearable."

Tribal friction was further aggravated by accusations of sorcery said to have been practiced in peyote meetings. That this belief should have created trouble is not surprising in view of the deep preoccupation with witchcraft in aboriginal Washo culture. Nothing could have been calculated to precipitate conflict more effectively than the injection of the old supernatural fears.

The leaders, of course, denied the accusations. They pointed out that peyote rendered witches impotent. The cult doctrinally repudiated the alleged power of the shamans. Shamans, indeed, were held up for open ridicule at the meetings.

But such apparently was the tenacity of the belief in sorcery that it persisted through all the iterations of peyote's theological opposition. Nor did it escape from the leaders' thought patterns. As we shall see, it constituted a scarcely concealed substratum in Sam Dick's world view. As for Ben Lancaster, for all of his derogation of shamanistic power and repudiation of aboriginal ideology, his very references to them as well as his whispered charges of witching at meetings were interpreted as a tacit recognition of their potency. Supernatural power, on the indigenous model, was ascribed to Lancaster himself. More than one informant said that people were scared of his power. There was reluctance to speak disparagingly of peyote, manifested especially by women, since all who did so might ultimately be destroyed through its power.

In fine, peyote did not reduce the fear of witchcraft. On the contrary, it may have stimulated it. Certainly the air was filled with charges concerning witching which emanated from peyote sessions.

Thus one woman, reputed to be a witch able to kill, related her grievances against Lancaster, who at a meeting had evidently "talked against" her, saying that she was witching everyone in the country. According to her story, she was in her house at the time, much troubled and unable to sleep. Her anger increased as she pictured how she was being victimized. Finally, she got up and went to the meeting place. Disregarding the ritualistic niceties, she boldly confronted Lancaster and warned him to stop telling lies about her. Obviously she was in a fury. "If I had had a gun," she related, "I'd have shot him right there."

Repercussions of the charges of witchcraft eventually reached the Indian Agency. After the Smokey family had left the cult, a report began circulating that in a meeting at which both Ben Lancaster and Sam Dick were present, they had been accused of killing people through witchcraft. Thoroughly aroused, Willie Smokey set about discovering who had made this dangerous accusation, dangerous because of the implicit threat of ostracism, to say nothing of possible retaliation by relatives of the deceased. In the web of fears automatically spun in a situation of this kind, it was no easy task to find an informer. Finally, however, through the intercession of the Agency superintendent, one was found. All interested parties were invited to the Agency, there to thrash out the matter face-to-face. At the dramatic session, Sam Dick was pointed to as the guilty one. He at once denied the accusation, claimed he was being persecuted, insisted he had nothing against Willie Smokey, who was his own cousin. Lancaster joined Dick in the denial, emphasizing that the beliefs inherent in the charge were in direct contradiction to the doctrines of peyote, which taught brotherliness and mutual love. If some members entertained benighted notions, it was merely indicaive of their incomplete conversion. They had not yet found the right road. The conference ended with stern warnings from the superintendent that the peyote leaders exercise caution in the dissemination of their beliefs.[32] That laymen like the Smokeys were thought capable of sorcery is another illustration of the Washo concept of the general diffusion of supernatural power among many members of the tribe.

To sum up, the introduction and spread of peyote had a most

disturbing influence on the social fabric of Washo life. It was a source of conflict dividing the tribe into two camps. It split families. It dislocated communities. It rearranged the hierarchies of political and religious authority. It intruded into the routines of everyday life so that whether someone was affiliated with the cult became a criterion of paramount importance in judging an individual. Its treatment of witchcraft, far from allaying fears, increased them, and this proved an added source of perturbation. Although only a small number of tribesmen remained faithful devotees, it can be said that the lives of few Washo were unaffected by the diffusion of peyote.[33]

But if peyote proved a dislocating and dividing force in the larger perspective, in a smaller sphere it became a unifying influence. It had a centripetal as well as a centrifugal influence. Peyotists, for all their fractional splits, were yet joined together in a group rendered cohesive by a common ideology, a common language. It was a unity, moreover, that transcended tribal boundaries. Washo, Northern Paiute, Southern Paiute, and even an occasional Miwok, assembled as brothers in peyote. Between peyotists, friendships were established which led to visiting. This in turn increased travel, to which members were already becoming accustomed through long journeys to meetings. Contact with broader horizons, cultural as well as geographic, was bound to have its assimilative influence.

THE ACCEPTANCE AND REJECTION OF PEYOTISM

Reasons for Acceptance

No account of the spread of peyote among the Washo would be complete without enumerating the reasons given for accepting and rejecting the cult. In the course of two summers spent in investigating the diffusion of the new religious form among the people, many natives were interrogated with special regard to their feelings and attitudes toward peyote. The great majority spoke freely. In fact, the subject contained such explosive possibilities that many found difficulty in discussing it without displaying deep emotion. Neither was such a discussion a rare occurrence. Everyone talked about peyote, this phenomenon which had caused such serious intratribal repercussions and constant preoccupation with it fostered fluency of expression.

Nevertheless, reasons given for either acceptance or rejection were, no matter how readily expressed, never too precise. Usually more than one reason was mentioned. The difficulty of making the concepts and categories of native thinking correspond with those of a more sophisticated culture was an expected obstacle to clarification.[34] Expressed reasons frequently masked real reasons, which became known only as the life history of the individual unfolded. For the present, however, a discussion of the overt motives, grouped under convenient if arbitrary headings, will suffice. These headings under which the ensuing material has been subsumed are: therapy, religion, ethics, Messianism, visions, economics, personality of leader, prestige, extravagant promises, kinship, and social and emotional by-products. The following discussion of the various categories of peyote appeal provides a fuller picture of the manner in which the cult was adopted, as well as a clearer insight into the consequences that came to the culture and to the people with the impact of the new religion.

The power of peyote to cure physical sickness was perhaps its strongest manifest attraction. It is a sick person who most often requests a meeting, and it is he and his family who will act as hosts. Stewart estimates that 90 percent of the peyotists joined the cult hoping for some cure.[35] There was virtually no organic ailment that peyote could not allegedly cure. Many were the testimonials offered in behalf of its therapeutic efficacy. Some had been cured of tuberculosis, others of rheumatism, still others of headaches, colds, goiter, and blindness.

Peyote, however, is not itself the curative agent. It helps in the diagnosis, enables the leader to discern the course of the illness. Sam Dick's testimony concerning the case of Raymond McBride, a twelve-year-old boy, whose cure is celebrated among Washo peyotists, will serve to illustrate this concept. Raymond had tuberculosis and had spent three years in Tucson. Upon returning to his home in Owens Valley, he became seriously ill and was given four months to live. In an effort to save his life, it was decided to try peyote. Dick's ministrations were sought.

> I try anything to save his life: white doctor, Indian doctor, peyote. I never saw anyone feel bad when he come to a peyote meeting who didn't leave feeling better. . . . At the meeting last Saturday night I saw that the boy may get better. I saw lungs. There were blue spots, scars—three small ones, and down below all blue. It looked like it was freshening up, healing.

Other interesting clues are herein revealed concerning the exact role of peyote in curing. For one thing, other curing agencies are respected, at least by some adherents of the cult and are not felt to be in conflict with it. It will be recalled that Willie Smokey was being treated in the Agency hospital when his family called for a meeting in Dresslerville. In fact, it was his sickness that occasioned the request. Although peyote was reputed to be capable of curing any ailment, the feeling existed that some maladies had better be left to other therapies. Susie Dick said: "I was pretty near paralyzed. Peyote fix me up fine. It also fix up my stomach. Peyote is good for the stomach. Peyote may not be good for appendicitis or a broken leg. White doctor fix that. But peyote good all right."

But over all is the conviction that the peyote alone is not enough. It must go hand in hand with faith. One fails to grasp the function of peyote as a cure unless one reckons with the indispensable religious associations. Thus Ben Lancaster: "Faith in God is the important thing. Jim of Mono Lake was a boy, a cripple. He didn't realize there is a God. He didn't pray to him—the Master who can overhaul you, take you apart and put you together again, then leave you running better than ever." Thus the religious appeal of peyote went hand in hand with the curative, and it would be artificial and arbitrary to separate the two. As might have been expected, Lancaster was one who had no patience with white doctoring. He condemned it at great length, accusing white practitioners of fraud and greed. Most interesting, however, in the present context is this blanket charge of his: "Medical practice today is wrong. It is done without the word of God. It is just like a butcher killing a cow, stripping it, and cutting it up for steaks." That such practice was divorced from the supernatural was the cardinal offense.

For some the curative aspects of peyote predominated; for others, the religious. Among the latter Willie Smokey finds his place. As we have seen, he enjoyed a considerable prestige among both Indians and whites. He spoke English well. Frequently he represented the tribe in dealings with the Agency, which regarded him as reliable and trustworthy. Conscious of his uncommon status, he assumed many of the symbols of the dominant white culture. He took pains with his speaking. He took pride in his family and the family establishment at Dresslerville, ruling the roost in characteristic white (and non-Washo) fashion. (Because the feeling for bilaterality was manifest in the Washo family, this prevented any patriarchal domination.) Willie Smokey's desire for knowledge was strong, and he was never reluctant to display his learning—another accommodation to white culture. He was also a "good Christian." He was for years the pillar of the Dresslerville Baptist mission, and when it no longer attracted the people, he was saddened and disappointed.

When peyote came to Nevada, Willie Smokey saw in it a substitute for mission religion. He was drawn to "the Christian part of it." To him, peyote was the "Indian church." "I'm a God-fearing, churchgoing man," he declared more than once. "I was always a faithful worker. I learned much in the church and from the Bible that I couldn't have learned outside." In the same eloquent breath he spoke of the virtues of churchgoing and peyote. Then he added, "We went also because of ailments, especially rheumatism and troubles." Clearly it was the religious elements in peyote that chiefly attracted him. Hence there was nothing inconsistent in calling a meeting for him while he lay sick with bladder trouble in the Stewart hospital. He also held to the belief in therapeutic specialization: "I don't say that Indian medicine men are no good. They are good for what they can do. An Indian has his right to go to Indian doctors." Neither was he by any means opposed to white doctors. He had been hospitalized several times.

Peyote won adherents not only because of its formal religious elements but also because of its moral religious tone. Exhortations to walk the "right path," to be brotherly, to be kind, to help one another, became ritualized into a monotonous formula. George Snooks said of Ben Lancaster, "He is there to make people good." The idea was sometimes expressed that peyote does not automatically transform the individual into a righteous being, but it rather guides him, makes him aware of the difference between good and evil and, after due contrition and penitence, helps him attain the worthier life. Lancaster said:

> Peyote guides you in your right and normal mind. It guides you in the right path of life—cleaner morals. In the meeting, when you feel good you pray, and you get into a new channel of life. Then you condemn your old deeds. It's up to you. You have your choice. It makes you realize right and wrong. Then it's up to you to choose.

Here we come to the doctrine, central to the cult, that one cannot take peyote and drink at the same time. The injunction against liquor is part of the cult's ethical component. Peyote purges one's being of all impurities—moral as well as physical. "It cleanses your evil thoughts—the poisons, the filth accumulated within you." And liquor is a primary source of such accumulations. Dire were the consequences of those who "mixed" peyote with liquor. Lancaster said it brought "everlasting darkness." Even peyote's strongest antagonists admitted that most of the cultists stopped drinking. But it was not true as some maintained that if one ate peyote, the imbibing of liquor became an impossibility. There were those who did wander from the stern antialcohol position[36] and who, as a result, sank into a state of guilt-laden misery. One individual, after a heavy drinking bout in Reno, was ridden with feelings of guilt and could scarcely wait to return to the meetings, at which through zealous participation and sincere repentance he might be returned to grace. His reaction is typical of the delinquent peyotist. The feeling of guilt and shame was concomitant with such transgression because one of the main tenents of the faith had been violated.

The Indian's unhappy economic and social lot was also attributed to liquor. The Washo had been cheated of their patrimony because they had succumbed to liquor, it was held. Ben Lancaster waxed vehement on this issue:

> Liquor makes them greedy because when under the influence of anything alcoholic, you want the whole sack of potatoes. That's how this country was gotten—get 'em drunk and make 'em sign. Average deals with the Indian were done that way. Take this Washo country. Washo territory is from the Lake [Tahoe] to the [Carson] Valley. If there's justice, the government has no title. It would have been different if there'd been no liquor. White man drinks it and makes false promises. Those promises are never fulfilled.

Lancaster was sensitive to the injustice that had defrauded and impoverished his people. He spoke of it at the meetings, and this espousal of Washo rights must have won some to his cause. George Snooks spoke approvingly when he said, "Ben is interested in the future of the tribe. He will go to Washington and look into Washo land difficulties." Lancaster must have loomed as the leader long overdue who would be instrumental in redressing the old wrongs. The overtone of Messianism here discernible, reminding us of Ghost Dance doctrine, was projected into the visions that accompanied peyote. Sam Dick, whose point of view was oriented toward the supernatural, emphasized the otherworldly aspects of Messianism: "Indians and white men would one day stand as equals before God."[37]

Vision experiences during the sessions constitute an important element of peyote and for some become a strong attraction. Such visions are not understood as sources of power; they are not dreams in the strict aboriginal sense, although, in conformity with the old pattern, peyote songs have been received in the visions. Rather are they instructive revelations—prognostications and warnings. Visions are, of course, of infinite variety. Some are of an intense apocalyptic character in which scenes of the days to come are disclosed in colors and action most vivid. At the other extreme are found a few individuals who see no visions despite liberal peyote stimulation. Some revelations are of dead relatives, of the creation of the world, some of a Messianic age when Indians will be united with all peoples in brotherhood. Some visions are of an erotic character. All are perceived in brilliant colors and a great many bring the beholder deep satisfaction and pleasure. On the other hand, macabre and revolting visions are experienced, and these are interpreted as punishment for sins. One person had visions of this sort shortly after his straying from sobriety. Sam Dick's dreams frequently dramatized the conflict between good and evil, between God and the devil.

Monetary rewards and economic advantage came to many peyotists. That pecuniary considerations animated Ben Lancaster there can be little doubt. For him it proved a primary motivation, and for others, too, who attached themselves to him and benefited from the largesse he distributed to his helpers. Hansen Pete and Leeman Miller, both from Woodfords, were learning to conduct meetings and become leaders under Lancaster's tutelage, and both were aware of the material gain that would derive from such offices. Ray Fillmore mentioned that the leaders, the would-be leaders, and the hangers-on "hadn't done a bit of work since taking up peyote." Most of them certainly made enough to live on. Sam Dick, however, had a difficult time making ends meet.

Lancaster's followers paid the tribute exacted quite willingly, eagerly even, and considered the return altogether worth the expenditure, especially when they compared their present benefits with those derived from the discredited shamans. Moreover, shamanistic curing had always been a financial burden on the people. The nominal voluntarism of peyote contributions in the light of the shaman's unyielding coercions must have had a special appeal. Improvements in economic status naturally went with abstinence from alcohol, always the cause of Washo financial profligacy, and this must have led not a few into the cult. People spoke of the economic betterment which had come to them. A family could now buy more groceries, more clothes, even an automobile.

Lancaster's personality was a powerful drawing card. Men and women reveled in his favor, were aggrieved and made jealous by his neglect. They concurred in his judgments, lived vicariously in his exciting narratives, joined in his jibes, laughed uproariously at his jokes. Prestige accrued to those who attached themselves to this man of prestige. For he had been around, had mingled with the great. He had met and spoken with John Collier, Commissioner of Indian Affairs. He had addressed the Minden Rotary Club and had talked on peyote at the 1938 Carson Valley Fair, for which he had arranged a peyote exhibit. At the 1939 Fair, Sam Dick spoke, and this public recognition by the whites did much to rehabilitate Dick's shaky reputation in the eyes of his own tribesmen. The opportunity to bask in reflected glory brought its quota of men and women into the cult.

Extravagant claims made in peyote's behalf by Lancaster and others constituted an initial inducement to affiliation. Belief in the validity of these claims was probably a function of the power of the leader's influence. When he first appeared in Dresslerville, he declared what he would do—with the aid of peyote: he would make the people stop drinking and fighting "so they could live happily in this country"; he would cure them of their illnesses; he would expose their native doctors. The belief got about that "no jail could hold you" if you took peyote. Equally bizarre was the notion that if a peyotist saw a bottle of whiskey at fifty feet, he would vomit.

While kinship cannot be said to determine membership in the cult, it can be stated that in a good many cases family connections proved an important stepping-stone to membership. Lancaster's own initial moves were undertaken through the agency of kinship with Sam Dick. The Smokeys were in turn won through relationship with Dick. However, although kinship was a coalescing factor in some cases, we have already seen how other families became bitterly divided over peyote.

What we might call the social and emotional by-products of the peyote meetings carried an undeniable attraction for the members. Once a devotee, one became a member of a select group, one "belonged." One was in league with other choice spirits and members of the fraternity called one another "brother" and "sister" effusively. Fellow feeling with other peyotists was for some rendered even more piquant by the sense of persecution. When Harry Jim, a Shoshoni working in Smith Valley, was fired because of shiftlessness allegedly due to peyote and was told by his white boss that he could return to work only on the condition that he give up attending meetings, he retorted, "So you too are against peyote." Cultists were joined in a brotherhood of the oppressed. But there were compensations. There were the exciting preparations for the meetings, making the rattles and fans; there was the eager anticipation days before the meeting and the tense expectancy just before entering the meeting place; there was the undergirding emotion of joyous well-being. Outside meetings, members would visit and sing the peyote songs together. Thus did peyotists draw together in common emotional and social ties. Thus by the same token, did the schism between peyotists and nonpeyotists widen.

Such, in sum, are some of the more manifest aspects of peyote which won converts. It appealed because it cured sickness, provided a formal religious setting for curing in which faith was enlisted as an indispensable aid, stressed the worth of ethical conduct with emphasis on the evils of liquor, revived hopes for a restoration of native rights through natural and supernatural agencies, provided visions which were instructive and satisfying, brought economic advantage, conferred prestige and promised extravagant rewards validated in the personality of the leader, was approved and propagated by kin, and united devotees in compensating emotional and social bonds. Peyote thus represented a constellation of attractions from which the individual might select those elements that promised to satisfy his particular needs.

REASONS FOR REJECTION

We now turn to a consideration of the reasons articulated for opposing and rejecting the cult—reasons given by the majority who did not join the movement. These can be grouped under much the same headings as those cited in support of peyote, for obviously every justification for peyote brought forth its corresponding indictment, every testimonial of beneficence and success its obverse testimonial of maleficence and failure. Consequently, the ensuing discussion of manifest reasons for opposing the cult will be in effect not merely a refutation of all claims made by supporters, but in addition a chronicle of its baleful results.

Far from curing sickness, peyote aggravates it, according to the opposition. It kills people. Many examples of both Washo and Northern Paiute victims were cited to prove the charge. At least twenty individuals were said to have died from peyote during the first two years of Ben Lancaster's ministrations. There were the three boys in Fallon who died shortly after attending a meeting. When the parents wanted to know why they died, peyote was shown to be the cause. Some members were said actually to have expired at the meetings. In other cases death came later but the cause was not far to seek. Martinez Kyser in describing the deleterious action of peyote said, "It makes your heart swell up. It presses against your ribs until it can't pump no more." These reports, undoubtedly exaggerations, yet contain that modicum of verisimilitude sufficient to convince all who hated and many who had remained undecided about peyote. Dr. Fred Anderson of Carson City, who had conducted postmortems on some of the Indians supposedly killed by peyote, was of the opinion that while peyote could not have been the sole cause of death, it might have been a contributing cause—and not so much for its intrinsic constituents as for the violent and turbulent circumstances which surrounded its ingestion. Plainly a person suffering from a severe cardiac or hypertensive condition took no small risk when he participated fully in a peyote meeting.

A second serious charge against peyote is that it makes people crazy. The following is Steve Earl's accusation:

> Peyote makes you go loco. Leonard Moore [one of Sam Dick's fire chiefs] was a good strong fellow. He always worked steady. At Home Ranch he suddenly went crazy. He saw visions. He had begun to sing songs and eat peyote while working on the ranch. He burned up a new hat. Now he has quit work for peyote.

The example of Harry Jim has already been cited. After he turned on his boss and accused him of being in league with the opponents of peyote who were persecuting the faithful, he then proceeded to upbraid and warn his employer. God, he said, was outside that very room and was listening to what they were saying. Punishment would, he predicted, come from on high.

Every antipeyotist related the story of a man from Fallon. Peyote had driven him into all sorts of crazy actions. A fanatical convert to the cult, he had sold all his horses for three hundred dollars and had turned the money over to Ben Lancaster. He had had incestuous relations with his daughter and had then forced his son to do likewise. This man seems to have been emotionally disturbed. He was known and feared for his uncontrollable temper, which had led him to murder his wife, cripple his son, and beat a cow to death. In the 1920s he had ardently embraced Christianity, and it was with comparable zeal that he took up peyote. He became a passionate proselytizer. In the course of the meetings, he confessed the dreadful deeds that had crowded his life—murder, wanton cruelty, incest. When, in spite of his appeals, white merchants refused to contribute money to peyote, he threatened them. This led to his arrest. Peyote can hardly be blamed for driving this disturbed man "insane."

Information secured from both Indians and whites point to past histories of insanity and personality dislocation in the majority of those cases in which derangement is said to have been caused by peyote.

It was claimed that temporary derangement came to some users. During the meetings they would behave queerly. "I stood outside the meeting place for three nights," said John Mack, "when peyote first came to Dresslerville. I saw crazy things. Peyote makes you crazy."

A number of informants explained peyote's apparent cures as caused by the narcotic properties which brought temporary relief. According to Mike Dick, "It is eaten, goes through the system, and makes part of the body numb like dope, aspirin." But it is no cure. Martinez Kyser said, "Peyote deadens your nerves. That is why it 'cures.' Rheumatism is just deadened, postponed. I'd get the same effect with a bottle of whiskey."

Some believe that the old curing methods are more effective than peyote. Cases were cited in which shamans cured persons who had received no help after taking peyote. Susie Rube looked upon peyote as a new herbal remedy inferior to ancient varieties. To it she ascribed the sickness of a girl in a neighboring encampment: "Long time ago she eat peyote. No good for Indian. *Nawi* [a root, ground and used as a 'tea'] good for Indian. All Indians take it for stomach."

Certain features of the ritual provoked disgust. The leaders' practice of masticating the peyote buttons for those who could not chew, and the communal drinking of peyote tea and of water from the drum were two such items. The objection to such activities was on sanitary grounds. (To anyone familiar with native life, this is an obvious rationalization.)

Peyote's status as a formal religious cult was assailed with various arguments. There were those who could see little to distinguish it from the Christian church. Ray Fillmore, who had joined the

Baptist church at the age of seventeen, "saw no reason to leave the church and join peyote, which is the same thing except for peyote, which makes you see visions." Oklahoma meetings he had known as a student were "the same as church meetings." Steve Earl scornfully asked, "What do they know about God! About punishment! Me, I don't know about God. But they say they know everything." This skepticism was further reflected in the belief that Ben Lancaster included the stereotypes of Christian worship merely to beguile the naive. For such individuals impressive embroidery had both prestige and propaganda value.

Far more specific and serious was the challenge to peyote on ethical grounds. First, many found difficulty in squaring peyotist practice with cult doctrine. How could one reconcile the reiterated emphasis on brotherliness, kindliness, and mutual helpfulness with the actualities of intracult relationships—envy, bickering, backbiting, strife? Families were divided, friendships broken up, husbands estranged from wives and parents from children—all because of peyote. Peyotists hated not only nonpeyotsts but also members of dissident factions within the cult. The very leaders from whose tongues dripped the moralistic admonitions were the worst offenders. Ray Fillmore summed up a widely held view when he said, "More people would follow peyote if those who use it practiced what they preached."

There were specific ethical transgressions of which peyotists in general and Ben Lancaster in particular were accused. One everywhere reported was sexual excess. Lancaster was said to have turned some of the early meetings into sex orgies. Accusations in this category ran all the way from the charge of his making the fire blaze in order to see the girls' genitals when they crossed their legs, to the definite assertion that sexual intercourse took place at the meetings. Ray Fillmore, an informant of cautious judgment, said: "In the second year Ben started fooling around [sexually] at the meetings. He told people to have a good time, to get acquainted, to be sociable. Ben himself went in for it. He had many wives—young girls. But there's no more of it since some people left. They didn't think it was much of a religious meeting. That's why most of the people in Dresslerville didn't want Ben to hold meetings there."

It was difficult to verify these charges. Fillmore was not a bitter opponent of peyote, and as an informant was temperate and reliable. The Agency authorities, who were concerned with the reports of licentious behavior, watched Lancaster closely. On several occasions his car was searched for narcotics at the California-Nevada border. The presumption was that the greater success of Lancaster's meetings, as compared with Sam Dick's, may have been due to the surreptitious use of sexually stimulating drugs. During the time that I was with the Washo, the federal agents did not find anything to substantiate their suspicions.

Stewart (1944) doubts whether narcotic stimulants were added to peyote. Lane Dixon, a Northern Paiute who informed for the authorities, was a discredited character, hence, an unreliable witness. Some Indians believed that the sack of powder into which Lancaster dipped while rolling cigarettes, mixing a little with the tobacco, was marijuana. Actually it was finely ground sage.

The veracity of the charge, however, is not so important as its psychological implications. Lancaster's sexual exploits were the subject of much talk. There can be no doubt that he enjoyed considerable success with the women, and more than one husband found his place supplanted by peyote, which by an obvious transfer became Ben Lancaster. Accusations of sexual irregularity at meetings may well have been the expression of a displaced aggression aroused by envy at his sexual conquests.

The claim of the peyotists that liquor and the evils which came from it were cancelled by eating the sacred cactus was ridiculed by antipeyotists. Some maintained that for many, peyote was nothing more than a substitute for liquor, and like it, taken for its intoxicating effects. Moreover, it was an illusion to believe that peyote effectively stopped the addiction to liquor; there were too many examples to the contrary. One accustomed to heavy drinking might stop for a while, but after a time the old bibulous habit would be resumed. In the meantime, there was always the chance that peyote would enslave the user with its narcotic properties, and this was certainly worse than habituation to alcohol. Thus did the opposition refute the moral and ethical potency ascribed to peyote. Why, they argued, join the cult if promised moral reforms fail to materialize; worse, if peyote produces consequences more harmful than the conditions it is supposed to relieve? Again, it should be noted there is no conclusive evidence that peyote is habit-forming or seriously harmful. La Barre agrees with Hrdlička that the effects of peyote are of the same order as those of nicotine.[38]

If there were some who saw in Lancaster and in peyote a cham-

pion for social and economic rights, there were others who saw in
them nothing but a snare leading to present troubles and future
disillusionment. Lancaster was bitterly denounced as a mercenary
rogue bent on ruining his gullible tribesmen. At their expense he
was obviously prospering, his new car a particularly blatant and irri-
tating symbol of affluence. It was not only the large sums of money
that he took from the meetings; it was also the fact that the economic capacity of cult members was often impaired. "A man who
takes peyote," it was said, "is not fit for a couple of days after a
meeting. Maybe he works three days a week." (In this regard also,
peyote was compared unfavorably with liquor. Whatever one might
say of the hazardous results of whiskey, one informant observed, it
was not as lasting in its effects as peyote. Then this parting shot: "I
prefer ninety proof whiskey any time.") Instances were cited of men
who were fired for lack of efficiency on the job. Ranchers around
Coleville were for this reason said to frown upon peyote's use by the
Indians. Lancaster, of course, was held responsible for all of this.
Contradictory evidence was offered by Ray Fillmore. Peyote does
not militate against a worker's effectiveness, he said. The objection
of the ranchers is based upon disapproval of their helpers leaving
the job early on the day of a peyote meeting, a practice often
necessary because of the distance to the place of meeting. On the
contrary, "men who ate peyote on very tough construction jobs
could 'take it.' White huskies couldn't 'take it.' But peyote users
who took peyote every day were whistling around." This refers to
the practice of taking peyote as a daily stimulant. "They take it in
the morning. It's supposed to last twenty-four hours. When that
goes they're all in. But when they take it, they can go." In other
words, shiftlessness on the job was due not to any physical ill-effects
occasioned by the eating of peyote but to the creation of attitudes of
restlessness and instability as the result of too serious a preoccupation with the cult. As for Lancaster's concern with tribal rights
and the securing of justice for long overdue Washo claims, did not his
ruthless materialism directed toward personal enrichment give the lie to
his declarations of concern for the tribe? In the economic sphere, then,
there also seemed to be an unbridgeable chasm between preachment
and practice.

   To some leaders and would-be leaders in the tribe anxious to
preserve whatever temporal authority they possessed, peyote presented
a serious threat. The new cult brought a new authority in the persons of

Ben Lancaster and his disciples. Naturally, those who saw their prestige challenged by the new religion rejected it. In many cases they were joined by kinsmen in the organized resistance which eventually took shape. If this was true of those who fancied themselves temporal leaders, it was even more true of the shamans whose position was directly menaced. They and their kinsmen constituted in the main a formidable part of the opposition. These aspects of the dissemination of the cult will be discussed more fully later. For the present it will suffice to say that tribal leaders of the old regime, both temporal and religious, joined by kinsmen, for the most part opposed peyote.

SUMMARY

In summarizing the avowed reasons for accepting or rejecting peyote, it should again be emphasized that this is far from presenting the full story. When we deal with such phenomena as the replacement of deep-rooted sanctities such as ancient medicoreligious forms, we must reckon with forces which do not operate on a conscious level. Unconscious motivations conditioned by all manner of hidden, repressed factors play a crucial role.[39] The whole subtle and complicated structure of relationships between members of the tribe, the roots of which reach back into the past, must as far as possible be known and considered.

However, a discussion of manifest motivations in reacting to a new cultural form is not without ethnological significance. The conscious causations no less than the unconscious have their persuasive power with the individual as with the group. Furthermore, to list and describe them does give something of a picture of the spread of the institution, if only a two-dimensional one. We do see people actually caught up in the disturbing current of new forms—how they behave among themselves and toward outsiders, what they tell each other, what they tell the investigator from an alien culture.

What emerges is that the individual Washo could find plenty of justification for either espousing or denouncing peyote. On the one hand, there were medical, religious, ethical, economic, social, emotional benefits to be derived from peyote. On the other, peyote was a snare and a delusion not one whit better than established forms, leading often enough to grave medical, religious, ethical, economic, social, and emotional ills. Plainly, pure logic was not important. You believed what you wanted to believe. When you knew what you wanted to believe, you would find enough supporting reasons in a well-stocked arsenal of justification, with facts and figures galore. The concern thus far has been with *what* people wanted to believe, with the rationalizations trotted out. *Why* they wanted to believe, what conditioned them in this direction, the crucial third dimension in the picture is covered in the next chapter.

5. THE CLASH BETWEEN SHAMANISM AND PEYOTISM

THE PROBLEM

The spectacular career of peyotism among the Washo will inevitably raise two questions in the mind of the student of culture: What were the factors that made for its rapid and widespread acceptance? What were the forces that contributed to its swift decline? A satisfactory answer to these questions must obviously involve a consideration both of the cultural circumstances that conditioned peyote's introduction and of the personalities of those individuals whose role in the conflict was crucial.

Our primary concern here is with the process of culture change. The operations of this process have been a matter of historic interest to anthropologists, and studies in the dynamics of culture have constituted a notable contribution to the literature of anthropology. But nearly all such studies are later reconstructions based on data made available by more or less remote human and documentary sources. The noteworthy historical reconstructions of Spier, Radin, Nash and Du Bois, to name a few, have, for all their excellence, been created out of such bits of secondhand evidence.[1]

The opportunity to study the process of culture change at first hand is seldom afforded the field ethnologist. It was my good fortune to be on hand when a new institution was brought to an Indian tribe. During a period when both people and culture were seriously shaken by the appearance of new forms, I was lucky enough to be there, notebook and stopwatch in hand, so to speak. (Remember: This was before the time of tape recorders.) The cultural analysis and assessment which derive from such intimate observational study may present fresh and authentic insights into the complex operations of culture change, and may, as such, provide pertinent comparative material toward a deeper understanding of social dynamics.

From the anthropologist's vantage point, what can be said about the initial acceptance and ultimate rejection of peyote by the Washo? Looking beyond the manifest as expressed by the tribesmen themselves, what strikes the student of culture as determinant factors directing peyote's course? Without in any way discarding the data offered by the Washo themselves, data which, for all their component of rationalization, give valid and illuminating guidance, let us consider the forces inherent in the impact of the new on the old, the conflict between peyotism and shamanism.

BREAKDOWN OF THE ABORIGINAL CULTURE

The relationship between the rise of revivalist cults and the dislocation of native life because of the crushing impact of a more powerful culture has been noted repeatedly, and, indeed, must be apparent to every student of history.[2] The Washo suffered the fate of all American Indian tribes who stood in the way of the advancing white frontier. Perhaps their hardships were unusually severe because their territory fell within one of the main avenues of westward expansion.[3] Neither they nor their institutions could withstand the pressure imposed by dominating intrusive pioneers.

That the first stages of acculturation were attended by extreme subjection is revealed in the early American chronicles. The Washo were regarded as a rather despicable adjunct to the animal kingdom. This is Bancroft's description:

> Of the miserable root and grass eating Shoshones (among whom the Washo are counted)—those who have seen them unanimously agree that they of all men are lowest. Lying in a state of semi-torpor in holes in the ground during the winter, and in spring crawling forth and eating grass on their hands and knees, until able to regain their feet; having no clothes, scarcely any cooked food, in many instances no weapons, with merely a few vague imaginings for religion, living in the utmost squalor and filth, putting no bridle on their passions, there is surely no missing link between them and brutes. Yet as in all men there stands out some prominent good, so in these, the lowest of humanity, there is one virtue; they are lovers of their country; lovers not of fair hills and fertile valleys, but of inhospitable mountains and barren plains; these reptile-like humans love their miserable burrowing-places better than all the comforts of civilization; indeed, in many instances, when detained by force among the whites, they have been known to pine away and die.[4]

The bewilderment and fear that seized the Washo in the face of white encroachment are vividly portrayed in a chapter of Sarah Winnemucca's *Life Among the Paiutes.* Interesting too is Sarah's own attitude toward her ethnic kinsmen. Mournfully she refers to them as the "poor, poor Washo." Either she had absorbed the prevailing white attitudes or she, a Northern Paiute who had arrived, so to speak, was indulging the luxury of pitying former neighbors (the Washo and the Northern Paiute were never too friendly).[5]

From the catastrophic days of early white contact until most recent years, the tribe as a whole had been victimized by acute deprivation. The invasion of white settlers, come to farm the valleys east of the Sierras, drove them from traditionally frequented terrain, narrowed the scope of seasonal tribal movements, and by presenting opportunities for employment disrupted age-old Washo economy.

Unlike their eastern and northern neighbors, the Washo offered no resistance to the tide of invasion. They never took up arms against the whites. They seem to have accepted the yoke of oppression passively. Even their verbal protests were timid. Beyond an occasional visit to the legislators at Carson City by a "Captain" mumbling scarcely intelligible grievances, little was heard from the sorely harried tribesmen. Consequently government concessions, invariably won under pressure, were not forthcoming. The Washo were not placed on a reservation. Between white economic paternalism and rapidly shrinking aboriginal subsistence resources, they barely managed to maintain a hand-to-mouth existence.

Conditions gave promise of improving at one point but the hopes aroused at the time ended in disillusionment. A Captain Jim, who was briefly recognized as chief during the first decade of the century, actually undertook a journey to Washington.[6] He pleaded the cause of his people and was successful in winning land grants for them. He had asked for unlimited access to Pine Nut Range where the Washo repair every fall to gather pine nuts, chief item in their food economy. Shortly after Captain Jim's return, allotments of forty acres were parcelled out to every Washo family. However the fancied Utopia failed to materialize. The pine nut crop is at best capricious—one in four fails. It became apparent that no watered land had been allotted, these desirable tracts having been preempted for whites. As a result, the soil could not be turned to farming. It had also been prudently provided that no Indian could prospect on his land, potentially rich in ores. All the Washo had were pine nuts, and they found out soon enough that they could not rear a stable economy on a pine nut foundation. When the crop failed and they were hard pressed, they cut down the trees and sold them for timber. In this extremity, they had neither trees nor pine nuts.

Only in the last few years, with the application of new policies fostered by the Collier administration, has the economic condition of the Washo improved. But as often happens, the legislation of policy no matter how enlightened is no panacea for those profound ills that spread, in the last analysis, from a shifting, unstable cultural base. Four years ago (1937) the government purchased 795 acres of farmland for the tribe; government works projects have relieved unemployment to a degree; the old folks get adequate pensions. But the Washo are still poor, dissatisfied, and the beneficent measures of the government have only succeeded in generating new conflicts and exacerbating long-standing animosities.

The Washo feel they have been badly used, cheated. Whenever they speak of the past they are full of bitterness at the treatment received from the whites. Yet they do not stop here. They turn upon themselves, upon their leaders, in bitter recrimination. Why didn't they fight like the Northern Paiutes? Why didn't they demand a place on the reservation? Why didn't Captain Jim ask for a reservation rather than for the useless pine-nut strips? And so on. Their aggressions turn inward upon themselves[7]

Obviously the scene of such profound and pervasive frustration is ready for revivalist religion. We have learned that the ashes of a crumbling culture prove fertile soil for the growth of nativist cults. In 1871–72, the Ghost Dance came to the Washo.[8] In 1936 peyote arrived. It may be noted in passing that both had brief careers in this tribe. The probable explanation will be given later. For the present suffice it to say that if deterioration of the aboriginal culture and the advent of revivalism are correlates, the appearance of nativist cults among the Washo was inevitable.

RESEMBLANCES BETWEEN PEYOTISM
AND SHAMANISM

It is approved anthropological theory that the acceptance of a new culture complex is facilitated by the presence of cognate symbols and practices in the aboriginal pattern. This had often been verified with respect to peyote. Radin early indicated the similarities between Winnebago peyotism and shamanism. Indeed, the only distinctive elements in the former were the peyote itself and a few Christian teachings. The rest was cut in the pattern of the already existing religious institution. Shonle hazards the suggestion that the speed of peyote acceptance is coterminous with "the underlying belief in the supernatural origin of visions." Petrullo sees striking similarities between Delaware peyotism and aboriginal Delaware Big House ceremonialism, and the Oplers adduce Mescalero and Southern Ute examples as illustrating the same principle. The prior practice of the mescal bean cult is mentioned by La Barre as paving the way in the Plains for the adoption of peyote.[9]

Ritual and ideological resemblances between peyotism and Washo shamanism were observed. Both are curing ceremonies combining social as well as religious features. The session in both cases begins around nine o'clock in the evening; no one is excluded, men and women are accorded equal status, and all participate in the singing and smoking. The festive meal that is shared at the conclusion of the all-night peyote meeting is reminiscent of the less elaborate repast eaten during the fourth night of the shaman's curing séance. Eagle feathers, rattle, and a bird-bone whistle are used in both. So it is with the pattern number four and the clockwise circuits. Sam Dick compared peyote with "old Indian herbs" used in shamanizing, which he claimed were also nonhabit forming and which upon occasion would first be masticated by the shaman.

Visions are part of both peyotism and shamanism—Ben Lancaster's and Sam Dick's conversion experiences were both accompanied by a vision in which an animal appeared. God the Creator mentioned in peyote meetings was a belief familiar to the Washo. "The old Washos believed in it," said Lancaster, who would often relate peyote beliefs and practices to shamanism. Though apparently scorning the old way, he nevertheless sensed the value of resemblances with forms carrying age-old supernatural sanctions. Both the shaman and peyote diagnose sickness and both reveal the location and cause of sickness "like an X-ray." Peyote is more than a medical specific, its ingestion must needs be accompanied by faith; shamanism, while somewhat different in its component beliefs, is also a combination of natural therapy and supernatural intercession. In a word, both constitute a medicoreligious complex.

Other peyote beliefs resemble not so much particular items in shamanism as rites and beliefs in the larger aboriginal context. Thus the peyote chief's staff suggests the staff held by the singer at a girl's puberty rite. Eating sage and perfuming the body with it have parallels in the old culture. Sam Dick called sagebrush an "old friend" of the Washo. The seven marbles wrapped into bosses on the peyote drum reminded the people of the seven stars that travel together at night. Incensing at the peyote meeting finds its analogue in the old Washo ritual fumigation that played an important part in aboriginal ceremonialism. All these resemblances were clearly recognized by the people on a conscious level. Undoubtedly such recognition tended to allay anxieties aroused by the feeling that in serving peyote, one was betraying the old sanctities.

The force of patterning must also be reckoned with here. The dynamic adaptation of new or borrowed traits to local cultural forms has been described classically by Goldenweiser. Wissler and Lowie have recognized this principle as operating in various aspects of Blackfoot and Crow cultures.[10] That the same principle was at work in the acceptance of peyotism among the Washo is dramatically evidenced in the concept of witching. Even though peyote repudiates sorcery and all its works, and in spite of his own objections, Ben Lancaster was looked upon as possessing supernatural power, power cast in the aboriginal mould with its witchcraft implications. To Ray Fillmore it was inconceivable that one in Lancaster's position should not have power. When Steve Earl walked into a peyote meeting presided over by Lancaster, the power of Earl's mother left her and went into the drum. Lancaster was held responsible for thus destroying the power of the most feared "witch" in the tribe. And it was of course his power that had been the agent of deliverance. The imperatives in the culture pattern ordained that these phenomena be interpreted as manifestations of supernatural power even though such interpretation flew in the face of basic peyote doctrine.

Once the substratum of supernatural power was discerned in peyote, the pattern of development could be foreseen. For now, connected imperatives are brought into play. Thus having recognized the presence of witching in meetings, the accusation of witching—a serious matter—would follow. As Park says, "Accusation of witching is tantamount to conviction." Accusation in turn would lead to bad blood, counteraccusations, rifts, upheaval, The pattern becomes scarcely distinguishable from the sorcery-ridden scene of pre-peyote days. This development might be subsumed under the term "culture drift," coined by Eggan.[11]

Illustrated in this chain of imperative patterning is the "integrative process" operating in all culture. As Murdock writes, "A people tends to adopt, out of the various new elements offered by its neighbors, those that fit best into its own culture, and to modify or transform them, if necessary, to adapt them to the native cultural framework."[12]

MECHANISMS AIDING DIFFUSION

In her study of the 1870 Ghost Dance, Du Bois makes the observation that while the concept of diffusion has been employed constantly by anthropologists and historians, little has been done toward describing its actual functioning. She pleads for a livelier concern with diffusion as a dynamic process rather than as a cold measuring rod for historical reconstruction. Even though the instruments at her disposal are the somewhat remote human and documentary sources mentioned before, she attempts an anatomy of the diffusion of the 1870 Ghost Dance. She concludes that the following mechanisms made possible the spread of the religion: intertribal marriage, language, reservation systems, transportation, and employment of Indian labor.[13]

The mechanisms governing the introduction and diffusion of Washo peyotism may be subjected to similar analysis. With the singular advantage of personal observation and participation, it will not be necessary to resort to postmortem reconstructions, cultural autopsies, armed with the blunt scalpels of doddering informants and unverifiable documents.

Some of the instrumentalities which promoted the introduction and diffusion of peyote among the Washo may be said to resemble those enumerated by Du Bois. Ben Lancaster's facility with languages proved an undoubted asset. He could make himself intelligible to both Washo and Northern Paiute, to say nothing of other Shoshonean-speaking Nevadans. In addition, his command of English provided valuable prestige symbolism. Rapid transportation, easy in his flashy car, made for the initial contacts as well as for the swift spread of the cult through western Nevada. Traveling to other parts of the state by individual Washo, unheard of in earlier times, brought acquaintanceship with a new religion that had come to eastern Nevada peoples. Intertribal mingling, fostered by such agencies as marriage, attendance at the Stewart Agency school, employment by whites and other by-products of acculturation, served to broaden the people's cultural outlook—softened people up, so to speak, for the invasion of new institutions. Having come in contact with non-Washo culture, they would no longer recoil from the new and the strange.

In the last analysis, however, these factors seem to be of secondary importance. They are the mechanical supports for the spread of institutions impelled by more fundamental drives, steered by more purposeful forces. A rounded picture of the diffusion, it is true, demands a recognition of these aids. Nevertheless, it would be a distortion to overemphasize their significance. Lancaster's ill-starred predecessors, Leo Okio and Lone Bear, were both favored with these supporting diffusion mechanisms. Yet they failed to strike fire. The reasons, it would appear, are to be found in other spheres.

THE ROLE OF BEN LANCASTER

It has already been indicated that one of the chief influences in the adoption of peyotism among the Washo was the proselytizer Ben Lancaster. Linton and Mandelbaum have pointed out how decisive a role "particular personalities may play in the acculturation process," "in mutations of the social mass."[14] In the attempt to convert the Washo to peyotism, a weaker personality would have failed, as Leo Okio and Lone Bear failed prior to Lancaster's arrival on the scene. Without ignoring the social forces which were silently preparing the ground for some form of revivalism, it is still possible to say that Lancaster took full advantage of the propitious setting, that his personality was the spark which kindled the tinder of tribal deprivation and frustration.

Lancaster's hold on his followers has been described. In the eyes of the staunch believers he could do no wrong. It was of no significance to them that their leader was mercenary. Either they did not recognize pecuniary preoccupations or, recognizing them, deemed them of no importance, even justified them. The psychological mechanism at work here should be familiar to the student of religious conversion.

Lancaster is no aberrant phenomenon in the diffusion of nativist American cults. He takes his place with a whole species of proselytizers whose personalities cannot be dissociated from the causes they helped to spread. Many bear arresting resemblances to him, especially with regard to what appear as materialistic motivations.

However, we should be cautious in judging native institutions by the apotheosized values of white culture. The nexus between gain, whether in money, goods or prestige, and the religious office conforms to many a prior native pattern. Moreover, in white culture the linkage is not uncommon.

Who were some of these personalities? A number of zealous proselytizers are connected with Ghost Dance diffusion. The 1870 Ghost Dance was brought to the Washo by Frank Spencer, also known as Weneyuga, a Northern Paiute who eventually carried the cult to the Southern Paiute and to the Klamath reservation. Novelputus, Paitla, and Homaldo are perhaps the most important figures in the dissemination of the 1870 Dance. An elaboration of the movement in the form of the Earth Lodge Cult is attributed to Novelputus, a mixed Wintu–Northern Yana. Another extension is seen in the Bole-Maru Dance, a development variously ascribed to Charlie, a River Patwin dreamer, and to two Long Valley Hill Patwin, Lame Bill and Tele. In all, sixteen individuals are mentioned as proselytizers responsible for the spread of the 1870 revivalist movement.[15]

The 1890 Ghost Dance is also bound up with the personalities of powerful leaders. Wovoka, a Northern Paiute (also known as Jack Wilson), immediately comes to mind not only as the prophet of the Dance but also as one of its leading missionaries. Mooney ascribes to the Arapaho, Sitting Bull, the spread of the movement among the Kiowa, Kansa, Osage, Oto, Missouri, Iowa, and Ponca. The Pawnee version is inevitably associated with Frank White, and the Caddo with John Wilson, who later became a peyote leader.[16]

Personalities are integral with the spread of the peyote cult. John Wilson, successively connected with the Ghost Dance, mescalism, "old Algonquian 'shooting' ceremonies," and finally peyotism, carried it to a number of tribes including the Shawnee, Quapaw, Delaware, Osage, and Potawatomi. John Rave, the Winnebago, having brought peyote to his own tribe, preached the new religion in South Dakota, Minnesota, and Wisconsin. Quanah Parker, Jim Aton, Jonathan Koshiway, and Sam Lone Bear (Sam Roan Bear in some of the early publications) are but a few of the leaders to whose missionary zeal much of the diffusion of peyotism must be attributed.[17]

Lancaster's success in winning the Washo to peyote unquestionably stems from a shrewd and colorful personality developed through a host of tempering experiences in the larger non-Washo Indian and white world. To his fellow tribesmen he represented an awe-inspiring combination of the new and the old. His life was a confluence of two streams of culture; and the teachings that flowed from them, living water bedded in an old channel, carried their irresistible appeal to the people.[18]

THE ATTITUDE TOWARD SHAMANS

The factors thus far mentioned as contributing to the acceptance of peyotism among the Washo may be characterized as essentially extraneous to the aboriginal pattern. A brief recapitulation of these factors shows how they derive from an acculturative base, from impulses generated by nonaboriginal components: the old culture breaks down, new forms bearing reassuring resemblance to the old are welcomed, the process is facilitated by familiar diffusion mechanisms and by the personality of a resourceful leader. The point of departure, be it noted, is the catastrophic impact between Indian and white. The acceptance of peyote is the corporate expression for fulfillment after the acute deprivations attending the process of acculturation.

There was, however, another factor that contributed to the rapid absorption of peyotism by the Washo. This factor is the attitude which the people as a whole entertained toward the shamans. It is my contention that this was as powerful an agent in the acceptance of the new religion as any which derived from debilitating white contact. It was a force that inhered in the aboriginal culture, and it can be comprehended only as one understands the political structure and the social controls of primitive Washo life.

The position of the shaman in Washo society has already been assessed. In brief, through the power of sorcery, he possessed sovereign influence, wielded unchallengeable control. But there was an obverse side to high status won through uncanny means. As manipulator of the supernatural, he was held in awe, sometimes feared, sometimes hated. And as one who often exploited his power to gain material ends, his motives were constantly suspect. The layman expressed his antishaman aggressions in highly charged attitudes of suspicion and hostility. That these attitudes reached deep into the consciousness of the tribe was disclosed by the general agreement of informants in expressing them.

It will be understood, of course, that antishaman reactions were expressed only after friendly relations between natives and investigator had been established for some considerable time. Individuals had to feel confident that no word or deed of theirs would redound to their hurt. Always in such matters the native had to exercise the greatest caution, for he never knew into what remote fastnesses the power of the shaman might penetrate. So it was to be expected that the great majority of individuals would avoid any discussion of witchcraft.[19] Others could be led into a discussion only through devious ways, and then their comments on shamans would be in the nature of whispered asides, implications. But whether directly or indirectly revealed, popular judgment of the shaman was couched in attitudes of unmistakable antipathy.

The antipathy is, to be sure, often screened by brave professions of faith in the shaman and in shamanistic practice. One does hear of shamans who cured, who counteracted a sorcerer's maleficence. But eventually one is likely to hear of the identical shaman cast in the role of witch. Scarcely a practitioner but that he "turned bad." One gets to suspect that any word of praise accorded a shaman is motivated by fear of his pervasive power. "Everybody liked the chief," said Charlie Rube, "but there were only a few doctors everybody liked." My notes fail to disclose a single example of a shaman who was regarded with trust, much less affection. One never knew when the shaman, whoever he was, might strike. In George Snooks's eyes Mike Dick was a "good doctor." The men were friends. Yet Snooks always kept his distance. At times he advised me against questioning Dick on the subject of religion. On a few occasions his reluctance to act as interpreter in this phase of the investigation, conscientious and sophisticated though he was, became so apparent that it was necessary to terminate the session. Snooks's ambivalent feelings toward Dick were undoubtedly paralleled by the reactions of many Washo toward their shamans.

This ambivalence is further demonstrated by the practice indulged by a number of informants of contrasting contemporary shamans with the shamans of old.[20] In the comparison, the former invariably suffered. Peyotists like Sam Dick would, in justification of their religious defection, reiterate the generalization that whereas "doctors were good in the old days, they're no good any more." Even the steady and sophisticated Ray Fillmore expressed this nostalgic view of shamanism. But it appears obvious that such expressions are merely calculated to assuage the anxieties aroused by religious *lèse majesté*. M. K. Opler describes how among the Southern Ute this attitude seeped down to the shamans themselves.[21] Their diminishing influence led to self-derogation. Although definite data on this point are lacking, there is reason to believe that Washo shamans would reveal the same self-denigrating tendencies. In the wake of the conflict over peyote, the Washo shamans, sensing their insecure status, assumed, if not a self-denigrating posture, then a conciliatory, almost ingratiating one toward the people (see "The Impact of Peyotism upon Shamanism" below).

The guilt feelings precipitated by inner disrespect for and rebelliousness against shamanism must have proved a heavy psychological burden, one which required the relief that came with paying tribute to the hated institution's pristine form. By creating this fantasy one could reject the contemporary shaman with impunity.

Fear and hatred of the shaman were beyond question instinct generated out of the old pattern. What is important here is to recall that the means for resolving these feelings were also part of that old pattern. Under the old order a shaman who caused too much trouble, created too many anxieties, would in time be liquidated. Vengeance would be executed by the kin of a sorcerer's victim. The social sanctions which accompanied such action were also integrated in the aboriginal way. Thus were deep-seated hostilities resolved. The culture provided a release for aggressions directed against the shamans, against those who wielded a terrifying authority in the ultimate questions of life and death.

Of more recent times, however, this channel for the release of hostility against the shaman has been blocked. Not in thirty years (as of 1941) has a shaman been murdered for witching. The reasons lie, of course, in the process of acculturation. Murder of shamans, while still sanctioned by native culture, was not sanctioned by a more powerful law, that of the intrusive whites. Moreover, as assimilation to white ways increased, the people for the first time began to move out of the orbit of shamanistic domination. It was a slow process, at first hardly perceptible. The religious complex, of all aspects of the culture, would be least susceptible to alien influence. But the tide was running and the old moorings were beginning to weaken. Hence, while the murder of witches could no longer be executed with impunity, the need to murder them was beginning to lose its force. In any case the murder of sorcerers ceased.

It must not be imagined, however, that hostilities against the shamans came to an end or even diminished to any appreciable degree. As long as shamanism is practiced, it is bound to carry with it those patterned responses which have made hatred of the practitioner an almost necessary corollary. Modifications in the complex will occur, and indeed have occurred, but they will come slowly and, as we shall see, only under pressure. (They came more quickly than might have been anticipated when this was written in 1941.) The point is that shamans were feared and hated thirty years ago, when the last one was murdered; they are feared and hated today (1941). But the traditional mechanisms for coping with shamans have broken down. Within the span of one generaton, the "arbitrary inheritance of problem solutions" which delineate a culture have proved an insufficient solvent for the issues at hand.[22] Murder can no longer provide release for the lingering, persistent fears. Where can such an outlet be found?

The answer came in the peyote cult. Here was an opportunity to defy and challenge the shamans. By affiliating with the cult one plainly rejected the shaman's chief stock-in-trade for preferred supernatural merchandise. Every time he dropped a contribution into the basket, the peyotist was striking a blow not only at the shaman's purse, but also at his power. He knew the money gathered at the peyote meeting meant that much less for the shaman's pocket, proper requital for the ruthless exactions which had made the shaman the economically elect of the tribe. Furthermore, by paying honor to a peyote chief, he was by implication derogating the shaman. The visions that came in the course of the sessions, although not strictly analagous to power visions, were yet comparable with them and as such constituted another challenge to the shaman's unique status.

But the overt behavior of cultists at meetings is the indisputable proof that peyote was a channel par excellence for the release of pent-up aggressions. No meeting passed but that it saw ridicule heaped on the shamans.[23] Ben Lancaster would begin talking in seeming innocence about the failure of some shaman to effect a cure. This would be the signal for those assembled to howl in derision. Lancaster, a master at this sort of demagoguery, would lead them on. What was all too apparent was that he was giving expression to sentiments which everyone seemed profoundly to share. To the investigator familiar with the old religious way, which surrounded the shaman with an aura of dread and squelched any whisper of disrespect, the sight of a gathering of tribesmen laughing to scorn every mention of this quondam sacrosanct figure comes as something of a shock. We can only imagine the psychological trauma sustained in such circumstances by the people. When in their foolhardiness Mike Dick and Ruth Calley, feared and hated Washo shamans, ventured into meetings and were made the butt of Lancaster's insulting witticisms to the raucous delight of all assembled, serious damage must have been done to the inherited hierarchy of values. Murder was one method for liquidating shamans. Peyote was another, which, if it did not eliminate them as effectively, at least drastically reduced their stature.

It is important to bear in mind that the dynamics of rebellion against the shaman smoldered constantly in the aboriginal culture. It was prevented from reaching the point of combustion by the existence of recognized channels of release—chiefly, murder of sorcerers. When the process of acculturation blocked this release, another had to be found. It appeared with the advent of peyote.

THE ATTITUDE TOWARD WHITE CULTURE

A curious ambivalence is encountered with respect to the symbols of white culture in relation to peyotism. Revivalist religions are usually interpreted as an attempt "to restore the original value pattern" of a culture.[24] They are in effect revolts on a fantasy level against the dominating and suppressing milieu. From this viewpoint, one would expect to see in peyotism the derogation of white culture, of its symbols and carriers.

This was not the case. Certainly Washo peyotists were not unfriendly to whites. With Lancaster giving the cue, every consideration was shown to whites. They were welcomed to meetings, where they were often placed in the seats of honor. They received prominent mention in prayers, were taught songs and given rattles, were taken into the cult and called "brother." One might reason that these acts of friendliness may merely have been stratagems designed to win the support of members of the dominant culture. After all, the opposition of whites to peyote has been long and bitter, and Lancaster, knowing this, might be expected to exert every effort to conciliate potential adversaries.

But peyotists themselves adopted some of the common conventions of white culture; they made a great show of bidding their fellow-cultists hello and goodbye, social gestures without precedent in native life. On a less conscious level it seemed that rapprochement was being attempted with important symbols of white distinctiveness. Thus the theology of peyote, for all its resemblances to older lore, still contained fundamentally alien features. The Christological and biblical components, even though less important than in other tribal versions, were yet obviously identified with the whites. And it was these very elements which proved a major allurement to the acculturated Willie Smokey and a worthwhile feature to the neutral Ray Fillmore. The use of English, the obvious relish with which it was employed, the distinction attached to its fluent command, bespeak anything but a rejection of the value pattern of the "suppressing" group.

On the other hand, the outcroppings of Messianism with its hope for a better day for the Washo, would indicate an attitude of resentment, if not hostility, to the whites. Other facets of this hostility are to be seen in the low regard expressed for white medical practice and for white education generally. Every meeting led by Lancaster found the white doctor portrayed as an ignorant bungler. At a meeting that I attended with Will Christensen—young Washo premedical student and my interpreter—the peyote chief, for all his deference to me, took the opportunity of holding Christensen up to public ridicule. He was thus made to pay a heavy tribute for contemplating a career in white medicine; he dropped out of college the following year. Here it might be argued that Lancaster was simply being practical, inuring his followers against the blandishments of any rival therapy, protecting his own interests. The impression we gained, however, was different. His repeated jibes at white education left the feeling that in this context he wished to point out the superiority of native forms. Lancaster became himself a symbol of native superiority. To his fellow Washo he embodied many of the tokens of success won in the white man's world. Had he not made good in competition with whites? Had he not beaten them at their own game?

The attitude toward white culture was, then, an ambivalent one. On the one hand, features in peyote stamped unmistakably with the seal of the whites were approved—constituted, in fact, a decided attraction—and conferred prestige upon those who mastered them. On the other, reactions of hostility to white symbols manifested themselves in a number of interesting contexts. It should, however, be emphasized that the whites never called down the vehement hostility reserved for the shamans. This is an additional datum indicating that antishaman antipathies proved more decisive than antiwhite aggressions in the development of peyote receptivity.

THE INDIVIDUAL

We have seen how peyote served to relieve anxieties that flowed from two sources—one implicit in the process of acculturation, the other embedded in the aboriginal culture. The conflicts and deprivations attending acculturation precipitated the customary insecurities. Shamanism had been an age-old fashioner of fear and aggression. The cumulative result of the mounting anxieties was a groping quest for some release. Peyote promised such release.

Stated in these terms, the dynamisms of societal change are defined as cultural entities. However, many of the deeper implications of this development are missed if we fail to grasp the significance of the individual in the unfolding process. That an adequate understanding of culture cannot be achieved without a recognition of the role of the individual, "the carrier of institutions," is an axiom of contemporary anthropological study. "It is difficult," writes Sapir, "to see how cultural anthropology can escape the ultimate necessity of testing out its analysis of patterns called 'social' or 'cultural' in terms of individual realities." It has been agreed that the very term "culture" needs to be redefined in terms of the individual. As Linton says, "Culture, insofar as it is anything more than an abstraction made by the investigator, exists only in the minds of the individuals who compose a society."[25]

If we truly seek a three dimensional picture of the impact of peyotism upon shamanism, we must inquire into the relationship between the individual and the institutions under discussion. "The culture is expressed through personalities, and the personalities are expressed in the culture."[26]

"An institution 'means' one thing to one man and something else to another," says Murray. This in a sense sums up the role of peyotism in the lives of many individual Washo. The reactions and attitudes of the people toward the new institution were as variable as the differentiated personality types found among them. The people were not regimented in their reactions by impersonal, superorganic cultural constructs. They were moved by individual personality drives. Horney's comment is apropos: "There are, however, variations not only in customs but also in drives and feelings."[27]

The appeal of peyote was manifold. Students of peyotism have attempted to define the "basic," "most important," appeal of peyote. Thus Schultes concludes that "the therapeutic and tonic properties of peyote are fundamental and of primary importance," a view that harmonizes with Radin's of the Winnebago. On the other hand, La Barre and Shonle seem to agree that "instruction and power through a peyote vision . . . is the primary motive, with doctoring second." As protector from witchcraft, peyote won adherents in Taos and among the Mescalero.[28] Peyote as a religion, as agent for introduction to the Native American Church, as cure for alcoholism, as bringer of rain, as prognosticator—all these and more have been assigned as the dominant attractions of peyote in different tribes.

To speak of "basic" or "dominant" peyote appeals is, however, a somewhat restricted and arbitrary approach. There is the question as to whether the investigator can ever be certain as to what is the primary appeal of peyote in a given tribe or over a given area. The disagreement among anthropologists would indicate that there is no certainty. Perhaps there can be no agreement. For we come to grips here with the problem of the relativity of cultures. We cannot separate into the neat categories of white cultural concepts abstract entities from a primitive culture. As Kardiner points out, "The relationships existing among our institutions are poor guides for . . . understanding . . . a foreign culture."[29] The appeal of peyote is so diverse and complex as to defy classification in terms of our own tidy categories.

Basically the appeal of peyote is definable in terms of the individual. Every attraction that La Barre mentions for all the tribes among which the cult spread was specified an attraction by different individual Washo. Undoubtedly some of these specific appeals were culturally clustered with the cactus itself, were spread along with peyote as a diffusing complex of traits. These were, perhaps, "learned" from Ben Lancaster or from others who had elsewhere come in contact with the cult. But it is quite as true to say that each individual took from peyote what satisfactions it could offer in terms of personal need. Ray Fillmore spoke more penetratingly than he knew when he declared, "Here they take it for what thrills they get out of it—that's all I can see." This, it would seem, is the key to an understanding of peyote's appeal to the Washo. As La Barre has written, "A descriptive account of a ritual pattern, however meticulously detailed it be, must always fall short of reality unless supplemented by further information regarding its functioning in terms of individuals."[30]

Beyond the cultural, members of the tribe had personal anxieties which peyote promised to mollify. Peyote as a powerful mechanism for the "liquidation of manifold anxieties," for the solution of lifelong problems, has been recognized by La Barre. These anxieties might arise as the result of "controlling ideas" within the culture, like the fear of death in the Plains or the fear of sorcery among the Washo.[31] But they might also grow out of conflicts and frustrations of a highly personal nature, which are either removed from the cultural sphere or tangential to it. Exhaustive personal histories of devotees would be required to verify this suggestion. Perhaps it is in order to cite a few cases that tend to validate peyote's role as solvent of personal anxieties, of lifelong problems.

Emory Arnot is in his sixties, dignified, robust, industrious, universally respected and well liked. A man of sober habits, he has become one of the more prosperous members of the tribe. Recently he and his son bought some wool-shearing equipment that cost over two thousand dollars. "We're staying with it," said Arnot, eloquent indication that the confidence of white merchants in him is not misplaced. He gives the impression of being reliable, stable, normal.

One would not think of Emory Arnot as suitable material for the peyote cult, yet he was an ardent devotee. One of Lancaster's most substantial supporters, he was in evidence at every meeting. During the early morning confession period, he would give expression to feelings that came, uninhibited, from deep within him. Dignified old fellow though he was, he would break down and weep unashamedly.

Eventually I learned the story of his life. The great tragedy of his days had been his children. Ten had died, some when adults. Sorrowfully he spoke of his "bad luck with children." For his eighteen-year-old daughter, Hilda, he had an especial fondness, a feeling sharpened no doubt by her sickliness, for she was an epileptic. She had attended a peyote meeting, and the peyote seemed to help her. Arnot was overjoyed. Then one day the girl went down to the river, was seized with a fit and drowned. The father was grief-stricken. His only consolation thereafter came from peyote. At meetings he would see her in the visions. His yearnings would be gratified, his sorrow eased.

Obviously peyote's appeal with Emory Arnot was rooted in the deeply personal. Only an understanding of his personality organization can lead to a proper appreciation of peyote's protean function.

Sam Dick is another case in point. His insecurities arose from physical deformity and more or less continuous sickness. Since the age of eleven, when he fell out of a tree, he had been a hunchback. "I was sick for four years then," he related, "and I've been sick ever since. When I was about twenty, a wind came along when I was working on the ranch. It smashed my leg, broke it on the hip. I lay in bed for two months and never moved."

Additional frustrations came to him in connection with his aspirations to shamanistic office. He was considered a shaman, but evidently had not achieved full-fledged status. He prayed, sang and smoked, but he did not suck out disease-objects. "I didn't go that far yet," he said. "Maybe I do it about this time, but I stop before I went this far." The basic insecurity of his personality is further revealed in his statement, "I worried over sick people. I felt bad. When they went down, I went down."

Peyote brought him the fulfillment he failed to achieve with shamanism. His dissatisfaction, deriving from a basic instability, made him easy prey to missionaries of a new faith, and even before Lancaster, the nondescript Lone Bear had won Dick to the cause. Here again the underlying causation stems from intimately personal components.

No less intimate are the compulsions that brought Roy James into the peyote fold. He is the victim of an inferiority obsession. In a family distinguished for its economic and social achievements, Roy James is a cipher. His father, Ben James, is reputed to be the most prosperous Indian in Carson Valley—his credit rating at the Minden Bank is ten thousand dollars. He is highly esteemed by the whites, sought as guide and companion on hunting and fishing trips. His two older brothers, Earl and Roma James, enjoy a reputation among both Washo and whites equal to their father's. Both are well-off, successful in their own right; have many white acquaintances; are tall, strapping physical specimens. Perhaps their chief distinction comes from having enlisted in the Army in 1918. No one fails to give prominent mention to this symbol of honor when talking about the "James boys."

In this context of brilliant achievement and distinction, Roy James is the forgotten man. He is dependent on his father, has none of the easy graces of his brothers, is slovenly and unprepossessing in appearance, claims few white friends. In addition, he was too young to join the Army during the war. Wherever he goes he hears the merits of his brothers and father extolled, is reminded of his own inadequacy. His lot is that of "younger brother"—psychologically disadvantaged, thwarted. In time he became a heavy drinker, a role which only served to drive him deeper into public disapproval and private self-abasement.

When peyote arrived, he saw in it a possible release from the psychological pressures that were undermining his stability. In joining the cult he would assert his independence from family; he would fly in the face of paternal and fraternal disapproval. His yearning to rebel is further indication of his insecurity. As Kardiner states: "The security system of the individual depends on how effectively he can conform.[32]" He would also gain a certain degree of power in stimulating family anxiety. Moreover, peyote would liberate him from liquor, bring him up to the level of sober respectability his brothers had achieved, thus restoring another segment of his shattered self-esteem. Finally, Ben Lancaster's visits were especially soothing to Roy James's ego. Lancaster was, of course, motivated by the desire to win the support of any member of the prestigious James family. To succeed here would mean considerably enhanced status for the cult. For Roy James's part, it was no small thing to be singled out for special visits by the celebrated peyote chief.

In these several ways—and they might be elaborated further— did peyote mitigate James's anxieties. He became a fervent believer. At last he "belonged." Now he too was a member of an elect brotherhood. It might be noted that his peyote experiences were loaded with neurotic projections. "If you eat more peyote, you can read the mind of one who eats less," he once said. "You can find out how others feel about you." He was still anxious about his position in society, haunted by insecurity; but peyote, he knew, would provide the answer, would bring release. His visionary hallucinations were macabre, full of blood and excrements. His was also an acute consciousness of the penalties that would come with infractions of peyote mandates. After a bout in Reno, in which he had lapsed from abstemiousness, he was extravagantly remorseful, determined to make amends by being more faithful than ever in clinging to cult demands. With the ecstasy of a repentant sinner, he returned to the bosom of peyote. Here at last was forgiveness, surcease from the buffetings of a hostile world.

The cases of Emory Arnot, Sam Dick, and Roy James are alike in that the anxieties and fears which led them to peyote are discoverable in the realm of the highly subjective and personal. It might be argued that, under aboriginal conditions, mechanisms were available for coping with such dislocations of the individual psyche and that, to this extent, the causes are lodged not in the individual but rather in the acculturative drift. But it seems clear that whereas acculturation has undoubtedly taken its toll in psychological stability, individual derangements were in no wise liquidated by pristine cultural forms.

Crashing Thunder, a Winnebago, is an illuminating example of the native who is frustrated in the aboriginal culture. The vision experience denied him so long came only with conversion to peyote. In his case, too, the cult was informed with deeply personal meanings. Hallowell has shown how among the Berens River Indians of Canada the causes of anxiety with certain individuals "are of a different order than the culturally constituted fears of the general run of the population. In contrast with the latter, the situations that provoke the fears of these individuals are emotionally structured by highly subjective meanings that are personal and unconscious." The situation is no different with the Washo. To borrow a metaphor from Benedict, peyotism was an arc representing a wide range of satisfactions from which the individual selected a segment in terms of personal needs.[33]

Mandelbaum has shown how the same process as that described for the Washo with reference to peyotism operated among the Kota of the Nilgiri Hills in southern India when a new religious cult was introduced. Three key characters, who epitomized varying tribal attitudes toward the intrusive religion, reacted to it in consonance with highly subjective needs. The Kota study and the Washo study were both undertaken with people who had become familiar to the investigators, into whose personalities valuable insights had been gained. Hence the significance of the individual in the intepretation of these cultural phenomena.[34]

Sapir has remarked, "Under familiar circumstances and with familiar people, the locus of reference of our interest is likely to be the individual." In both the Washo and Kota cases, as Dollard put it, "the institutional form is seen as a pattern and drape for the individual emotional life." Viewing the societal scene thus, one perhaps gains a deeper, more realistic awareness of the nature of culture. "Cultures," Sapir has written, "are merely abstracted configurations of idea and action patterns, which have endlessly different meanings for the various individuals in the group and which if they are to build up into any kind of significant psychical structure . . . must be set in relation to each other in a complex configuration of evaluations, inclusive and exclusive implications, priorities and potentialities of realization which cannot be discovered from an inquiry into the described patterns."[35]

ANTECEDENT CONFLICTS

Inner psychological drives were not the only forces motivating the individual in the peyote conflict. Still on a personal plane but less subjective, perhaps, were considerations revolving around the concept of temporal prestige, of political power. These were also largely of a noncultural category, running in personal, noninstitutional channels. We have already alluded to the fact that some Washo championed peyote because others denounced it, and vice versa. Alignment on one side of the fence or the other, with one leader or another, was frequently in terms of political interest and alliance. Behind the high-flown ideological disputations, some of the combatants were engaged in a grim struggle for power.

The sordid realities of intratribal politics, like the hostile attitude toward shamans, are not always apparent. Deep-seated conflicts, profound social ferment, hostile relationships within a tribe sometimes escape the notice of even the observant student. Hallowell mentions the aggressions in Salteaux society which actually stamp the culture but which have been overlooked by generations of observers. One would never suspect that politics are rife in the Pueblos from reading the standard accounts of that "nonindividualistic," "Appollonian" culture, yet that they are of marked significance is authoritatively attested. Park was unaware that peyote had been introduced among the Northern Paiute according to La Barre, yet one of Park's chief informants, Joe Green, told Stewart that he had "joined the cult in 1929, continued believing in it, and re-affiliated with it in 1936." Said Green: "I didn't tell Willard Park about peyote because he didn't ask me." The reason for such oversights may be found in the dichotomy already mentioned between white and native conceptualizations. Our own arrangement of culture categories does not coincide "in the manner with which they are functionally integrated in the native mind."[36]

That conflicts which may best be characterized as political did exist among the Washo prior to the advent of peyote is learned from various sources. The conflicts centered in Dresslerville in the persons of Willie Smokey and Steve Earl. They had been rivals for years. Both had their allies, but until the coming of peyote Willie Smokey was unquestionably the more powerful. He was singled out for responsible missions by the Agency, while Steve Earl received no such favored assignments. Smokey was a member of the Tribal Council, had been its chairman, an office to which Earl aspired in vain.

Steve Earl's claim to leadership was based on the former chiefship of his father, Captain Earl. Now many Washo deny that Captain Earl was ever their rightful chief, maintaining that Captain Jim had been the real leader of the tribe. Thus the conflict over the office of tribal leader was not new. Steve Earl's pretensions were looked upon as a special piece of arrogance by those who had never regarded his father's claims as legitimate. When Captain Jim died, bewitched as many believed by Earl's close relative, Becky Jack, his popularity did not increase. Hostility toward the Earl family, in fact, reached such a pitch that they were forced to leave Dresslerville. They erected a shack about a mile from the colony and lived there in relative isolation.

When Willie Smokey became a peyotist, Steve Earl saw his chance for recouping lost prestige and proceeded to make the most of it. Smokey seems to have joined the cult because he viewed it as charged with white status symbolism. "I've always been a God-fearing, churchgoing man," he said. "I never took one puff of marijuana or opium. I was mainly responsible for the church in Dresslerville. I've been a faithful worker of the church. The church is working for our interests. Peyote is the Indian church. Churchgoing is good and peyote is good." He may not have reckoned with the possibility of a powerful opposition to peyote. When it did form, organized out of a combination of powerful interests, it found as its most vocal leader Steve Earl. Always a voluble talker, Earl was suddenly cast in a role for which his ambitions and talents fitted him. He was restored to favor, his family permitted to return to Dresslerville. Rapidly gaining strength, the antipeyotists under Earl soon made life uncomfortable for cultists living in Dresslerville. Petitions were circulated calling for expulsion of the cult. A movememt was actually started to oust the Smokey family from the colony, doubtless suggested by Earl, who must have had an ïtch for poetic justice. So great was the pressure that Willie Smokey and his family finally withdrew from active participation in the new religious movement.

Willie Smokey was bitter at the turn events had taken. His explanation is a telltale disclosure of the part played by intratribal politics in bringing about the conflict:

> Captain Earl was Hitler and Mussolini around here. He was in control until the new deal. After Captain Jim died, he thought he was captain and he wanted to control like Hitler and Mussolini.
>
> They all say that peyote is no good, that it makes you crazy. But none of them have been to meetings. They don't know what they're saying.
>
> It will lead to a mixup. The classing of people is beginning. It must come to a showdown. I can only stand so much. If they want to get me out of here, it'll come to a showdown. If they want to run me off here, it'll come to a split. Two parties will come. They'll have to prove me guilty.
>
> Martinez Kyser is circulating another petition to put out peyote users, and I haven't been to a meeting in two years.
>
> Steve is naturally against me because I stood up for the right of the people. During the war the County Commissioners got together with Steve and made a law to run the Indians out of town [Gardnerville] after six [P.M.]. I fought against that law and we won. Since then Steve has been against me. Now they're fighting me. They're not doing this for the benefit of the people.

It may be reasonably concluded that antecedent frictions and conflicts on a political plane offer an explanation for some aspects of the peyote struggle. The rivalry of Willie Smokey and Steve Earl for temporal status was a potent factor in the development of the conflict. There were undoubtedly other rivalries of similar character which found oblique expression in the peyote phenomenon. Peyote, in other words, was a rationale for airing old conflicts, a pretext for trotting out old grudges, a catalyst precipitating long-standing envies and hatreds. Geertz reminds us that "political conflict . . . tends . . . to focus around ostensibly religious issues," and Firth that "religion can operate as a system of political maneuver."[37]

THE OPPOSITION OF THE SHAMANS

By far the most powerful factor in the decline of peyotism among the Washo was the opposition of the shamans. To this force all others are subsidiary. How powerful an influence it is can be measured by the fact that with so many factors conspiring toward the rapid and widespread acceptance of a new religious dispensation, the shamans were still strong enough to turn back a tide which at one time threatened to sweep all before it. Hated as they undoubtedly were, less dominant though their position was becoming, they yet exercised sufficient control to abort the development of a rival religion.

The shamans opposed peyotism for obvious reasons. It threatened their status, politically, socially, economically. Should peyote under the leadership of peyote chiefs gain too much headway, their power might be permanently eclipsed. How did the shamans propose to maintain their position? By playing on people's fear of their prime weapon, witchcraft. This had been the means for preserving their status in the old order; it would be employed in this critical contingency. It would constitute the nucleus around which the antipeyotist opposition would form.

It was not the first time that the shamans had been forced to reckon with an intrusive religious movement. The 1870 Ghost Dance was, as has already been related, brought to the Washo in 1871 by Frank Spencer, a Northern Paiute known more commonly as Weneyuga. But from Du Bois's account, it is clear that the movement made little headway in the tribe. In spite of the fact that the Washo lived contiguously to the Northern Paiute, source of the cult, and, as documented earlier with Tom Snooks's illness, knew them intimately enough to call in their shamans for curing, the new religion lasted "only one summer in the vicinity of Carson Valley." It appears that the cult affected only Northern Washo. There is no mention of its presence among the Southern Washo. Nor were the Washo in any sense channels of diffusion. "It may be confidently stated." writes Du Bois, "that the Washo are debarred as transmitters of the cult to the west."[38] Du Bois's account is bolstered by my experience in failing to secure any information from Central and Southern Washo informants about the 1870 Ghost Dance. Obviously its adoption was both restricted and transitory.

The same forces at work in opposing peyote seem to have been operating against the 1870 revivalism. From Du Bois we learn that "when his [Weneyuga's] prophecies failed to materialize, the local Washo shamans met and denounced him as an imposter." That was undoubtedly the *coup de grace*. The movement collapsed.

According to Du Bois, "it left in its wake a few persons who continued to believe in a deferred advent but who maintained no active cult practices."[39] The shamans had succeeded in liquidating the upstart religion.

No better reception awaited the 1890 Ghost Dance, also disseminated from the proximate Northern Paiute. "In recent years," writes Du Bois, "Washo attended Jack Wilson's meetings out of curiousity and gregariousness, but very few believed his prophecies."[40] In Washo territory the 1890 revivalist cult did not strike root. Yet Jack Wilson (Wovoka) was well known to many Washo both socially and in his professional capacity as shaman. It seems logical to infer that in this instance also Washo shamans exerted sufficient influence to prevent the diffusion of a rival faith.

The Washo are not the only tribe in which the spread of peyotism has been squelched by the shamans. At Taos the same thing happened, and there is an unusual degree of correspondence between the two cases. In Taos the introduction of peyote resolved itself into a struggle between vested religious interests, the shamans, and the protagonists of the new faith, the "peyote boys"; here too the people's fear of witching and its exploitation by the shamans played a decisive role. The claim that peyote was antiwitch prophylaxis, that it cured bewitchment, was enough to rally the established religious professionals against it. It was not difficult to organize an opposition, a step undertaken by the powerful shaman, Porfirio Mirabel, since the individualistic aspects of the new cult were in many ways not congenial to the "general temper of Pueblo ceremonialism." Ultimately, however, the "peyote boys" were brought to heel through employment of the omnipotent weapon of sorcery. As with the Washo, the charge of witchcraft was made against the rebellious peyotists. It is a parallel example of the "witchcraft complex serving for a standardization of control."[41]

The case of the Mescalero is basically no different from that found in Taos and among the Washo. Peyotism was taken over by the Mescalero shamans lock, stock, and barrel and closely woven into the indigenous culture. Here the shamans made peyote their own possession and turned the meetings into grim witching bees. The important fact is that the shamans retained the mechanisms of social control. Having absorbed the new cult into the old, their status was in no way impaired. Parsons has suggested that the difference in approach to the intrusive faith by the Mescalero on the one hand and at Taos on the other, is to be explained in terms of the "personalities" of the two cultures. Whereas among the Mescalero the individually centered peyote cult could be reconciled with the "individualistically minded shamans," in Taos it came into too fundamental a conflict with the "communal ritualistic performances" of Pueblo religion.[42]

Among the Southern Ute the power of the shamans is no less commanding. M. K. Opler has described the interesting division of the tribe into two distinct reservation communities, one at Towoac and the other at Ignacio, the former conservative and still close to the old way of life, the latter in the process of becoming assimilated to a progressive agricultural economy. Two levels of peyote acceptance have been discerned in the respective communities. At Towoac it has been wholeheartedly approved and "flourishes in the soil of cultural reaction." At Ignacio it exists feebly. What is of importance for our present purpose is the disclosure that in Towoac the shamans enthusiastically support the cult, while in Ignacio they vigorously oppose it.[43] While the variant levels of acceptance may in some measure be due to economic and social differences stemming from variant rates of acculturation, the role of the shamans as a determinant force in the fate of a religious institution cannot be ignored.

The actual mechanisms employed by the Washo shamans in combating peyotism centered in the direct and indirect exploitation of witchcraft. We have seen what profound intracult agitation was created by the accusation that sorcery was being practiced at meetings. The source of the agitation was unquestionably the shamans. They assiduously circulated the impression that peyote meetings were charged with supernatural danger. When peyotists died, it was the shamans who designated the cause as the unearthly power inherent in peyote. During the period of interreligious struggle, there could not be a shamanistic curing séance but that it brought forth the diagnosis that peyote may have caused the sickness. Shamans would seize the opportunity presented at these sessions to deliver stern homilies against the wicked cactus. No wonder that many of the people, oriented to a world view traditionally dominated by the fear of the supernaturally sinister, were filled with misgivings and severed active affiliation with the cult.

Neither did the shamans hold aloof from more tangible methods of expressing opposition. The exercise of control through supernatural means might not impress some individuals of little faith. But everybody would be impressed by the use of force. The drunken gangs that broke up cult meetings, persecuted active peyotists, and signed petitions of expulsion were organized around the shamans. Steve Earl became the gang leader. He could be depended upon to champion the cause of the shamans because his mother was one. Furthermore, peyotists were arrogantly asserting that her power had vanished since the night he had gone to a peyote meeting. Not to be forgotten also was the comforting knowledge that in fighting the shaman's fight, he was promoting his own political fortunes.

It may be wondered how the shamans, hitherto riven by mutual antagonisms and rivalries, could act in concert in this instance. Not that they suddenly banded together into an organized guild. But that they did sink their mutual suspicions and work in tacit concord in behalf of the same end, there can be no doubt. The explanation is to be found, of course, in the nature of the emergency. Failure to unite might have meant defeat. As Mandelbaum remarks in connection with a similar development among the Kota, "Dissident factions within a group suddenly consolidate when the security of the larger group is menaced. . . . This seems to hold true for all units of society." And this from Sapir: "Personality organizations . . . psychologically comparable with the greatest cultures or idea systems . . . have as their first law of being their essential self-preservation."[44] The individualistic Washo shamans, who were faced with the serious threat of peyotism, exemplified this pattern of self-preservation.

It would seem, then, that the shamans when accorded high and powerful status in the aboriginal pattern, can exercise dominant control over intrusive religious movements. The fate of revivalist cults is often determined by the will of the professional religionists acting in behalf of their own vested interests. When the shaman occupies a position of unique and unrivaled preeminence as among the Washo, a position secured through the agency of witchcraft, new religious movements may receive summary treatment. As long as the shamans rule Washo life, revivalist religion may stand no more chance of gaining a foothold than did the Ghost Dances of 1870 and 1890 and the peyote cult.

THE IMPACT OF PEYOTISM ON SHAMANISM

A movement like peyotism which created such a profound disturbance in the life of the people might properly be expected to leave its mark on many aspects of the culture. The effects will become more palpable, in all likelihood, as time goes on. While I was with the tribe, the peyote conflict was still too immediate and absorbing a concern to permit a gauging of its possible influence on future cultural modification. If we think of the indigenous culture as a pool and of peyote as a stone dropped into it, we may say that the impact had been too recent to allow the resulting ripples to radiate far.

In one branch of the culture, however, certain interesting mutations were perceptible. Shamanism, the institution directly menaced by peyote's impact, did give evidence of undergoing change, which, although not spectacular, was nonetheless profound.

Specifically it was the shaman who, in his attitudes and reactions, embodied departures from tradition. From having been unyielding and arrogant, the shaman became conciliatory and constrained. Mike Dick, who curtly refused to allow me to witness a curing during my first year in the field, was without difficulty prevailed upon to do so twelve months later. It was no different with Bill Wilson of Loyalton. Peyote had swept through the tribe in the interim.

The shaman's latter-day restraint is further seen in a curious liberalism toward other therapies. It is inconceivable that the shamans of old would have given sanction to alien medical practice. Yet in 1939 Mike Dick was recommending that some of his patients consult white doctors. On one occasion he spoke approvingly of Chinese medicine. During this period, he stressed his willingness to cooperate with white practitioners, with the Agency hospital, although my notes reveal that he spoke contemptuously of white medical practice just two seasons earlier. M. K. Opler records an almost identical case of a White Knife shaman, struggling for existence in a rapidly acculturating scene, who offered his services to an Agency hospital.[45] Henry Rupert admitted that shamans "can't cure everything" and spun elaborate rationalizations in defense of shamanistic curing methods. In these interesting dialectics he employed the borrowed terminology of the whites—"high psychology," "will power," "mind over matter." There can be little doubt that these developments received a potent fillip from the peyote impact.

But Mike Dick's quest for justification is perhaps the most persuasive datum pointing to the growing feeling of insecurity on the part of the shamans. It was with a great show of self-righteousness that this most powerful shaman of the region showed me two documents drawn up at his dictation by a young Washo, Donald Wade. These were his charter, he felt, his diploma. It was a symbol of security—borrowed from another culture. Couched in language designed to impress those whose approval he seeks—and needs—these documents become in effect an *apologia pro sua vita*:

> I, the undersigned, Blind Mike Dick, in this day of our Lord, July twenty-fourth, one thousand nine hundred and thirty eight. I will explain my autobiography in the following paragraph:
>
> I have been given the power which I possess, known as supernatural power. My power is a miracle one. When I am at work on my patient, I would have visitors attending my performance and on the third night of my work the spirit would whisper above my head which that every one in the room would hear.
>
> This spirit talk is like radio which we hear every day. It explains the condition or the cause of the patient's sickness. During all my four nights of doctoring this spirit would give power which would make visible all germs in the body of the patient and then I would draw the germ out of the patient's body through pores and I have found many different kinds of life germ. The germs which I draw I would exhibit to the audiences.
>
> I am about sixty-six years of age, native of Carson Valley, Douglas County, Nevada. I have been practicing on my people and many other races for thirteen years. In all these years I have been very successful in healing the sick. I believe my power is beyond the power of many. The sick people would come many miles to visit me. My record has been very favorable among my tribe and others. I heal my patient without using any kind of medicine. My work is scientific healing. I have many more things to say but I believe this will be all.
>
> Blind Mike Dick
(written by D. T. Wade)
>
> I, BLIND MIKE, have been practicing this course for years. I have no hard feelings against the white doctors. They have helped us a lot, such things as broken arms or legs, or operations that I can't do.
>
> All the dead persons have been erased out of the last list, and this present list contains all living individuals.
>
> Since March 1922, so far I have doctored in rough count 225 persons; that is, persons living now. All dead persons not counted in the following list:
>
> Emory Arnote; Seymour Arnote; Hilda Arnote; Hattie Arnote; Minnie George; Carrie George; Jimmy George and boy; Lilly Barber; Amy Barber; Pete George; Archie George; Leland James; Tom Barber; Bennie James; Enie Cornbread; Mable Washoe; Magie Washoe; Dolores Washoe; Harford James; Irene James; Earl James; Effie James; Roye James and boy; Doris James and 2 boys; Roma James and 3 boys; Emory Dick; Lucy Dick; Willie Jack; Maggie Jack; Marguitte Jack; Louina Jack; Tom Sango; Louisa Sango; Jenny Henry; Irene Henry; Jim Winters; Franklin Mack; Jerry Dick; Lissie Johnson; Arlene Bobb and boy; Maggie Joe; Em Dick; Johnson Walker; Berdie Dick;

George Orange; Charlie Nevers and 2 grandchildren; Bernice Nevers; Julia Nevers; John Henry; Harry Jim; Willie Jim; Ada Jim and 2 boys; Fred Mike's son; Lula Mike; Mena Mike; Frank Peter and 2 daughters and son; Lizzie Pixley; Annie Brown; Francis Brown; Cora Washoe; Viola Washoe; Lincoln Pete; Alma Winters; Pansy Wadsworth, daughter and son; Sammy Dick; Susie Dangberg; Mandy Smoky; Willie Smoky; Carnegie Smoky; Tommy Smoky; Sadie Smoky; Teresa Smoky; Dorothy Wyatt; Lucile Smoky; Geraldine Smoky; Mayde Johnson and 2 sons; Nita Wade and daughter and sons; Cecil Wade; Mathen Harris; Harry Fillmore; Leona Fillmore and son; Hazel Fillmore; Mandy Joe and son; Maggie Tom; John Walker; Tom Walker and daughter; Mena Walker; George Snooks; Memo Snooks; Isabelle Snooks and 2 daughters; Tillie Snooks; Mike Holbrook; Marion Holbrook; Delphine Holbrook; Marie Holbrook; Goldie Holbrook; Herman Holbrook; Clara Frank; Garfield Frank; Charlie Dressler; Durman Fred; Kitty Fred; Alma Fred; Agnes Fred; Mary Jean Pete; Minnie Teacot and daughter; Amy Teacot; Dorothy Teacot and son; Murphy Teacot; George Dutchy; Elaine Dutchy; Mabeline Ellis; John Mack; Rosie Mack and boy; Cleveland Mack; Howard Mack; Jermna Pete; Tillie Pete; Alvina Dick; Arlina Dick; Ed Rufe; Willie Hecke; Elsie Bobb; Maddy Dutchy; Dewey Dutchy and son; Rosie Henry; Minnie Henry; Nancy Pitts and daughter; Hattie Joe; Velda Joe; Winnie Christensen; Jennie Shaw; Tuney Bagley; Walla John; Molly Wade; Bessie Wade; Cesar John; daughter and son; Ott Bagley; Bronco Bagley; Ed Mack; Lena Frank and daughter; Tillie Frank; Annie Fillmore; Susie Maxwell; Nancy Wyatt; Evan Wyatt; Robert Wyatt; Maggie Pitchwood; Jessie Frank; Judie Jake; Elve Hopper; Edison Hopper; Florence Hopper; John Christensen; Mamie George; Ernest Fillmore; Burna Sally and mother and 3 children; Perry Nevers; Lytel Palmer; Doon Cornbread; Whitney Washoe; Ben Moose's sister; George Orange and wife; Charlie Miller; Rubell Miller, son and 2 daughters; Annie Sally; and besides these counting about 45 children.

Also:

May John; Conner James; Vernita Wade; Verdder Smoky; Maggie James; Jackson Snooks; Juanita Dick Higgen; Maidie Johnson; May Abe; Moose Joe; Charley Dick; Lula Esau; Wanie Pete; Doda Mack; Maggie Merrill; Mamie George; Agnes Elwania; Jack Wiltse; Gertie Jack; Roy James; Burna Sally.

And the following Paiutes:

Rosey Jack; Lizzie Jackson; Jake Williams; John Alston; Jimmie Tibbetts; Wesley Keno; Minnie Kene; Roy Higgin; Lorine Kane; Mack.

The change in attitude apparent with Mike Dick and his colleagues is significant in that it indicates a serious dwindling of shamanistic prestige. When the shamans make concessions, show themselves eager to compromise, their star is declining. They are at last beginning to sense the instability of their position. The struggle over peyote demonstrated that their hold on the people was uncertain. Never before had they met with such open and prolonged defiance. It was clear that they no longer wielded the control which had formerly dragooned the tribesmen into submission.

What lies ahead can be dimly apprehended. A recent communication from Carson Valley tells of the firm belief in peyote maintained in the very center of tribal conservatism—the Dresslerville colony. The fires of peyotism still smolder. In some of the steadfast the faith probably burns more brightly because it burns in secret. It may be that the Smokeys still carry on their clandestine devotions. Perhaps Emory Arnot and Roy James still chew an occasional peyote button and mutter a fervent prayer for the return of the cult. Should propitious circumstances arise, the revival might again ignite. Should Mike Dick die, should Steve Earl fall to fighting with his henchmen, should some leader of the opposition become newly discredited, peyotism might once more enter Washo life and become firmly established. It flourishes in neighboring Northern and Southern Paiute camps. It remains a symbol of release to not a few individuals who found in it a solvent for crushing problems. The process of cultural deterioration has not been stayed, the pace of assimilation is becoming accelerated. The shamans are in retreat. A revivalist cult may yet find in the valleys immediately east of the high Sierras a fruitful soil for flowering.

Dresslerville Indian colony, Nevada, 1938.

Pool near Bijou, California, where George Snooks saw the footprints of water babies (1938).

George Snooks, interpreter, informant, at Myers, California, 1937.

Blind Mike Dick (left) at Myers, California, 1938. In his right hand is his shaman's staff on which is notched the number of patients he attended. Dick (right) sitting outside his winter house at Coleville, California, 1937.

Charlie Rube (left), antelope shaman, near Bijou, California. He was in his eighties when photograph was taken. Susie Rube (right) making a basket. They would spend the summer at Bijou, following the old Washo tradition of moving from Carson Valley to Lake Tahoe for the summer.

Brush enclosure or "corral," for peyote meeting, Coleville, California, 1939.

Long Pete, Southern Washo informant.

Sam Dick (left) at peyote altar inside enclosure. Sam and Ida Dick (right) holding paraphernalia. The drum is not tied; this is done only before meetings.

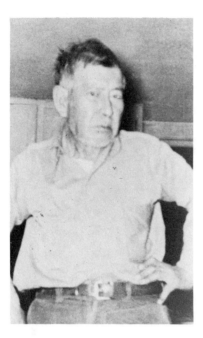

Henry (Moses) Rupert. Photograph by Don Handelman sometime in the 1960s; in earlier years, Rupert did not permit having his picture taken.

Ramsey Walker, veteran peyotist, near Dresslerville, Nevada, 1981.

John Frank, healer, dreamer, at Carson City, Nevada, 1981. He was in his nineties when photograph was taken.

EPILOGUE

WASHO SHAMANISM SINCE 1939

Washo Experience and Washo Personality

Over the past forty years the changes that have taken place in Washo life are commensurate with the ferment that has agitated American life in general during these decades. Vine Deloria, Jr., has suggested that the Second World War is a useful bench mark for measuring the recent progress of racial minorities. Certainly since the mid-forties the material condition of the Washo has improved. Many Washo are still plagued by economic insecurity and social disability. Recent statistics show that American Indians are among the poorest, unhealthiest, least educated, and worst housed among America's ethnic groups.[1] Nevertheless it remains true that the grinding poverty and pariah status the Washo once knew are now largely gone.

Forty-five years ago the Washo were impoverished, disdained, shunned, their life an unremitting round of restriction and denial. Most of the men eked out a living working as seasonal ranch hands, the women as domestics. Some men lucky enough to work on highway crews were counted among the elite. The old people subsisted on canned foods distributed by the government. No Washo was served in a restaurant. Washo children were barred from attending public schools. In conversation with whites, Washo were usually dismissed as shiftless idlers given incorrigibly to drink. Until recently no Indians were allowed by law to be seen after dark in Gardnerville, five miles from Dresslerville Indian colony. Only in 1974 was the law abolished.[2]

With increasing white settlement in the foothill valleys of the Sierras and along the eastern shore of Lake Tahoe—Washo territory since pre-Columbian times—new jobs and added income have become available. It is said that the Washo are becoming urbanized. Furthermore, with the growing disapproval and proscription of social and economic discrimination, Washo can begin to move and share in the life of the general community. Social distance between Washo and white is not exactly approaching the vanishing point and an egalitarian society is not about to be born in western Nevada. Yet in Dresslerville, once a scabrous tribal settlement where a white would seldom set foot, there is now a clubhouse where Washo and whites eat, play cards, and socialize together. In 1978 Warren d'Azevado could write, "The wretched conditions of the recent past seem all but obliterated, and many young people are scarcely aware of the quite different world in which their parents and grandparents clung to a precarious existence."[3]

Changes in the external life of the Washo have been due in large measure to the Pan-Indian movement for native rights. The revolution of rising Indian hopes demanding justice for wrongs inflicted since the white intrusion and asserting pride in being Indian has invested the tribe with a new élan. It has rearranged the hierarchy of tribal authority and carried younger Washo to new positions of leadership. Land claims have been resolutely pressed in the courts, where white champions, anthropologists among them, have signed declarations and given testimony in their support. In 1975 the federal government settled a Washo land claim with a payment of $5,523,536, the result of which a recreation and camping area on the Carson River was created as a commercial venture and each authenticated Washo given $2,000. (Jo Ann Nevers, a Washo, has written a tribal history which contains a précis of the history of the Washo claims case.)[4]

The 1975 land settlement stands out in astonishing contrast to past responses by the government to Washo claims. In 1892 when Captain Jim led a delegation of tribesmen to Washington D.C. on the last of a series of frustrating missions, the Washo finally won a government concession: individual forty-acre Pine Nut Range allotments. But restrictions on the use of the land made the allotments of little value. In the late thirties during the benign administration of Indian Commissioner John Collier, the United States government gave 795 acres of farmland to the Washo "in trust," adding it to the

Dresslerville colony. But since the Washo had had no experience with agricultural pursuits on this scale, the farm was a failure. Historic government response to Washo claims, when it had not been devious and unjust, was ill-advised and bungling. Little wonder that as late as the early forties, the mood of most Washo was one of frustration, apathy, resignation. All that has changed.[5]

The mood of disenchantment and defeat that marked Washo-white relations since earliest contact revealed itself in the posture of nonresistance to white intrusion. The Washo yielded passively to the encroachment and advance of white settlers on their lands, never giving armed resistance. Thereafter they squatted on the fringes of white communities begging for handouts. In the process of submissive response to white domination, much repressed hostility may have been generated.[6] But in the absence of any tradition of violence, the Washo demonstrated no combativeness or belligerence.

It is curious that in the early chronicles recounting the steady penetration and continuous traversing of Washo territory, the Washo themselves are mentioned only rarely. The reason is to be found in their tendency to avoid whites, to flee from them, to give them no trouble. They would hide in the hills, watching the intruders pass their concealed camps. Washo scouts saw the beleaguered Donner Party in their extremity but did not come near to help. Their timidity and fear brewed a numbing inferiority. They accepted this status of inferiority and did not begin to overcome it until more than a century later.

The passivity and quiescence which characterized the Washo stance toward whites seems to have marked their attitude toward neighboring Indian tribes as well. "Wars" with the Northern Paiute, Miwok, Nisenan, or Maidu were conventionally limited skirmishes. Feuds were seldom sanguinary. To the Northern Paiute, closest neighbors, who had horses, who fought battles with the whites, and who for their pains were placed on a reservation where they learned successfully to farm and to breed stock, the Washo, horseless and landless, were poor, bedraggled relations. There is a tradition that the Northern Paiute humiliated the Washo by banishing them to the highlands and forbidding them to ride horses. Whether for this reason or another, the Washo never adopted the horse for either hunting or warfare.[7]

The Washo have been portrayed as displaying among themselves contentious and quarrelsome behavior. A brooding distrust

which fostered disunity and factionalism is said to have marked
intratribal relations. Perennial discord has prevented unified tribal
action at every stage of Washo history. It is said that only once have
the Washo acted as a unified tribe—in 1902 when their land allotments were menaced and Captain Jim was chosen tribal leader.
Even the achievement of a Washo tribal council failed to heal the
traditional divisiveness, and deep schisms developed over the land
claims case. The "pervasive factionalism" ascribed to Taos and to
the Western Shoshone would seem to apply to the Washo.[8] A white
resident born in Carson Valley and respected by the Indians spoke
to me of the "jealousy, spite, backbiting and hatred" among the
Washo. The explanation for this Washo personality cast probably
lies in the sources of deprivation and humiliation caused by the
years of traumatic contact with whites and Indian neighbors.

That the personality flaws attributed to the Washo should be
accompanied by a frayed and stunted self-image should occasion no
surprise. Washo self-denigration with its neurotic sequels seems to
be a leitmotif of the tribal outlook. (This psychological state has
been called the "grasshopper syndrome." In the biblical account of
the first reconnaissance of Canaan by the ancient Hebrews, scouts
brought back a defeatist report on the chances for occupying a land
inhabited by the giant "sons of Anak." They said, "We looked like
grasshoppers to ourselves, and so we must have looked to them.")[9]
"Some of them other tribes don't have much use for the Washoe,"
related a Washo peyotist. "Say they are kind of hard to get along
with—keep to themselves." Quite a few are embarrassed and
ashamed of their native ways, even of their aboriginal artifacts. The
young will not speak Washo and only a few old women make the
baskets for which the Washo are celebrated. They will affect a dis-
like for old Washo foods and will even hide the bedrock mortars
from view. Leaders who tried to bring innovations into the life of
the people have been ridiculed, despised as tools of the whites.[10]

The novel, *Rabbit Boss*, by Thomas Sanchez, published in 1974,
is a fictional account of the Washo encounter with the whites over a
four-generation span. The book describes at harrowing length and
in grim detail the treatment of the Indians at the hands of the brutal
whites. All the younger Washo who mentioned the book praised it,
verifying its accuracy by reference to what their parents and grandparents had told them. What is of interest in the context here is the
tone of much of the book—a long plaint bewailing the docility and

impotence of the Washo in facing their oppressors. Lamentation over the helplessness of the victims is a continuous counterpoint to the condemnation of their persecutors. Throughout the book one hears echoes of Sarah Winnemucca's dirge over the "poor, poor Washo."[11]

A reading of the Washo attitude toward their neighbors, as well as toward themselves, will help in better understanding their approach to the changing scene of the decades following World War II. With new opportunities for forging a better life as individuals and as members of the Indian community, they might be ready to accept the tokens of change and renewal and to discard the symbols of dependency and submission. In this light we may comprehend their response to shamanism and the shamans, as well as to peyotism and the roadchiefs. We may understand the reaching out to the white world as well as the quest for some significant link with their Indianness. We can anticipate that the road to these objectives will not be smooth. Conflicts and ambiguities will make the journey fitful and uncertain.

The Ambivalence Toward Tribal Culture

With the change in Washo status has come a progressive erosion of the tribal culture. The rising tide of acculturation has cut Washo life adrift from its aboriginal anchorage. Some of the old customs and usages survive. The card game *bengeli* is still played; there is a reluctance to mention the Washo names of individuals, and a disinclination to speak of the recent dead. Old Washo still point with their lips. In the summer of 1981 the girl's puberty ceremony was still held, and in the fall some of the people traveled to Pine Nut Range to gather pine nuts. But the Washo way of life which gave the tribe its self-conscious corporate being now lives mainly in memory. This fate is no different from that of other specific tribal societies which have felt the impact of powerful intrusive cultures.

Symbolic of the fate of Washo culture is the present condition of the native language. This primary datum of tribal identity may now be said to be disappearing. Young Washo no longer speak Washo. The universal complaint of the old people runs, "They don't speak Washo anymore." Recently attempts have been made to teach the Washo their language but the response has been feeble. The instructor who journeys from Reno to Dresslerville for each class session is not a Washo but Professor William H. Jacobsen, Jr., of the University of Nevada, authority on Washo and Hokan languages.

This attitude of Washo toward their tribal heritage is marked by an unhappy and confusing ambivalence. They profess pride in being Washo and drive around in cars that display bumper stickers reading, "I'm Washo Indian and proud of it." Yet they feel that their Indian identity together with their failure or tardiness to embrace the favored white culture has proved a serious, if not crippling handicap. Sometimes they speak bitterly about being a Washo.

Leroy Rupert, grandson of the shaman, Henry Rupert, spoke for many Washo when he said, "Pride in being a Washo will get you nowhere." He operates an auto-body repair shop with his father and brother in Carson Colony, and had just returned from a hunting trip in a new truck and trailer which stood outside his recently built house. He spoke with the nonservile assurance of younger Washo leaders:

> The Washo need a lot of things but what they need more than anything else is education so they could compete with whites for jobs. That's the main thing. Being a Washo is not that important. If he can read and write, then pride is good. If he can't, it's for the birds.

But a little later he spoke of his grandfather, who at bedtime would tell his grandchildren tales of the past, of monstrous animals in the mountains ("like the abominable snowman"), and small mountain people "you could hear laughing and talking but who would disappear if you came too near." His mood of cynical realism had changed as he savored the memory of the old Washo tales traditionally told by grandfathers at bedtime.

The Washo are proud of the basketmaking reputation of the tribe and particularly of Datsolalee, famous Washo basket maker, examples of whose work are found in some of the leading American museums.[12] Yet basketmaking is a vanishing craft. "No one makes baskets any more," bemoaned Fred Richards. Some of the older women still do. Marvin Dressler's wife was making a cradleboard when I visited her in Dresslerville, and I saw a number of young mothers carrying their infants in cradleboards. But the young ones no longer make them. Viola Brenard took me to the nearby house of her elder daughter, who opened an old trunk and proudly drew out some rabbitskin blankets, the stick on which they were "woven" and a pine-nut-soup stirrer. No one is making these artifacts any more.

These physical tokens of the aboriginal life are now only relics, museum pieces that have survived the assault of the white culture juggernaut because they were stored in trunks. And because the language, like the artifacts, has a low evaluation in the marketplace, it will soon cease to be spoken. As a leader of the Nevada Inter-tribal Council said:

> Our language is too much. There's not enough time [to learn it] when you want to be like Americans. We want to preserve the native languages, but it's not easy. My folks didn't care if I learned the language. They told me, "It won't help you earn a living."

When making your way in the white world, your Indian culture is likely to have a hard time surviving.

It is, then, an unresolved ambivalence that clouds the attitude of Washo toward both their own and white culture. A Washo will reject his own culture because it handicaps him in the climb to success in the working world. At the same time, he may yearn for the old ways, for the stability, serenity, and comforting sense of identity they provide. But his response to the white world is no less equivocal. He may want to reject it for its harsh and callous treatment of him since the first contact 150 years ago. But while recoiling, he will embrace it for the material rewards it can bestow. Thus are the Washo, like Indians everywhere, trapped in a perplexing and disturbing conflict.

The Eclipse of the Shamans

The religious life of the Washo in particular has undergone profound change. While Washo may still feel that there is a spirit world which is the source of power, the formal vehicles for the expression of religious belief and practice have been radically altered. The religious scene among the Washo today bears little resemblance to that of forty years ago.

The most conspicuous and dramatic change that has occurred in the Washo religious scene is the eclipse and demise of the shamans. The shamans who once dominated the religious world of the Washo are no more. There is no full-fledged shaman among the Washo today. In 1939 there were ten Washo shamans; in 1956 there was one;[13] today there is none. Neither is there any sign of an aspirant to the shaman's office. One old man does some simple healing, perhaps calling upon a spirit helper in dreams, but he is more properly classified as a healer or curer, than a shaman. The last Washo shaman who embodied the supernatural power associated with the traditional shaman was Henry Rupert, who died in 1973. For the last twenty-five years of his life he was the only living Washo shaman.

A Washo family will on occasion call in a shaman from another tribe for "the old-time healing." Such a shaman may come from a considerable distance—Wyoming (Wind River), the Dakotas (Pine Ridge, Rosebud), Utah. Intertribal healing was a rare occurence in the old days. A Washo shaman would attend a Northern Paiute, or a Northern Paiute a Washo, but only in exceptional circumstances. Now for lack of a Washo practitioner, shamanistic curing over a Washo can be conducted only by a non-Washo shaman.

Additional Causes for Decline of the Shamans

The abrupt decline of the shamans in Washo life was aided by factors already delineated in chapter 5. We have seen how in the late thirties the shamans were strenuously challenged by the peyotists. It was noted that as a result of the devastating blows to their authority and prestige, the shamans were in retreat, their hold on the people weakened and their star in decline. Yet they had stopped the spread of peyotism, the peyote leaders were banished, the shamans remained. Shamanism and its traditional practitioners still gave promise of remaining a fixed body in the constellation of the tribal culture. No one would have hazarded that within a few years they would pass from the scene. Yet within fifteen years there were no more traditional shamans. Henry Rupert remained the lone Washo shaman, but he ministered with such novel techniques and exotic concepts as to have separated himself from the mainstream of Washo shamanism. Perhaps the exceptional case exemplified by the Washo of a tribe seeming to repudiate in the short span of less than a generation an institution so venerable and sacrosanct as shamanism bears further examination.

The ruin of native institutions as the result of contact with whites is an old story. In the case of the Washo the destructive process was accelerated and aggravated by the prolonged and uninterrupted symbiosis of whites and Washo. Beginning in 1825, when Jedediah S. Smith and his party of trappers crossed the Sierras, down to the present, Washo territory has been a favored thoroughfare and stamping ground for pioneers, homesteaders, ranchers, miners, vacationers, and gamblers. Contact with white culture in all of its protean guises has been continuous and intense. It is doubtful if contact in such dimensions was experienced by any other Great Basin tribe. Price believes that because of their "relative isolation" in a mountainous habitat, the Washo "seemed to retain their cultural integrity longer than other Great Basin Indians." At the same time, he chronicles in some detail the numerous encounters with frontiersmen, travelers, and settlers, noting that in 1858 an estimated twenty thousand people entered Washo territory in the celebrated "rush to Washo" and that by 1859 whites outnumbered Washo by as much as fifteen to one.[14] This would indicate that the Washo were less than isolated and that the process of acculturation began early with its inevitable erosion of the native culture.

This sustained exposure to the aggressive white culture could not but devastate the structure and substance of native life. A highly placed official of the Nevada Indian Agency in Stewart, himself a Washo, gave as the main reason for the eclipse of shamanism the constant stress toward cultural assimilation:

> The Washo became more rapidly acculturated than other Indian tribes. The old culture is practically gone and no one cares about reviving it. Our young people no longer make baskets or even speak Washo. That's what happened to the old religion. The young people adopt white ways, white medicine. It's different in other tribes (conversation 5 October 1981).

There can be little question that another factor which hastened the decline of shamanism was the growing recourse to white medicine. In 1961 Downs reported that "most Washo are willing patients of white doctors," and Leis records that the healing function had been taken over by white doctors and peyote roadchiefs.[15] Today it would be hard to find a Washo reluctant to consult a white doctor. With their main raison d'être preempted by rival curing techniques, the shamans found themselves bypassed. Resort to white medical help, easily available in the developing communities of western Nevada, made it easier for the Washo to forsake the traditional modes of doctoring. Thus was the shaman's professional status undermined.

Turner has suggested a close nexus between sorcery and "the high rates of morbidity and mortality that affect most tribal societies."[16] When many people die, sorcery flourishes. On the other hand, when people enjoy good health, the sorcerer languishes. To the extent that white medicine effectively cured illness and prolonged life, to that extent were the services of the Washo shaman/sorcerer likely to become superfluous.

The question may be asked why the Washo did not give their allegiance to more than one religion. Primitive peoples have commonly found no conflict in belonging to two or even more religions simultaneously. The Pueblo Indians have belonged to the Roman Catholic church since the sixteenth century and have at the same time practiced their elaborate native religious complex in the kivas with the annual round of Kachina dances. When peyote came to Taos, some pueblos began practicing three religions. Joe Green, well-known Northern Paiute shaman, was simultaneously shaman, peyotist, and Episcopalian deacon. Stewart points out that giving allegiance to one religion is a "European tradition" and that American Indians "have been able to give wholehearted allegiance to two, three, or even four different religions at the same time.[17] It is no different in other primitive societies. The Washo, however, seem not to have practiced religions in parallel, coordinately. Some "belonged" to Protestant denominations but this was at best a superficial contact with mission churches in Dresslerville. Willie Smokey's boast about being a good Christian was a rare admission for a Washo. Hence the people were either followers of the shamans and shamanism or devotees of the roadchiefs and peyotism. While there were tribes where members could be both, this was not true of the Washo. Belonging to the peyote cult meant a rejection of shamanism.

HENRY (MOSES) RUPERT—THE LAST OF THE SHAMANS

The eclipse of shamanism and the disappearance of the shamans among the Washo is a striking cultural phenomenon. In no other Great Basin tribe has this occurred. Among neighboring Nevada and California tribes the shamans' influence may have waned, but they still operate within what remains of the traditional cultural framework. It is indeed these shamans who now travel to Washo settlements when asked by an occasional member to administer the old-time healing. (Northern Paiute shamans have diminished in number in recent years but they still have "more authority . . . than anyone else . . . in this society." From Bean one gathers that in California shamanism still functions effectively. While the number of practicing shamans is fewer than twenty years ago, "the status of the native doctor has risen considerably within the past few years" [personal correspondence]. Elsewhere he and Vane have observed, "Among American Indians . . . there is a resurgence of shamans." Bean notes that Governor Jerry Brown of California appointed a Kashia Pomo shaman, Mabel McKay, to the Native American Heritage Commission, evidence of the shaman's "new cross-cultural legitimacy."[18]

In viewing the decline of Washo shamanism, it is instructive to consider the life and times of Henry (Moses) Rupert, the last of the Washo shamans.[19] Rupert was also known as Henry Moses. He was given the latter name because of an incident said to have occurred when he was a boy. Out hunting one day, he was almost drowned when a torrent of water released by a flash flood came hurtling down on him, only to divide at his feet at the last moment and roar past him. Like the first Moses, the waters parted for him. During my earlier field sessions, the Washo referred to him as Henry Moses. His officially recorded surname seems to have been Rupert.

Rupert's long span of life coincided with a period of turbulent change in the life of the Washo. In a sense his life encapsulates the trends and forces which contributed to the breakdown of the native culture, and his career as a shaman may be seen as a response to the winds of change which swept through the fragile abodes of his kinsmen.

Henry Rupert was born in Genoa on the western edge of Carson Valley in 1885. His father deserted the family when Henry was an infant. His mother worked as a servant for one of the Carson Valley ranchers. His uncle was a well-known shaman, Welewkushkush, who lived nearby, and his older sister's husband was Charley Rube, an antelope shaman. As a child Rupert spent much time with these kinsmen, who served as "models of behavior based on kindness and sympathy."[20] He would also watch his uncle cure. He had few friends and would wander alone in the desert and foothills of Carson Valley under the brow of Job's Peak in the high Sierras. Some of his earliest dreams were of a bear and a flight to the moon. By his seventh year, he had had the first intimations of the shaman's calling.

When he was eight, he was taken to the Stewart Indian Agency school, ten miles north of Genoa, where he remained for the next ten years. Education at Stewart was supervised by the United States Army and lasted through the eighth grade. In contrast to the freedom he had known since infancy, Rupert was now subjected to a harsh, sometimes brutal discipline. He did well in his studies, read a good deal, and learned the printing trade. He was baptized and exposed to missionary Christianity in a daily schedule of prayers, hymns, and Bible study. In his seventeenth year he had a power dream indicating that his spirit power would be water, an uncommon familiar to Washo. The nosebleed that followed the dream confirmed its authenticity as a spirit visitation. Before leaving Stewart the following year, his true vocation was assured: He would be a shaman.

During the next ten years he lived in Reno and worked as a typesetter on the *Reno Evening Gazette.* From books he learned how to hypnotize and would display his prowess as hypnotist in monthly sessions at the Reno Press Club. It was at this time that he began shamanizing, and when he was twenty-two achieved his first successful cure aided by his spirit helper, water. Not long afterwards he acquired another familiar, a young Hindu whose spirit, lodged in a skeleton he came across in Carson City High School, "got on" Henry.[21] Water and the young Hindu remained his helpers in curing for the next fifty years.

When he was twenty-five, Rupert married Lizzie Smith, a Northern Paiute girl he had met at the Stewart school. Marrying a non-Washo was frowned upon but characteristically he kept his own counsel and went his own way. Four children were born to the couple. As the years went on he became well known as a healer. With the children away, Henry and Lizzie Rupert moved to Carson Colony, where virtually no Washo resided. Here he lived as a recluse, spending much time in meditation and introspection, at the same time growing strawberries and raising turkeys, turning a good profit in their sale.

Rupert's reputation as healer began to spread beyond Washo territory, and patients from many ethnic groups sought his services —Indians from other tribes, Hawaiians, Filipinos, Mexicans, whites. He had already developed his own philosophy of curing, having formulated a new cosmogony as the metaphysical framework of his shamanistic practice. When he reached his fifty-seventh year, he decided to spend his full time curing.

A restless curiosity had always prompted him to search for new and better curing techniques, and when he was seventy he began to cure in abbreviated sessions which never lasted longer than four hours. Now he had a third spirit helper, George, bequeathed to him by his friend, George Robinson, a Hawaiian and curer himself.

Robinson had introduced Henry to the brief healing séance. After almost fifty years of shamanistic practice, Rupert discarded the old methods and adopted a radically new one.

Rupert continued to live in Carson Colony. Members of his family in time moved into the Colony in order to be near him. He cured until the end of his life. In 1973 at the age of eighty-eight he died. The local newspapers wrote up the story of his life, called him "a well-known Nevada figure," and carried his picture. Both whites and Washo respect his memory and no one disparages him. A year before he died he was chosen grand marshal of Nevada Day ceremonies, and a street in Carson Colony was named after him. Washo will tell you he lived to be more than one hundred.

Henry Rupert's career and influence as shaman may have been a significant factor contributing to the demise of the traditional Washo shaman. Although a shaman himself, Rupert introduced changes into the shaman's office which made "the traditional components . . . quite unrecognizable to contemporary Washo."[22] Motivation for these changes derived in part from Rupert's personality, from strong subjective needs and drives. But it was also due to the forces of cultural accommodation of which Rupert was the agent. He was both the bold and imaginative initiator of change and its ineluctable instrument. He was the paradigm of the acculturated man, as much bound by the symbiotic cultural strands in which he was entwined as propelled by his own personal drives. His personal metaphysical and ethical restructuring of traditional healing, together with accelerating acculturative trends, may have contributed significantly to the undermining of traditional Washo shamanism.

THE INNOVATOR

Rupert's life was fashioned in considerable measure by the larger world beyond Washo horizons which his curiosity and venturesomeness led him to explore. Tribal perspectives were broadened to encompass both Washo and white worlds. Elements from other cultures were also incorporated into his world view, particularly in his shamanistic practice. Unlike previous Washo shamans, he did not consider these dissimilar strands mutually incompatible. His life may, in fact, be seen as an attempt to blend them into a consistent harmony, thus creating a synthesis that marked a fundamental departure from traditional Washo ways and outlook.

The capacity to yoke together disparate worlds is clearly disclosed in Rupert's easy movement from one cultural realm to another. He mingled at will in the white world—as printer, hypnotist, farmer, business man. Whites were unfailingly impressed by him. A rancher who had known him over the decades characterized him as "thoughtful, intelligent, well-spoken."

But he was also integrated into his tribal world—eating, collecting the aboriginal foods (locusts, fly grubs), withdrawing into the seclusion of a private Washo world for meditation and introspection, using the old paraphernalia in curing, and ordering them hidden in a riverbed after his death. He left instructions that when he died, his house was to be destroyed.

The urge to harmonize different traditions is also revealed in Rupert's way as a shaman. His first power dream, while validating Washo values, permitted the quest for outside knowledge. During a curing session when Rupert was twenty-five, his shaman uncle, Welewkushkush, drew from Henry's forehead a piece of printed matter, symbolic warning that his nephew should not dabble in white learning. Rupert disregarded the warning, justifying the rejection by asserting a common moral objective for both Washo and white belief systems. His three spirit helpers, drawn from widely different sources—water, the young Hindu, and George—could coexist in his spirit world because all subscribed to an "ethic" summed up in the Hindu's "law of nature": "to be honest, discreet and faithful; to be kind and do no harm."[23] All were, after all, working toward the same goal: healing.

It was in his approach to shamanism that Rupert made his far-reaching, perhaps revolutionary, impact on the tribal culture. For it was his adoption of new practices and development of new beliefs which may have altered the form and substance of Washo shamanism, the sacred core of Washo life. In 1967 Handelman could remark, "For most contemporary Washo the traditional form of shamanic healing is almost non-existent."[24] For this profound change in the fabric of tribal life Henry Rupert was in large part responsible.

The scope of change that Rupert introduced into Washo shamanism can be demonstrated by citing some of the more dramatic components of his practice. His pantheon of spirit helpers included a Hindu and a Hawaiian, an unprecedented exoticism. He would minister with a handkerchief wound around his head, simulating a Hindu turban. When called he would treat patients without asking for payment, a radical change from the traditional shaman's crude cash-on-the-barrelhead demands. As his reputation spread, his clientele became more diverse, and in his later years, non-Washo comprised 45 percent of his patients. In his seventieth year, he suddenly adopted a drastically shorter curing session.

But the more important innovations were those which invaded and transmogrified the realm of shamanistic belief and outlook. In developing a new philosophy of healing, Rupert changed Washo cosmogony, locating the source of power in the third and highest level of the spirit world. From this source, he said, the prophets of Israel, Jesus, and shamans all drew their personal power for working miracles and for healing. The spirit source was wholly beneficent, leaving no room for evil, for the sinister, whether in the form of ghosts or witchcraft. Thus sorcery plays no part in Rupert's theological or therapeutic scheme. He was the first Washo shaman to eschew sorcery.

This marks the sharpest break with antecedent Washo belief. Traditional shamanism held that power was morally neutral, that good and evil were both embedded in the structure of the universe. Shamans could thus be both healer and witch, capable at once of killing and curing.[25] Rejecting this moral Gnosticism, Rupert declared that power was "all-good" and that it could not be used for foul purpose. A shaman was obliged to be good, a state achieved by ritual purification and the fulfillment of the "moral compact" binding a shaman to his spirit helpers. In this state he would be discreet, kind, humble, and do no harm.[26]

Henry Rupert was unique in the annals of Washo shamanism in that he never practiced sorcery. Unlike other shamans he was "trusted and not feared by anyone." In 1981 he was remembered with reverence and affection as individuals told of the cures he had wrought. That he was able to develop a theological structure for shamanism that rejected sorcery represents a novel achievement and affirms his role as radical innovator. But his break with past belief and practice may have hastened the decline of the shamans. He was the first Washo shaman to shun sorcery. He was also the last of the Washo shamans.

IMPACT OF THE PEYOTE CULT

If traditional tribal shamanism was undermined by the impact of acculturation joined to Henry Rupert's radical innovations, the introduction of the peyote cult produced the shock waves which doomed it. For it was the advent of Ben Lancaster with his new religious way in 1936 which delivered the *coup de grace* to the old shamans and their dispensation.

Until Lancaster's appearance in Washo country, the feared and hated shamans were sovereign among the people. Peyotism at last offered a channel for the release of long-standing antipathy and simmering resentment against them. In the subsequent clash between the shamans and their supporters on one side and the peyote leaders and their followers on the other, an unprecedented pitch of intra-tribal strife and violence was reached. Neither side won the day, although at one point it seemed that the increasing camp of peyotists under the magnetic Lancaster might gain ascendancy. But the residual power of the shamans was sufficiently potent to prevent peyote from prevailing. By the time the conflict had abated, the power of the shamans was broken. The retreat of the shamans described in 1941, leading to their swift decline, ended in their defeat. In the power struggle with peyotism, the shamans were first denounced, then repudiated, finally eliminated.

WASHO PEYOTISM SINCE 1939

Peyotism Yesterday and Today

This study has traced the career of peyote among the Washo from its introduction in 1936 to 1939, when the thick of the conflict with the shamans had ended. A conspectus of peyote's course after 1939 in west-central Nevada follows.

Even at the flood-tide of peyote's popularity, only a minority of Washo became members of the peyote cult. In the first, fine, careless rapture following Ben Lancaster's initial dramatic forays among his tribesmen, meetings were packed by curious Washo, most of whom took the peyote. But few remained active cultists. The majority fell away—intimidated by the threatened shamans, disenchanted with the opportunistic Lancaster, troubled by the turmoil which was tearing families and the tribe itself apart. By 1940 peyote had so far receded in favor that meetings were no longer held in Washo territory. Lancaster followers had dwindled to a handful of mixed Washo and Northern Paiute who now met clandestinely, far removed from the centers of tribal settlement.

When Ben died in 1955, this pathetic remnant was split between the few still loyal to their leader and the larger faction of Tipi Way adherents.[27]

Peyotism never recovered its first enthusiastic vogue after the shattering blows sustained in the conflict which raged around Lancaster and his devotees in the late thirties. The number of cultists remained small, diminishing from 111 in 1938 to 78 at the time of Lancaster's death.[28] The Tipi Way sect managed to establish itself in Woodfords, California, a Washo colony off the beaten track, and meetings there have been held continuously until now.

The Tipi Way was brought to the Washo in the 1940s and was instituted as a branch of the Native American Church. Members would frequently travel to meetings in Idaho, Utah, and Oklahoma, and we begin to note in Washo-Paiute peyotism an orientation toward eastern models. Meetings were now held in a Plains-like tipi, women no longer participated in the meetings, much less presided as leaders, specialized peyote songs were now sung. Leaders, or roadchiefs as they were now called, using the eastern terminology, copied the liturgical style of their eastern counterparts.

This variant peyotism found the roadchiefs notably differentiated in character and function from their Washo predecessors. Lancaster had been the charismatic leader, supreme individualist, obliterating everyone in the blazing sun of his ego. At once prophet, preacher, and interpreter, he dominated every moment of the meetings he led. It would be hard to imagine him a member of any organized church or movement, following protocol handed down by distant hierarchical figures. Although his familiarity with peyote derived from experiences over a twenty-year period with Oklahoma and Utah Indians identified with the Native American Church, he never suggested such affiliation once he came to the Washo in 1936. No higher sacerdotal authority for him. He wore no man's ecclesiastical collar and was accountable—liturgically, doctrinally, financially—to no one but himself. Sam Dick and other Washo peyote leaders, far less flamboyant than Lancaster, tried to assume the style of the master.

In marked contrast, Washo Tipi Way peyotism disapproves any show of individualism in the roadchief. The roadchief becomes a priestly functionary representing the church, "working for peyote." Power resides in peyote, not in any roadchief. Neither does power inhere in a multiplicity of spirit helpers, nor in their human vessels, the shamans, as the old belief maintained. It inheres in peyote. Thus peyote becomes the most powerful of all Washo spirit repositories. In relegating the roadchief to a priestly role, any pretensions to overweening personal influence or temporal power were inhibited. Adherence to Tipi Way doctrine was thus a safeguard against both the rise of another Ben Lancaster and the recrudescense of the shamans.

It is not easy to estimate the number of active Washo peyotists today. At its inception in 1936, peyote meetings held in Washo territory were drawing not Washo alone but a mixture of predominantly full- and mixed-blood Washo and Northern Paiute, with an occasional Shoshone and Miwok also participating. As time went on and travel became easier, the tribal composition of meetings became more mixed. Indians living in the San Francisco Bay area, drawn from a variety of tribes, began coming over for the weekly meetings held in conveniently accessible Washo terrain.[29] They still do. Even the roadchief might sometimes belong to a tribe geographically and culturally distant from the Washo. Ramsey Walker, veteran Washo roadchief who lives in Woodfords, spoke of a Winnebago from Nebraska who served as roadchief at Woodfords meetings.

Lest this give the impression that the peyote cult is flourishing among the Washo, there is Roy James's testimony from the early sixties that there were approximately one hundred active members in Alpine and Mono counties in California and in Douglas and Ormsby counties in Nevada.[30] In 1981 Ramsey Walker was sure there were "less peyote members now among the Washo than at one time." This was also the estimate of Harold Wyatt, Washo executive director of the Inter-tribal Council of Nevada. D'Azevedo believes that while the number of Washo peyotists may be decreasing, the number of Indians coming to Washo meetings is growing.

Perhaps the relatively small number of Washo peyotists is attributable in a measure to the improved economic and social condition of the people, with the attendant political and psychological gains. Their steady upward climb from the lowest rung of the ladder could be interpreted as a fulfillment of peyote's promise. The paucity of Washo peyotists is discussed later in this Epilogue. When goals have been realized, the instrumentalities thought responsible for their achievement often suffer neglect and disuse. This may help to explain the career of peyotism among the Washo. But whatever the number and composition of cult members, certainly the status of to-

day's Washo peyotists has changed. Once storm centers of controversy, they are now accepted as part of mainstream Washo life,
respected members of the community.[31]

THE ETHICAL EMPHASIS

Another Tipi Way differentiation from both traditional Washo
shamanism and early Washo peyotism is the emphasis on ethical
behavior, as the received wisdom of white culture conceives it.
There is a strong ethical undertow in Tipi Way meetings. Members
are exhorted to follow the ethical way, and they look to the roadchiefs to exemplify it. In the theology of shamanism, ethics in the
western philosphical or religious sense was at best an unrecognized
category of discourse. The moral precepts of the golden rule and the
Ten Commandments may have been an irrelevancy in the scheme of
its religious concerns. Since shamans represented a doctrine that
was essentially amoral, it would scarcely occur to them to encourage
clients to lead a morally "good" life. They themselves were not
exactly its avatars. On the contrary, their lives exhibited a propen-
sity for gain and power which had little in common with ethical
norms and which always vexed, sometimes outraged, the people.[32]

Nor were ethical or moral concerns of particular relevance in the
early peyote meetings. The assembly was reminded to be "friendly,"
"brotherly," "sisterly," "to help one another," but the promptings
seemed an expected formality—formulaic stereotypes. The morning
after the all-night session, avowals of friendship, even between
former enemies, were exchanged, but this was part of peyote protocol, induced as much by a psychological, perhaps chemical, impetus as by ethical mandate. The overwhelming concern was with
the instrumental benefits of peyote—healing, telling the future,
purveying dreams, mediating personal problems, countering
alcohol. Prayers offered were almost wholly petitional, centered narrowly on the needs and desires of the individual supplicant. The
leaders were themselves preoccupied with affairs which were not exactly focused on moral or ethical considerations. Leo Okio was
recalled as a money grubber, Sam Lone Bear was convicted of
violating the Mann Act, did time in jail, and has been dubbed the
Elmer Gantry of peyotism.[33] Ben Lancaster was known as a
mercenary opportunist with a roving eye for the women.

One of the primary reasons for rejecting peyote in the late thirties had been the gulf between ethical preachment and practice as evidenced by both leaders and followers of the cult. Dissidents charged that all the noble precepts so volubly declaimed were being violated, as peyote precipitated family strife, intracult controversy, and tribal dissension. Leaders suspected of depravity, it was said, conducted meetings where moral license was condoned.

But in Tipi Way meetings there was a pronounced ethical stress. Here are excerpts from the accounts of four Tipi Way peyotists:[34]

> One thing I learned about this Church we got here is that you got to tell the truth. If you got the Medicine [peyote] in you, you got to do it or you feel worse.

> You got to keep your mind on living a good life and helping other people. The Medicine tells us that anybody trying to live right and follow this Peyote Way is like our own close family. We got no strangers in this tipi.

> Some people forget that sometimes you can't think about different tribes and different color people in this Church. We got to work with the new Way, now. This is the new Indian way—the New Tipi Way. It is for all people who want to come here in peace and good mind. We don't keep nobody away. If they are good people they are like our own brothers and sisters.

> He told everybody he was sick because when he was skinning a deer it kicked him in the chest. The people started to pray for him. But the Roadchief knew he wasn't telling the truth. He spoke right out and said this guy was having trouble with his wife and that's what hurt him in the chest. But that guy didn't want to admit it. If he only said the truth at that Meeting, it would really help him. But he lied that time.

The articulation of ethical values—truth, altruism, brotherhood, equality, peace—as significant and desirable, marked a new dimension in Washo religious perspectives.

One of the most conspicuous differences between the older Washo religious practice and the Tipi Way was the repudiation by the roadchiefs of monetary gain in the practice of peyotism. In contrast to the grasping shamans and the greedy early peyote leaders, the roadchiefs took no payment for officiating. They were self-supporting in a variety of occupations, taking no compensation save for travel, channeling all collections to the church treasury.[35] Few reforms could have proved more impressive to the followers or have more effectively established the ethical *bona fides* of the new religious way.

In the moral climate generated by the iteration of ethical values there was no room for sorcery. Witchcraft with its attendant brew of anxiety, fear, hatred, feud, and death was irreconcilable with Tipi Way peyotism, and its practitioners consequently became anathema. Earlier peyotists of Lancaster's day had ridiculed the shamans for their charlatanry and vilified them for their greed. The shaman/sorcerers had meanwhile vanished from the scene; but their memory still rankled and Tipi Way peyotists found occasion to disparage and deride them.

> . . . Them Indian doctors got different medicines for power. They have old time ways and are full of tricks. They don't care about the people. . . . They just want to show their power. They don't understand the medicine we use for the good of the people.[36]

In the summer of 1981, Ramsey Walker, Washo roadchief grown grizzled in peyote's struggle for acceptance, gave his evaluation of the old shamans.

> A witch could make you sick. He could take his spit and flick it any distance and no matter where you were it would hit you. It would feel like a pin pricking you and you would get sick. But we had enough of that bad stuff. Now there's no more witching.
>
> Peyote is four or five times more powerful than the medicine man [shaman].

He then recounted a catalogue of cures effected by peyote. "The drum," he said, "heals your body; the rattle, your mind."

The shaman's way was identified with "tricks" and witchcraft, the early peyote leaders with greed and opportunism. Tipi Way's emphasis was on truth, integrity, healing.

WASHO TIPI WAY AND CHRISTIANITY

What was the source of Tipi Way's ethical emphasis? The ready answer is the Christian character of the Native American Church with which Tipi Way was identified. Yet an examination of Tipi Way peyotism as practiced by the Washo raises a question as to the strength of its bond with Christianity.

Anthropologists have not agreed on the extent or depth of Christian influence on the peyote cult. Stewart holds that peyotism represents an amalgamation of aboriginal religious elements with Christian ceremonial-theological ingredients, that they diffused together from a southern source and that the Christian component of peyotism is as old as the cult itself. Against this view are ranged those anthropologists—Lumholtz, Radin, Petrullo, Opler, La Barre—who see the Christian elements of the peyote cult as a "thin and superficial" layer comprising "only secondary, adventitious accretions" to an aboriginal base and therefore of recent date.[37]

The history of Washo-white contact discloses that the impact of Christianity on the Washo had never been more than casual. The missions at Dresslerville were poorly patronized, sparsely attended except at Christmas, when seasonal bounty was dispensed. I have already referred to the rare incidence among Washo of giving wholehearted allegiance to more than one religion. When Willie Smokey described himself as a "God-fearing, churchgoing man," asserting that "churchgoing is good and peyote is good," there is reason to suspect that Smokey, prestigious leader with a practiced eye for white approval, supported the church for the respectability it conferred in the eyes of the whites. A similar reason may have moved him to join the peyote cult, feeling that membership was invested with status symbolism. He also had warm endorsements for "Indian medicine men" and white doctors. He apparently was ready to join all movements and support all therapies—native and white, old and new.

It is significant that Henry Rupert's shamanistic synthesis, woven of strands drawn from different cultures, contained no Christian elements, although Rupert was well acquainted with Christianity through years of church attendance and indoctrination at the Carson Agency school. One of his first rebellious acts took place when as a boy in class, he challenged the teacher's presentation of the Christian idea of theodicy. He absorbed much of what was taught at the school, but he "resisted" Christianity.[38] It may be that resistance to Christianity is an old theme in the tribal culture.

In personal contact with Washo peyotism, references to Christianity seemed incidental, when heard at all. In meetings attended, prayers were offered, but Jesus was seldom invoked, his name scarcely mentioned. "Some peyote doctors use Jesus in their meetings," said Ben Lancaster in 1938; "I use God." "We pray to Jesus and Mary the last time around," said Sam Dick. Merriam and d'Azevedo mention the diminishing emphasis on Christian elements, with the Bible no longer included in the roadchief's sacred gear and biblical citation becoming rare.[39]

In 1981 in the course of a lengthy afternoon's conversation about peyote, Ramsey Walker made only two references to either God or Jesus. He told how the Kiowa acquired peyote.

This woman went to Texas to find peyote. When she got tired, she laid down in the field and went to sleep. She dreamed of God, who told her she was sleeping in the shape of a cross with her arms stretched over the peyote plants. He told her to gather the peyote and take it to her tribe. That's how peyote came to the Kiowa.

Walker also mentioned God in explaining the curing efficacy of peyote. "God is there. God and peyote. He makes peyote work." When asked directly about the place of Jesus in peyote, he replied, "Jesus stands next to God." No other mention was made of either God or Jesus.

D'Azevedo's collection of narratives recounted by Washo Tipi Way followers is especially revealing for the light it sheds on the attitude toward Christianity. These personal testimonies reveal a surprising lack of reverence for some of the sancta of the faith—the Bible, prayer, Jesus. There is the lack of reference to Christian doctrine and symbols which has already been noted. When they are mentioned, more likely than not they will be compared unfavorably with peyote cognates.

One of the narratives treats the Bible and its God of creation with a disarming impiety. The familiar story is told of God trying to fashion man out of clay. After three unsatisfactory attempts, he makes one to his liking, baking it to just the right hue of redness.

He said, "Now this is the one that is good I wanted to make." So He breathed His life into it and made it come alive.

[The story] sounds right to me because that could happen. There's that story about the God making only one man and then He made a woman from a rib out of the man. It don't make much sense to me. . . . That's a white people's story . . . it don't explain much. It only explains one kind of people . . . the white people. This other story explain the four different kind of people in the world. It sounds like the real one to me.[40]

In another narrative white man's prayer is unfavorably contrasted with Indian prayer.

How can an Indian pray like a white man? The white man gets his prayers out of books . . . old books about things maybe thousands of years ago. He don't even have to think about it. He just says it and it is supposed to do him some good. He can be a drunk bum for a long time, do all kinds of no good thing, think all kinds of bad thoughts about people. But then he can walk right into that Church and pray one of them prayers and he gets away with it. . . .

But Indians here don't have no books, and they don't think about things a long time ago. We just have our own mind and our own thoughts, and we think about what happened today among the people. . . . We think about that and what kind of person we been that day. . . .

> It's hard for an Indian to pray. He don't have a prayer given for him to say.
> He has to think of it himself. . . . You just have to try to live right and then
> maybe it will come out of you.[41]

While white man's prayer is a sanctimonious formality, Indian
prayer is an arduous quest for meaning about the world and oneself.
Noteworthy is the ethical premise upon which Indian prayer is
posited: "what kind of person we been that day," "to live right."

There is a curious narrative in which Jesus is cast as little more
than a character in a farce. A man impersonating Jesus is exposed as
a fraud when a boy armed with a sharp stick prods the rump of the
donkey he is riding, causing the animal to throw its rider. When the
man "started cussing and chasing [that] boy around, the people
looked up and said . . . 'What kind of Jesus Christ is that?
. . . That guy is no Jesus.' " However interpreted, the story would
appear to make Jesus the butt of ridicule, hardly a figure for venera-
tion.[42]

The juxtaposition of peyote with church, Bible, and Jesus is
made to redound inevitably to peyote's advantage.

> An Indian can't go into his Church the same way as a white man. When you go
> into that Peyote Meeting, you don't just go there for a visit. You go there to
> work. . . . That Peyote ain't easy on you like that Bible is. Jesus was living
> thousands of years ago, but that peyote is living right now. . . . They say Jesus
> died and came to life again. That Jesus was a good man, they say. He was just
> a man like us. But Peyote was always there.[43]

The sancta of Christianity rouse no special awe or fervor in Washo
Tipi Way leaders or followers. Church, Bible, prayer, Jesus seem to
be viewed with a measure of tentativeness, of skepticism, as of inferior efficacy or authenticity to native models. We are not likely to
find the source of Washo Tipi Way's ethical emphasis in the external formalities of Christianity.

We may more plausibly find that source in the general moral
and ethical bias of the surrounding culture. Euro-American society
sets great store in the validity and sanctity of the moral and ethical
life. This is not to say that all Europeans and Americans live by the
Sermon on the Mount, obey the Ten Commandments, and follow
the golden rule. But if they do not practice these ethical codes, they
stoutly profess them. The dichotomy between creed and deed in
Christendom is not new and has often spawned awkward contradic-
tions and puzzling ambiguities. Recall that Savonarola was burned
to death because he "preached the unity of theory and practice,"[44]

and Voltaire, who seldom if ever crossed the threshold of a church, always tipped his hat when passing one. Whatever their practice, most Americans assert their belief in the moral charters of the Christian heritage. Formal, verbal endorsement of their norms is the *sine qua non* of personal respectability and social acceptance. Because of their close contact with whites, the Washo were probably not unaware of this.

White Ethical Norms

Two motives may explain why the Washo were drawn to the moral conventions of the dominant culture: The first was the need to provide a safeguard against the depredations of venal religious leaders; the second, the urge to find acceptance in the white world.

Protection against venal religious leaders became a pragmatic necessity for the Washo after the tribe had been torn asunder by the conflict between shamanism and peyotism in the late thirties. The rent fabric of tribal life badly needed mending.

When Ben Lancaster came back to his people with the peyote, he galvanized the Washo into open defiance of the shamans. This largely explains his brilliant early triumphs, for, as we have seen, the people had long resented the shamans. When the din of the conflict died down, the bells were tolling for the aboriginal religious practitioners, and most Washo heard the sound with few regrets.

But all too soon Lancaster demonstrated imperfections of character not unlike those of the shamans, which brought disillusion with his leadership and provoked factionalism among his followers. Later when Tipi Way peyotism came to the Washo, it signified a formal rejection of Ben Lancaster. With its new stress on ethical behavior derived from the moral bias of the majority culture, the new version of peyotism gave promise of assuring a religious way free from the corruption that had troubled the tribe in the past. After all, a moral system patterned after white models would tolerate neither venality nor sorcery, and without these the authority of both an old time shaman and a Ben Lancaster was a broken reed. It was reasonable for the Washo to see the appeal in such a system.

In this context it is of interest to remember that Henry Rupert's innovative shamanism had also incorporated ethical imperatives which were consonant with the professed moral values of the white world. His moral system was thus congruent with that of Tipi Way peyotism. Both had also repudiated sorcery, repugnant to white sensibility. Rupert's new shamanism may have been a response to the materialism of the traditional shamans just as Tipi Way was the rejection of Ben Lancaster. By incorporating beliefs which accorded with the ethical canons of the white world, both the new shamanism and the new peyotism served as a prophylaxis against old religious and social maladies.

A second motive for feeling drawn to prevailing moral and ethical norms may have been the desire by Washo to narrow the distance separating themselves from the white world. The Washo may have seen in the peyote cult an agent for achieving this. We have remarked that Tipi Way incorporated ethical components congenial to white sensibility. To embody the moral values prized by whites may have been an unwitting strategy of adaptation. It was perhaps an oblique way for reaching out for acceptance by the white world, leading to the process of socialization to values dominant in the larger society.[45]

Peyote's role as bridge between Indian and white cultures has previously been suggested by anthropologists. Barber characterized peyotism as oriented toward "conciliation and compromise with the existing world." Unlike the Ghost Dance with its Messianism intimating an apocalypse of uprising and overthrow, the peyote way was peaceful and nonthreatening, passively accepting the white world. La Barre has written that Plains peyotism, instead of articulating antiwhite sentiment, "preached conciliation instead." He has called peyotism a path to acculturation marked by a "peaceful . . . fairly complete syncretism of the cultures." Among the Menomini, peyote "sanctions . . . an integration of conflicting cultural patterns."[46] Dollard has proposed that joining the peyote cult may have been "an attempt to identify with white society . . . thereby acquiring some of the valued prestige symbols of the all-powerful whites" (correspondence 31 May 1941).

From the beginning the beliefs and rites of Washo peyotism were not without signs of reconciliation and outreach to the larger world. Ben Lancaster would regularly invoke blessing upon the president of the United States, the commissioner of Indian Affairs, and such other white officials as might come to mind. Sam Dick prayed for "our brothers and sisters, the white people, [who] are building a great, fine road . . . so that we be happy." Prayers and confessions breathed a fervent emphasis on the brotherhood of all men under the fatherhood of one God.

Both Ben Lancaster and Sam Dick urged me to attend meetings. I was welcomed with solemn punctilio, given the seat of honor next to the leader, and singled out for special prayer. Sometimes I got the uneasy feeling that I was being deferred to. At the time peyote was under attack from both Washo and whites, and my first reaction to the excessively cordial treatment was that Lancaster and Dick wanted primarily to demonstrate that, despite the ugly rumors, nothing untoward or sinister occurred at a peyote meeting.[47] My participation might provide a seal of respectability for peyote in the wider community.

But the deeper motivation may have been the groping quest for identification with the people and values of the life out there. In 1939 Willie Smokey, Washo leader, became a member of the cult because he viewed it as charged with white status symbolism. There can be little question that other Washo were similarly motivated. Downs has described many of Lancaster's first followers as "acculturated and successful [Washo who] had gone the white man's way."[48]

The common bond with whites was symbolically reinforced by bringing the similitude of Christian sancta into peyote ceremonialism and by replicating Christianity's basic moral postulates in peyote theology. Could a more appealing, convincing common ground for Washo and whites be found than in religion's green pastures? As noted, there is disagreement about the depth of Christian influence on peyotism. But even if Christian elements were only a superficial gloss, they nevertheless resonated echoes of the sacred in white culture. In adopting venerated Christian symbolism, the peyote cult may have been an acculturative outreach to the wider white world.

Peyote's prohibition of alcohol may also have been an accommodation to the dominant moral culture. Indians know that the stereotype of the Indian as an unregenerate liquor addict demeans him in the eyes of the whites. As the title of Deloria's book has it, *Nobody Loves a Drunken Indian*. What better way for a Washo to rehabilitate himself in the eyes of whites than by giving up liquor? Peyote would be the agent to facilitate sobriety and the inevitable ascent to higher social and economic estate. There would be beneficent consequences in his psychological estate as well, for he would be raised not only in "their" eyes but also in his own. At last he would be able to achieve a long-denied respectability and take his place in the favored world of whites.

ACCULTURATION AND MESSIANISM

The apparent contradiction between two of peyote's important themes, acculturation and Messianism, has been discussed earlier. Further comment is relevant.

Acculturation involves the aspiration to shape native ways after white models. It is a coming-to-terms with whites, an acceptance, declared or tacit, of their culture. Messianism, projecting a future when white exploitation and oppression would be ended in the full restoration of native hegemony, symbolizes a rejection of the established order. How can two such conflicting themes coexist in peyotism?

They can coexist as they seem to if we realize that the apparent anomaly is less a contradiction than an example of the ambivalence often exhibited by primitive societies toward dominant cultures. Deprived peoples tend to copy and adopt the cultures they hold to be the agents of their degradation and spoliation. La Barre has noted that with the rejection of white ways, "there is often also a simultaneous . . . copying of white culture traits."[49] He cites examples of this process from widely separated parts of the world.

In Western society minority groups display a similar ambivalence. Blacks, Spanish-Americans, and Jews typically identify not with their own ethnic culture but with the culture—often discriminating and exploitative—of the larger environment. There is currently much discussion and some show of the return to "roots," but in the real world only a small number return. A few conspicuously tip their hats to their ethnic origins but most are swept along—hats flying—in the irresistible tide of acculturation.

In this connection it should be remembered that Messianism was a muted theme in Washo peyotism. Revival cults have not flourished among the Washo. Both the 1870 and the 1890 Ghost Dances failed to win Washo adherents, although their respective leaders, Weneyuga and Jack Wilson (Wovoka), belonged to the neighboring Northern Paiute and were personally known to many Washo. In the early meetings, Messianic visions were experienced and described by participants, and these were clearly a transparent mask for those protesting tribal wrongs and hardships. But neither Ben Lancaster nor Sam Dick indulged in revivalist fantasies. Lancaster was the pragmatist bespeaking the cause of Washo rights now rather than in an apocalyptic tomorrow. Dick included whites among those standing before God at the end of days. It was a bland, nonaggressive version of Judgment Day.

In Tipi Way Messianism was but faintly articulated. In d'Azevedo's narratives, only one reference could be interpreted as Messianic. The top of the tipi is said to stand for "all the people of the world and how they are going to end up the same place. . . . Some day they will all come together . . . one kind of people . . . one place. But that won't happen in our time. That is way off . . . a long time from now."[50] Not exactly a flaming eschatological vision. In Washo peyotism the Messianic theme became progressively muted and in Tipi Way was far outbalanced by the acculturation theme.

PEYOTE AS AGENT OF ACCULTURATION

It is an interesting coincidence that the improvement in the social and economic status of the Washo began to occur not long after the introduction of the peyote cult. We have seen how the Washo have climbed from pariah status to a surprising level of acceptance by whites since the advent of peyote in 1936. To what extent this was due to the impact of peyotism on the Washo view of the world and of themselves, can only be conjectured. Other factors have been at work, particularly the general social ferment which began to stir in the country with the coming of World War II and which has increasingly benefited that part of it where the Washo live. That peyote has contributed to bettering the lot of the Washo by encouraging individual and communal responsibility and by restoring tribal and personal self-esteem, may well be true.

It may be asked why the peyote cult does not presently command the support of more Washo, given the steady improvement of the tribe's status over recent decades. Perhaps the relative paucity of Washo peyotists can be explained in part by the accomplishment of some of peyotism's principal goals—shamans eliminated, social and economic sufficiency increased, personal and communal self-regard strengthened, old tribal wrongs righted, Washo patrimony recovered, a place in the sun secured. There is no longer the need to mount the protest which animated some of the first peyotists as they gathered in their brush enclosures in the chill desert nights. There are more effective channels of protest: the Nevada Inter-tribal Council, the Pan-Indian movement, the United States government. There is no longer the urge to manifest, however obliquely, the desire to identify with the white world, for Washo have already made their mark and will continue to do so with or without the devices of religion. With the government distributing five and a half million dollars in settling a land claim, with Washo occupying positions of communal leadership and with their upward social and economic mobility, the urge to protest and the need ritually to affirm fellow feeling with whites loses its insistent edge. All of this would appear to validate peyote's role as successful agent of acculturation. It also explains why peyote's appeal today is less compelling than it was forty years ago.

DIFFERENCES BETWEEN WASHO SHAMANISM AND PEYOTISM

It has been suggested that Washo peyotism is organically linked with shamanism, that it is a lineal descendant of shamanism, a later religious dispensation of the same order. According to this view, the ritual, theology, and function of peyotism are in significant ways comparable to those of shamanism. Peyote curing is alleged to differ only in detail from shamanistic curing. "To the Washo," writes Downs, "the changeover from the aboriginal religion to peyote is viewed as simply the addition of a new element of supernatural power provided to assist the Indian."[51] There was a "merging of shamanism and peyote"; the roadchiefs took over and began functioning as shamans. It is the contention of this study that peyotism was not so much an accretion to shamanism, an organic development of shamanism, a shamanism redivivus, as it was the subverter and supplanter of the old native religion.

In the initial contact with peyotism, the Washo were no doubt impressed with rituals and symbols reminiscent of shamanism. These have already been enumerated. To mention some of the more conspicuous: vision experience, eagle feathers, bird-bone whistle, prechewing of wild parsnip, clockwise circuits, "X-ray" location and diagnosis of illness. But these were resemblances rather than similarities, their functions in the rituals of shamanism and peyotism respectively quite different.

For someone seeing and participating in a peyote meeting for the first time, these resemblances would have been enough to relieve the prickly discomforts of strangeness and to rouse the reassuring responses of compatability. But the comparable elements in shamanism and peyote were superficial at best. Downs, who had written that peyotism was merely an "addition" to shamanism, later observes that Washo peyote paraphernalia were "inspired by modern peyotists and do not represent aboriginal Washo survivals."[52] Likenesses of peyotism with shamanism are analogies rather than homologies, and in anthropology we have long been warned not to confuse the two. Things which look alike, even when sharing the same name, are not necessarily alike. Totemism is a classic example of a phenomenon bearing one name and taking a variety of forms, some having little or no relationship with others. To subsume all forms called totemism under one name is to deprive the concept of coherent meaning.

In the attempt to liken shamanism and peyotism, the vision experience of the aboriginal Washo has been equated with the visions of the peyote cultist. But if we compare them in a realm of factual discourse, we at once become aware of their wide divergence. In the aboriginal experience, dream is synonymous with spirit and power, and it assumes a rich variety of animate forms— birds, animals, reptiles, water babies. Dream visitation comes involuntarily and is heard rather than seen. It has a will of its own, strong and capricious, and could instruct the dreamer to perform certain acts; and no matter what the course of action indicated, it had to be executed. The exception was in the call to shamanism, when the ultimate decision lay with the dreamer after consultation with a practicing shaman.

The peyote dream experience occupies a realm of experience far removed from old Washo dream visitation. These visions are not sources of power. Induced by a psychotropic substance, panpeyotl, it is a hallucinatory experience with particularly intense visual kaleidoscopic content. Although there are sometimes faint Messianic or other components springing from a historic base, the visions are conditioned as much by personal as by cultural determinants. Power is not in any spirit world but in the peyote, and it is the peyote alone that purveys power. To compare objectively the aboriginal vision visitation with the peyote vision experience is to recognize that apart from the term "vision," they have little in common. To assert that the "comparability" of their "visions" argues for compatability or an inherent connection between shamanism and peyotism is to confuse appearance with reality.

La Barre, following Shonle, believes that peyote's visions are based upon the "aboriginal vision quest and the religious and ideological premises of the quest." Yet he seems to acknowledge the difference between the aboriginal and peyotist visionary experiences when he cites as a reason for peyote's decline among the Washo the "conflict of peyotist theology with [their] spirit-guidance concepts." Barber concedes that a similar divergence may exist among Plains tribes: "There may or may not be some relation between the importance of the vision in Plains culture and the Peyote Cult." Stewart, who knew the Washo case intimately, substantiates Schultes in dismissing the peyote vision as "incidental and of little significance."[53]

Other differences between shamanism and peyotism only serve to illustrate the distance that divides them. A Washo shamanistic session is a curing séance called for a single individual and attended primarily by his family. Participation by the company in the proceedings is incidental. It is the shaman who is the indispensable central figure. Until the abbreviated sessions pioneered by Henry Rupert in the last years of his life, most curing séances were of longer duration, and for serious illness lasted invariably for four nights. Since the purpose of the séance is healing the sick, it inevitably involves participants in the aboriginal theological framework — contact with the awesome spirit world, and concomitantly, concern for the fell caprices of witchcraft, feared source of illness. The emotional mood of the sessions shifts from quiet restraint to relaxed sociability to grim anxiety.

Peyote meetings, on the other hand, are religious gatherings governed by a strict ritual agenda in which all present participate under the direction of a roadchief and his ceremonial assistants. They are also social get-togethers where like-minded devotees affirm common purposes and share mutual fellowship in an identity of faith. Peyote embraces a variety of attractions, with healing an important but not the only reason for calling a gathering. While a meeting may be called for curing a single individual, far more commonly peyotists come together for the varied individual gratifications that peyote proffers.[54]

The uneven course of peyote intoxication charts the moods of the all-night session—excitement, euphoria, depression, introspection, confession, serenity—ending with a festive repast where the spirit of fraternal goodwill benignly reigns. To participate in a peyote meeting is to traverse the widest emotional spectrum, including as it may a description of the peyote vision, a litany of personal confession, evocation of old Indian times, assertion of tribal rights, defiant ridicule of shamans, ethical exhortations, and fulsome praise of whites. At the end, a participant is likely to be emotionally and physically spent, but pleasantly sustained by the lingering effects of the sacred cactus.

Shamanistic and peyote meetings are different not merely in programmatic details. They are of a different order of religious experience. To think of them as cognate is to miss the essential nature of each. To describe a peyote meeting as the "latter-day counterpart of shamanistic curing," is hardly justified by the differences in content, meaning, and mood that have been observed in both ceremonies.

WASHO WORLD VIEW

THE SUBSTRATUM OF BELIEF

We have sketched the course of Washo religion over the past half-century as it underwent changes in its principal manifestations, shamanism and peyotism. We have seen that some of these changes caused upheaval and transformation in venerated tribal institutions. Some of the forces that contributed to these developments have been discussed: the magnetic pull of the dominant culture, the influence of persuasive leaders, the search for personal and collective selfhood. Over the past half century of Washo life, we have seen exemplified what Shonle has graphically described as "the restless and almost despairing need for the reorganization of religion to meet the needs of a new type of living."[55]

In the strong winds of cultural and environmental change, the aboriginal structure of Washo religion has been severely buffeted and has sustained lasting, perhaps irretrievable damage. But what of the ideological and conceptual substratum of Washo being? What of the notions and perceptions, the traditional cultural responses which are the ground of the Washo world view?

The Washo world view is structured on the conception of power described earlier in this study. Power, in brief, is an omnipresent, generalized force embodied in a galaxy of spirits which is felt to pervade the universe. Spirits are encountered in dreams and may bode good or ill, life or death, to the dreamer. The tribal culture is suffused with this overarching idea of power, and many of its forms and institutions are invested with it. The question arises as to whether its scope has been narrowed and its force weakened over the years of religious change.

There is considerable evidence which demonstrates that the conception of power remains both an assumption and a preoccupation of the Washo mind. Recent Washo ethnographers have reported on the ubiquity and seminal influence of the native perception of power. "The belief in the nature of power in the universe is still very real." "Everyone has a soul or personal spirit that is activated by a supernatural power."[56] I recall how my sophisticated interpreter, George Snooks, carefully felt the ground around a lagoon near Lake Tahoe for water baby tracks. Like other Washo he believed that water babies were part of the reality of his world. His sophistication could not dispel this belief. Meetings with Washo in recent years have yielded information which supports the conclusion that the belief in power and its corollary spirit-world is still held by most Washo avowedly, haltingly, or grudgingly.

From the moment peyote was introduced among the Washo, the cult leaders loudly vented their opposition to the aboriginal view of power and in their meetings laughed to scorn the chief exploiters of power, namely, the shamans, whose virtuoso mastery of it in the practice of witchcraft held the tribe in thrall. Yet Ben Lancaster, who preached the new doctrine and lacerated the shamans for incarnating the principle of power, was himself regarded as a prime possessor of power. For many of his followers there could be no other explanation for his position as leader. Despite the institutional edifice of shamanism crumbling around it, power continued to be a viable, durable, haunting rationale for both natural and supernatural experience. It seems a verification of the apothegm in biological science that environmental conditions do not change the nucleus.

Had the peyote leaders succeeded in proscribing the traditional conception of power, the practice of sorcery might have withered for lack of ideological nourishment. As it was, during the days of the early peyote conflict the air was alive with accusations of witching. It was charged that witching was going on in the meetings themselves. Participants accused one another of being in league with malevolent spirits and of causing sickness and death. Thirty years after the people first partook of peyote, Downs could write that the Washo are different from their neighbors in "their concern about witches."[57]

Today the concept of power and the spirit world reared upon it are still an immanent reality to many Washo. In 1981 Henry Rupert's daughter-in-law, Virginia Rupert, spoke about her father-in-law's efficacy as curer. "It was his power. Power is all around you. It's everywhere. But you got to know how [to use it]. It's up to you if you want to use it." One of the younger Washo leaders, college graduate, perceptive, worldly, moderate in his views, remarked that he believed in spirits.

> My grandmother explained that all peoples have their giants and midgets. The Washo had theirs—mountain men, girls with long hair who had a swing, water babies. But we wouldn't accept them as members of the tribe. Therefore they had to shift for themselves. But if you leave them alone, they won't harm you.

In casual conversation, Washo would sooner or later advert to the spirit world undergirded by the theory of power. Marvin Dressler believes "the old way." In 1974 he told of his encounters with bear, repository of particularly potent spirit power.

> I was sitting on the river bank when I suddenly saw a bear going into the bushes. I got up and went in after him. But he had disappeared. Who knows where he went? Bears can do things like that.

Another time while shepherding in the mountains, he was suddenly confronted by a bear. "That bear turned slowly and walked away. I ran, left those sheep. I swore I'd never shepherd again" (conversation 3 October 1974). The spirit world was, so to speak, the permanent proscenium within which much of the interior life and thought of the Washo was enacted.

An anthropologist commented in 1981, "Sorcery among the Washo is still alive. But the accusations of witching are indirect. They're made often but quietly." Dread of witchcraft may no longer be the frightening incubus it was in a former generation. After all, the shamans, professional purveyors of sorcery, are gone. Nevertheless, despite peyote's rejection of the old power doctrine, there remains a lingering uneasiness that out of the spirit world some power may strike at any time, to sicken, blight, or end a human life, which may be one's own.

Other signs of a circumambient spirit world alive with awe and mystery are discernible in the life of the people. Fear of the dead is an unaltered apprehension involving Washo of all worldly levels. Some will speak of dead kinsmen in muttered monosyllables, some not at all. Clara Frank, now in her nineties, an informant forty-five years ago, refused to talk to me about her dead children whom I had known well.

Henry Rupert died in 1973. In 1974 his daughter, Viola, would not speak of her father because too little time had elapsed since his death. Rupert had given instructions that no headstone was to be placed on his grave for four years, and there could certainly be no talk of him until that period had passed. His spirit was still alive and was not to be disturbed. No liberties could be taken with it. Consequently, the house where he lived had remained unoccupied and, in keeping with Washo custom, was being dismantled. His shaman's paraphernalia had been hidden, buried under water. It will be recalled that water was one of his familiars and, for the Washo, informed with great spiritual potency.[58] To further questions, his daughter answered, "We don't talk about those things."

Seven years later, Viola Rupert still demurred when questioned about her father. There was a note of pathos in her response. "We feel he's still here. We used to go to him when we [were] in trouble or sick. He'd help us, cure us. We miss him." His spiritual presence could hardly make up for his physical absence. Next door lay the scattered ruins of Henry Rupert's house, destroyed in compliance with aboriginal mandate.

John Frank — Healer

Something of the persistence of the Washo aboriginal world view and of the conception of power upon which it rests is inherent in the life and religious vocation of John Frank, an old Washo healer now in his nineties. In the fall of 1981 he was quite able to fend for himself, physically frail but mentally alert. He had a boyhood recollection of Captain Jim's visit to Washington and of the ensuing allocation of Pine Nut Range allotments to the tribe.

John Frank was a contemporary of Henry Rupert, and the course his life took undoubtedly owed much to Rupert's influence. The two were raised together, went to the Carson Agency school together, became lifelong friends, and were Carson Colony neighbors. At the Agency school, Frank learned the trade of carpenter and after finishing school became a carpenter in Reno. He joined the union and reported finding no discrimination among the members. He would work for a building contractor during the six or seven months of good weather. When winter came his life followed the schedule of tribal life. He was a skilled hunter.

Frank made his way easily enough in the white world and was well regarded by whites and Washo alike. He had two sons, both successful. One became a foreman, later supervisor, with a construction company; the other, Robert, head of the Washo Tribal Council. Frank apparently shared in both cultures without difficulty. Emblematic of the prestige he enjoyed among whites, he was asked to narrate Washo tales for the ethnology archives of the University of Nevada.[59]

When questioned about Washo religion, Frank showed little hesitancy in speaking of the old shamans, in describing the steps by which one became a shaman, and in delineating his own experiences in quest of the shaman's vocation. His willingness to speak freely of shamans and shamanism marked a significant change from the sullen reluctance or outright refusal to discuss any aspect of shamanism recalled from the early field experience. This was no doubt due to the passing of the old religious order and the disappearance of its chief functionaries.

John Frank was never a full-fledged shaman. I recall no mention of him in connection with the earlier investigation of shamanism in the thirties. It was only in 1974 when he was already an old man that I heard he had "begun to take up the old doctoring." This may be connected with Henry Rupert's death the previous year. He had watched Rupert cure over the years and had in fact received instruction from him in curing techniques. In 1981 a good many Washo spoke of Frank's success as a healer.

Frank's assumption of the role of healer was no sudden inspiration. As a young man he had received intimations of shamanistic aptitude. "I could have been a doctor years ago," he explained. "But it was too dangerous. Old Indian doctors never lasted too long." He then went on to trace the steps he took for determining whether to enter professionally into the shaman's world.

It was the classical quest for the decision on becoming a shaman. He encountered his spirit helper in a dream, fell sick, went to a shaman for direction in the four-year apprenticeship needed for acquiring full shaman status. "I went to Monkey Pete. He was an honest Indian doctor. Those Indian doctors had the power to do things. He had the most power." After washing Frank's face, Monkey Pete counseled with him at length as to "whether to go ahead or stay out of it. He knew me, knew what it meant to be a doctor." The decision was reached to go no further.

Monkey Pete lived in the early decades of the century and was highly esteemed as a shaman. In 1907 after receiving several spirit visitations, Henry Rupert went to him for advice about pursuing the shamanistic quest. In contrast to his attitude toward John Frank, Monkey Pete seems to have encouraged Rupert to "go on." Rupert's feeling for the older shaman parallelled Frank's. He called him a "great man [who] knew more than the rest put together." In 1926 Rupert had introduced him to Lowie as a "philosopher."

Not until old age, perhaps shortly before the death of Henry Rupert, his closest friend, did Frank again experience a dream encounter with his spirit helper. He began to be visited at night by two women clad in gray. These had appeared in some of Rupert's early spirit visitations. Rupert's Hawaiian friend and associate, George Robinson, who had persuaded him to adopt the short cure technique, began to instruct Frank, teaching him "tricks." "He taught me how to handle things, especially heart attacks."

Frank described the therapy he employed for heart seizures and the theory behind it.

> There are two neck cords, one for pumping and one for circulation. The neck is the whole system—two veins, coming and going. When you get a heart attack, the neck cords get tight. So you rub and massage the neck. You loosen the cords until the heart starts pumping and the circulation comes back. You work on that goddam neck. You rub till you open up the whole thing.

He reported cures not only for heart attacks but also for varicose veins, broken legs, and incontinence. He asked no money for his services. "They give what they feel like—one or two dollars."

Frank does not claim to be a shaman. There is no hint of the spirit world in his heart therapy. "I'm not a doctor but I help people." Whether he meant native doctor (i.e., shaman) or medical practitioner is not clear. One of his neighbors said, "He doesn't claim to be a doctor but he likes people to think he is. He dreams a lot."

When I last went to see him, his wife told me he was sleeping. I had come a considerable distance, and she thought of waking him.

She moved slowly toward his room, stopped for some moments, then turned toward me and said, "It wouldn't be safe to wake him. He dreams every afternoon." I was left in little doubt that his dreams were not of the world I knew but of the supernatural world of the Washo which he and Henry Rupert knew. For this reason his dream world was allowed to suffer no earthly intrusion.

The Unbroken Heritage

We come inevitably to realize that peyotism was a break with traditional Washo religion. Moreover it was a break of revolutionary impact. The advent of peyote precipitated a crisis from which the old Washo religion never recovered. It was the critical factor contributing to the dissolution of shamanism, the tribe's millenial medicoreligious complex. There were other factors, already noted, particularly the desire to identify with the white world, which made for the breakdown of the cherished ways of old. But it was the bitter, remorseless, violent struggle with the peyotists that left the forces of shamanism weak, disorganized, defenseless, and ultimately vanquished. When shamans—hitherto unassailable and unchallenged—were defied, reviled, and boycotted, the signs were clear that the old religious order had begun to totter.

To characterize the denouncement of the violent encounter between shamanism and peyotism as a break with the past may seem an exaggeration, perhaps simplistic. To those who participated in the conflict and its aftermath—or to those who witnessed it—the description is neither. The depth and virulence of the emotional storm that raged over the tribe and involved most of its members was without precedent. Rancor and resentment, bitterness and enmity, threats and imprecations were the more explosive for being compressed within a relatively small inbred community. Moreover, religious strife is not uncommonly conflict *in extremis*. Partisan feeling on both sides hardened into unyielding attitudes from which there was no retreat. No witness to the unfolding of such intratribal disruption could have been surprised when the embattled traditions and sanctities, which were the occasion for strife, emerged shattered and broken.[60]

Within a few years of the prodigious struggle for supremacy, the number of traditional shamans had begun to dwindle. No single Washo felt called to the role of shaman's apprentice. Soon there were neither traditional shamans nor aspirants to shamanistic office. Within a relatively short span of years the tribal structure of aboriginal religious life had withered away. Now, if an occasional Washo wanted an "old time" shaman to attend him, he was compelled either to travel to a non-Washo practitioner or to invite a shaman from a neighboring tribe to tend him in Washo territory.

One full-fledged Washo shaman was left. Henry Rupert, who was born and grew up in the old cultural milieu when shamans were the sole healers and preeminent power-brokers of the tribe, continued to heal as a shaman. Yet from the beginning he showed maverick tendencies to act and to believe out of private personality drives as well as out of responses to the non-Washo world. Called to the shaman's vocation, he pursued his own patterns of practice and belief. Eschewing sorcery, he developed a novel synthesis of healing and faith. In time he had so far departed from the old shamanistic disciplines as to be considered a radical innovator. He became a good, kind, helpful nonmercenary shaman/healer only remotely akin to the feared curer/sorcerers of earlier days. When he died in 1973 the last Washo shaman had passed from the scene.

No one today thinks of becoming a shaman. Someone reported that Rupert wanted to instruct his son in the ways of a shaman, but the son showed little interest. Old John Frank began to cure in his declining years, using the techniques of his lifelong friend Henry Rupert, who lived down the street. Frank makes no claim to being a shaman. He dreams and he cures the tribesmen who come to his door with their aches and pains. It may be that we have in these casual curing encounters of a ninety-year-old man the last murmurs of aboriginal Washo religion. What remains is the substratum of belief in a supernatural world peopled with spirits and animated by power. Older Washo still recognize this superterrestrial world as an encompassing reality. Some younger Washo acknowledge it in vaguer definition, others hardly at all.

Given this persistent substratum of belief, the question may be asked whether shamanism may not one day enjoy a revival among the Washo. Bean and Vane have written about a "resurgence of shamans" and describe a vigorous role for them among neighboring California tribes. In 1961 Downs believed it was a "mistake to say Washo shamanism is a thing of the past" and held that shamanistic forms may return to a place of importance in Washo life.[61] In 1941 I had described the retreat of the shamans from the high ground of tribal influence and power. My 1974 stay with the Washo confirmed that shamans were no longer visible on the cultural horizon. Neither was there any suggestion during my 1981 visit of the possibility that they might reappear. It is difficult to imagine that amid the centrifugal forces of Western society, in whose violent momentum the old Washo culture is inescapably caught, an order resembling traditional shamanism will again take shape.

The question may also be asked whether peyotism may not again come to assume the vogue it once had among the Washo. It has been said that the Indians who journey from the San Francisco Bay area to attend peyote meetings on Washo ground are demonstrating a desire to maintain ties with the old Indian ways and so to strengthen the native identity. It remains to be seen how long these journeys will continue. The highly charged political climate that currently prevails in the national Indian community would appear to favor this pattern of religious confraternity. On the other hand, the steamroller of urban assimilation may in time inhibit the impulse to affirm an ethnic singularity.

Meanwhile, the increasing attendance at the meetings comes not from Washo who live close by but from the medley of Indians who journey from contiguous areas. This may indicate a less compelling need on the part of Washo to affirm the Indian solidarity and a readier acceptance by them of the status quo. Here are awakened echoes of the Washo attitudes of passivity and quiescence which have marked their history since the first contact with whites.

In 1941 I suggested that some future revivalist cult might yet strike root in Washo soil and flourish. In forty years this has not happened. Tipi Way perseveres in Woodfords with a decreasing number of Washo followers. While no one can predict the turns of Washo fortune, the people's improved social and economic condition and the prospect for future betterment would seem to point to a continuation of the present low level of involvement in institutional religious expression. It is possible, however, that in the event of future deprivation or disfranchisement by the government, this may change. Indian lands, particularly those located in the Western states, are rich in the natural resources related to the production of energy—oil, gas, coal, uranium—which are and which will continue to be in great demand. The Great American Desert has been compared to the Arabian peninsula in its hidden wealth. It is projected that the future of the Indians living on these lands will depend on "who will ultimately control these resources."[62]

It seems that a new genre of religious leaders has lately made its appearance in eastern Nevada. None is a Washo, but following the now familiar pattern of intertribal meetings, Washo, Northern Paiute, Shoshoni, and other Indians come togther for what seem to be new departures in Indian ceremonialism. A Northern Paiute from McDermott, energetic and articulate, appears to possess impressive qualifications for leadership. He advocates and practices a novel religious synthesis that brings together elements of the Sun Dance, peyote cult, and shamanism, with peyote used as a purificatory agent for the Sun Dance. A Chippewa-Shoshoni living in Fallon is a teacher and curer whose ministrations center around the sweat lodge ceremony. A Shoshoni from eastern Nevada is a curer reputed to be able to control the weather. The appearance of such leaders may presage the rise of a new religious syncretism which merges cultural elements drawn from the melange of tribes represented in their assemblages. Someone has called them neoshamans.

Whatever their designation, they are a far cry from the shamans who held spiritual sway in western Nevada when I first encountered them almost half a century ago. The shamans of that day and the religious order over which they presided exercised dominant control over the lives of the people. If there is a connection between the old shamans of the thirties, the roadchiefs of the fifties, and the "neoshamans" of the eighties, between their followers and between their several approaches to the religious life, it may perhaps be found in the shared belief in a spirit world pervaded by power which is the ultimate ground of the Washo world view. This transcendent reality is the unbroken heritage and dateless framework of their native faith.

NOTES

Introduction

1. La Barre (1975) has described the culture of peyote, white style, in rich and diverting detail.

2. A cognate American Negro chic marked the years between the two world wars. With the publication in 1925 of Alain Locke's *The New Negro*, black intellectuals and artists heralded the arrival of a black generation proud of its cultural singularity. Young blacks aspired to becoming New Negroes. As Langston Hughes observed, "The Negro was in vogue."

3. Stewart 1973:41; Deloria 1970:83–84.

4. de Mille 1976:76; La Barre 1975:271–75.

Preface

1. Siskin 1938:626.

2. Linton 1940:470; Herskovits 1941:3.

Chapter 1. Sketch of Washo Culture

1. Kroeber 1939:137, 191, 208, map 7. Although referring in many instances to forms and conditions no longer found among the Washo, the present tense is used throughout the chapter.

2. Siskin 1938:626–27.

3. Kroeber 1939:142,137.

4. Freed 1960; Downs 1961 (1982 addition).

5. Kroeber 1906–7:312–17, 1925:569; Lowie 1939:301. (See also Freed 1960; Jacobsen 1966:113, 123. Jacobsen believes Washo is less "aberrant" Hokan than Greenberg and Swadesh suggest [1982 addition].)

6. d'Azevedo 1966:334 (1982 addition).

7. Freed (1960:362) affirms Barrett (1917:8) in declaring that "the social organization of the Washo is primarily based on the family unit." In discussing the "usual" socioeconomic unit among Great Basin Indians, Fowler (1966:62) proposes the use of Malouf's "kin clique" as preferable to Steward's "nuclear family" and Harris's "camp group" (1982 addition).

8. Using Murdock's terminology, Freed (1960:362) classifies Washo marriage as "non-sororal polygyny." In recent times polygyny, along with levirate and sororate, has been abandoned (1982 addition).

9. Lowie (1939:304) equates this institution with neighboring California moiety organization.

10. Culin 1907; Kroeber 1925:573.

11. Barrett (1917) has a comprehensive description of basketry types. (See also Gigli 1974 [1982 addition].)

Chapter 2. THE NATURE OF WASHO SHAMANISM

1. This was Mike Dick's tally. He qualified the inclusions by explaining that Sam Dick's status was uncertain since he had become a peyote convert and that Becky Jack, whose power was feared, had not shamanized for some time. Dick Bagley was said not to "take his work as seriously as others." However, all were generally regarded as shamans. Henry (Moses) Rupert enumerated twelve shamans for the entire tribe: three among the Northern Washo, one in Washo Valley, one in Carson City, five in Carson Valley (including Woodfords), one in Markleeville, and one in Antelope Valley. Rupert further remarked that there were formerly many more shamans than there are now.

2. Lowie 1939:318.

3. Downs (1961:367), who recorded the same story, mentions a parallel Yokuts narrative recorded by Hatch.

4. Lowie 1939:322. Under "Miscellaneous Notes," Lowie writes: "Sometimes Indians see a water baby by a spring, with the hair flowing way down" (1939:331). But on page 322, the designation "water baby" is not employed although, in effect, it is water baby who is described.

5. Lowie 1939:320.

6. Du Bois 1939:v.

7. Praying to the sun is not uncommon in Great Basin shamanism (see J. S. Harris 1940:56).

8. Well-known shaman mentioned by Lowie (1939:321).

9. Henry (Moses) Rupert is referred to by Lowie (1939:321) as a "sophisticated young Washo . . . a mystic credited with shamanistic ambitions." That was in 1926. He is now recognized by the Washo as a full-fledged shaman. I interviewed him a number of times, and his account of shamanistic preparation is derived both from my own and from Grace Dangberg's notes, which she kindly placed at my disposal. He was her chief informant.

10. Dangberg's field notes.

11. Park 1938:134-35.

12. Park (1938:34) mentions for the Northern Paiute a rattle consisting of "a drum of dried skin of deer's ears" containing small pebbles "gathered on an anthill," resembling the form described by Snooks.

13. Lowie 1939:331-32.

14. Barrett and Gifford 1933:277-88, 370, plate 73.

15. Barrett 1917:44, fig. 3.

16. Nowhere in western North America is drumming an important component of shamanism (Park 1938:133-34).

17. Steward 1933:265-66; Barrett and Gifford 1933:200-202; Beals 1933:344; Dixon 1905:168-70; Kroeber 1925:407-8, 447.

18. Barrett and Gifford 1933:200-202.

19. Park 1938:123.

20. Only two plants are used by shamans in supernatural curing: wild parsnip and tobacco. None but a shaman is permitted to gather wild parsnip. It is administered in the following way: The shaman takes the dried root (about one inch in diameter and very hard)—which, if eaten, will ordinarily poison a person—talks to it, chews it, and gives it to the patient to swallow. It has a bitter taste. Peyote, in its external character and manner of administration (in some cases), offers interesting parallels.

21. Lowie 1939:319–20.

22. Jack Wilson is the celebrated Wovoka of Ghost Dance fame. The date of this episode is 1912–13.

23. Said Mike Dick: "A lot of them get sick this way."

24. No precise description of these medicines could be obtained. "I never saw it," said George Snooks, who at one time owned a gambling medicine. "It was in a cane tube. My grandfather bought it for fifteen dollars from another Washo, who got it from a Miwok. He got it for me so that I could grow up and be a good hunter. My parents kept it for me." The Washo term for medicine means "sleep." Evidently its effect was soporific. "It made the animal go to sleep," asserted Snooks. "When you have this medicine, you can come up to a deer when it's sleeping." That it was "strong medicine" was attested by the fact that it occasionally sent Snooks himself into a deep sleep. "Sometimes I would go to sleep and no one could wake me up—until I woke up myself." Medicines were always carried on one's person.

25. See Sapir 1936:127–28.

26. Barrett 1917:40, 44, figs. 1 and 8.

27. There is one exception to this rule. If a shaman is called to attend a sick person while he is undergoing the four-day purificatory rites following the death of a patient, he doctors for nothing. But even in such cases the patient or the family presents the shaman with a "gift" of money or a basket—"if they can afford to." However, Mike Dick denied that a shaman ever doctored for nothing.

28. Lowie 1939:321.

29. Lowie 1939:303, 324.

30. The Washo shaman does not conform to the generalized type described by Radin: "We must remember, at the outset that a definite correlation exists between the simpler societies organized on a non-agricultural basis and the extent to which, in such civilizations, neurotic-epileptoid individuals predominate among the medicine men" (1937:105–8). No Washo shaman, so far as I know, approximated the "neurotic-epileptoid" type. In fact, they were for the most part disconcertingly "normal."

Chapter 3. THE AFFILIATIONS OF WASHO SHAMANISM

1. Spier 1930:239.

2. Spier 1930:239–79; Park 1938:72–147.

3. Primarily J. S. Harris (1940) and M. K. Opler (1940b).

4. Park 1938:15, 45, 75; Steward 1933:311–16; Kelly 1932; M. K. Opler 1940b:141; J. S. Harris 1940:56, 103; Loeb 1926:366; Kroeber 1925:373, 859; Beals 1933:385–86; Gayton 1930; M. E. Opler 1936a:146.

5. Park 1938:15, 76; Steward 1933:308; Kelly 1932:190, 1936:129; Densmore 1922:127, 1932:101; M. K. Opler 1940b:141–42; Lowie 1909:224, 1924:296; J. S.

Harris 1940:58; Teit 1900:354, 1906:283; Ray 1932:172; Spier and Sapir 1930:236; Spinden 1908:247–48; Sapir 1907:35; Spier 1928:276–77, 1930:100–101, 1933:249; Du Bois 1935:113; Dixon 1905:281, 1908:218; Beals 1933:379–80; Kroeber 1925:754–55, 1935:185–86; Forde 1931:182; Gifford 1933:309.

6. Spier 1930:245; Park 1938:77; Lowie 1939:320.

7. Park 1938:16–17; Densmore 1922:127; Lowie 1924:296; J. S. Harris 1940:60; Teit 1900:339, 1906:599; Spier 1930:104–5; Lowie 1922:322.

8. Dixon 1905:265, 1907:470; Kroeber 1925:198; Spier 1930:246; Beals 1933:381; Park 1938:78–79.

9. Park 1938:85, 86; J. S. Harris 1940:57; Kelly 1936:136–37; Teit 1900:354–55, 1906:283–84, 1909:605; Ray 1932:201–2; Spier and Sapir 1930:244–45; Spier 1930:122–23; Dixon 1907:486; Kroeber 1925:854.

10. Lowie 1909:224, 1922:344; Park 1938:95–97; J. S. Harris 1940:57, Du Bois 1932:256–57, 1935:50, 118; Kroeber 1907:419, 1925:63–64, 180, 497, 500, 680–81, 748; Spier 1928:276, 1930:107, 123, 250, 1933:236–37; Benedict 1922:10; Sapir 1907:42; Dixon 1905:267–68, 1907:472–73; Nomland 1935:168; Loeb 1926:320; Gayton 1930:388–89; Gifford 1932a:38–39, 1932b:233, 241, 1933:303, 309; Forde 1931:181–82, 201–2.

11. Park 1938:95–96.

12. Park 1938:20; Lowie 1909:228, 1924:291; Densmore 1922:127; Steward 1933:311; J. S. Harris 1940:57; Teit 1900:360, 1909:613; Ray 1932:200; Spier and Sapir 1930:107; Spier 1928:277, 1930:107–8, 1933:238; Kroeber 1925:63–64, 111, 117, 196, 1935:185, 1939:274; Du Bois 1932:256, 1935:88; Dixon 1905:274, 1907:471; Beals 1933:385; Curtis 1926, vol. 15:97; Nomland 1935:168; Gifford 1932a:50, 1932b:236, 1933:310; Gayton 1930:389; Mason 1912:183; Strong 1929:64, 253; Russell 1908:256–57.

13. Spier 1923:312, 1928:277–78, 1930:94–95, 247–59, 1933:236, 238, 244; Park 1938:108–9, 112; J. S. Harris 1940:57; M. K. Opler 1940b:141; Densmore 1922:128; Teit 1900:354, 1906:471–72, 1909:605; Kroeber 1925:63–64, 196, 604, 640, 680, 688–89, 779, 1935:185–86, 1939:292; Beals 1933:388; Gayton 1930:388; Gifford 1932a:49–50, 1932b:233–34, 1933:303–4; Gifford and Lowie 1928:344–45; Benedict 1923:36–37, 1924:382–83; Hooper 1920:345–47; Russell 1908:25.

14. Spier 1930:250, 1933:247; Park 1938:115–17; Kroeber 1925:754–55; Forde 1931:201–2.

15. Park 1938:117–18; Kelly 1932:190, 1936:129; Lowie 1909:223–25, 1924:291, 295–96; Densmore 1922:128; J. S. Harris 1940:57; Benedict 1922:12–13; Spier 1930:249–50.

16. Dixon 1905:297, 1907:489, 1908:216; Gifford 1932a:49–50; Kroeber 1925:68, 117, 513–14, 1935:186; Gayton 1930:388–89; Goddard 1903:66; Du Bois 1935:88–89; Spier 1933:244–45.

17. Steward 1933:311; Park 1938:120–22; Kelly 1936:130–31; Teit 1900:354, 1909:605; Gunther 1926:297; Spinden 1908:247; Spier 1928:277–78, 1930:97, 247–48, 1933:240–41; Dixon 1905:274–75, 1907:471, 477; Du Bois 1935:90–91; Gifford 1932a:50, 1933:309; Russell 1908:256; Kroeber 1935:185.

18. Park 1938:45–46, 122–23; Steward 1933:311–12; Kelly 1932:189–90; Lowie 1909:223–24, 1924:291–92; Spier 1930:259–67; Kroeber 1925:111, 197–99, 302, 361, 852; Dixon 1905:268, 280; Beals 1933:386.

19. Spier 1930:266–67.

20. Park 1938:134–35.

21. Kroeber 1925:106, 127, 314, 419, 420, 665, 723, 823; Steward 1933:278, 313; Park 1938:33–34, 131–32; Spier 1928:289–90.

22. Clements 1932:196.
23. Park 1938:135–39; Spier 1928:277, 1933:280; Kroeber 1925:775.
24. Kelly 1932:192, 1936; Steward 1933:313; Park 1938:45–60, 123–26; Lowie 1909:228, 1924:292; J. S. Harris 1940:57; Kroeber 1925:117, 197, 515, 775, 1935:187; Beals 1933:387; Dixon 1905:270, 1907:478; Du Bois 1935:104–6; Spier 1928:279, 1930, 1933:283; Spier and Sapir 1930:246; Ray 1932:204; Teit 1900: 360–61, 1906:287–88, 1909:612.
25. Park 1938:136.
26. Park 1938:50–41, 126–29; Kelly 1932:193; Spier 1930:113, 124, 268; Spier and Sapir 1930:246; Ray 1932:204; Du Bois 1935:107–8; Dixon 1905:271, 315–17.
27. Lowie 1909:224, 1924:296; Steward 1933:311; Kelly 1932:83–84, 189, 1936:129, 136–38; J. S. Harris 1940:54; Park 1938:60–62, 97–98; Gifford 1932a:49, 1932b:234–35, 239, 241; Teit 1900:303, 1906:287, 1909:612–13; Ray 1932:201; Spier and Sapir 1930:244–45; Spier 1928:277, 1930:108, 123, 1933:238, 285; Gunther 1932:298; Kroeber 1925:504–5, 854–55, 1935:185; Dixon 1907:484; Russell 1908:256–57.
28. Park 1938:62, 143–44; Kelly 1932:83–86; Steward 1933:253; Lowie 1909: 185; 1924:119; Spier 1928:110, 1930:158, 1933:69; Spier and Sapir 1930:180; Ray 1932:77–78; Kroeber 1935:61, 65, 68.
29. Gayton 1930; Herskovits 1930:400–405; Radin 1937:41–43; Thomas 1937: 476.
30. Park 1938:66–71; Steward 1933:304; Teit 1900:289, 1906:255, 1909:569; Ray 1932:200; Spier 1923:318, 1928:235–36, 1930:94, 1933:154–55; Spier and Sapir 1930:211, 247; Spinden 1908:256; Goddard 1903:82–83; Kroeber 1925: 53–54, 373, 745, 778, 859, 1935:185, 1939:342–43; Loeb 1926:355, 402; Dixon 1905:246, 267, 1907:451, 471; Du Bois 1935:118; Gayton 1930:398–99; Benedict 1924:383; Gifford 1933:303; Russell 1908:256.

Chapter 4. Washo Peyotism

1. La Barre 1975:109–23, 175–88.
2. Lumholtz 1898, 1902.
3. M. E. Opler 1938:271.
4. Shonle 1925:58.
5. In the forty years since this was written, peyotism has apparently not taken root in California. Bean and Vane make only one passing reference to "Peyote religions," speaking of them as being among the "many local smaller traditions" (1978a:662), The fact that Indians living in California travel the considerable distance to Washo territory in Nevada to attend peyote meetings attests to peyote's minimal impact on the California tribes (1982 addition).
6. Fully covered by Anderson 1980:133–56, 90–102.
7. Since 1941 when this was written, extensive research has succeeded in isolating "more than 55 peyote alkaloids . . . as of 1978. . . . Research on peyote continues so this number . . . is almost certain to increase" (Anderson 1980:119). Schultes has called the peyote cactus "a veritable chemical factory" (1938:698–703) (1982 addition).
8. This description of a Washo peyote meeting is largely a composite of five meetings I attended, two conducted by Ben Lancaster and three by Sam Dick. Since Dick was Lancaster's disciple, there were no significant differences between their methods of presiding.

Dick's meetings were known for the mood of contagious intensity and rapt involvement that they projected. As one of Dick's followers put it: "I heard about Sam Dick holding meetings down there. He didn't have no Tipi then . . . just put up some kind of blankets to hold out the wind. But plenty people came. I never heard nothing like it. I never heard songs like that. . . . [He] used to pray good. It was just like he knew everything in the world. He talked about the whole world, and he made it seem all right there in the Tipi. . . . It opened up a new life for me" (d'Azevedo 1978:45–46) (1982 addition).

9. Lancaster trained both Mary Creek and Louise Byers to act as chief drummer. Dick followed suit and made Ida McBride (whom he married shortly after his removal to Coleville) his drummer.

10. La Barre 1975:43–53.

11. La Barre 1975:60, 69.

12. Sam Dick cast longing eyes on the copy of La Barre's book I occasionally brought to our interviews. The pictures particularly fascinated him—and all the members of the settlement who gathered round for a coveted glimpse.

13. La Barre 1975:61.

14. La Barre 1975; Schultes 1938. However, Voegelin has reported the trait for the Shawnee, while Lone Bear and John Wright, the latter a Northern Paiute, both prepared cigarettes of sage and tobacco when singing with Stewart. The presumption is that they learned the technique in Oklahoma (Stewart 1944:101).

15. Petrullo 1934:53.

16. Bennett and Zingg 1935:293–94; La Barre 1975:7; Lumholtz 1898:8.

17. La Barre 1975:64; Petrullo 1934; Stewart 1944:80.

18. M. E. Opler 1936a:144.

19. M. E. Opler 1936a.

20. Also known as Raymond Lone Bear, Ralph Chapman, Ralph Kachumik, and Ralph Kochampanaskin, and not to be confused with Sam Lone Bear.

21. Also known as Grey Horse and Chief Grey Horse.

22. Lancaster's standing in the Native American Church is vague. Present officials deny any knowledge of his connection with the institution. However, to Mack Haag, former president, he is known and, in fact, esteemed worthy of pursuing missionary work (correspondence with Carson Indian Agency, Stewart, Nevada).

23. Correspondence with Carson Indian Agency, Stewart, Nevada.

24. My stay with the Washo happened to coincide with the period during which peyote rose, flourished, and declined. During three successive summers—1937, 1938, 1939—I was able to trace the progress and development of the cult not only numerically, but also, and more important, in terms of the bitter and sometimes violent conflicts which erupted between peyotists and nonpeyotists.

25. Under various items of government legislation, e.g., the Wheeler-Howard Act, a Tribal Council has been organized. It consists of seven members including a chairman. Three are chosen from the Dresslerville community, "headquarters" of the tribe, and four from the rest of the tribesmen. Elections are held every two years on the third Saturday in October (U.S. Department of the Interior 1936; 1937). In 1939 the members were Willie James, Willie Jim, and Willie Smokey—representing the Dresslerville group—and Ray Fillmore, Roma James, Jackson Snooks, and Donald Wade—representing the rest of the Washo. Ray Fillmore was chairman. All sorts of rivalries sprang up around the prized position of council member, and especially of council chairman. These rivalries were not without significance in the struggle that ensued over peyote.

26. In fourteen Washo and Northern Paiute communities, with a total population of 2,257, there were 300 members—14 percent of the adult population—during the 1936–1938 span of peyote's greatest activity (Stewart 1944:122).

27. Strangely enough, Willie Smokey was being treated in the Agency hospital. His belief in the therapeutic efficacy of peyote was evidently limited. Such a restricted faith, however, created no qualms either in the family that called the meeting, in the officiants, or in the other peyotists.

28. Ben Lancaster had met Mary Dutchman Creek shortly after arriving in western Nevada. She lived in Schurz, scene of Leo Okio's peyotism years before and where Lancaster held some of his first meetings. She soon became Lancaster's drummer, a radical departure from conventional peyote practice, in which a woman never attains such ritual distinction.

29. From Stewart's (1944) figures.

30. Bill Cornbread was one of Lowie's informants (1939:301).

31. Steve Earl was the son of a self-styled leader of the Washo, and also had pretensions for leadership. His mother was one of the powerful shamans of the tribe, so he had a double stake in the preservation of the old culture, political and religious. Joe Ryder was antagonized because of a family rift caused by peyote. His brother had had his favorite grandson taken from him and brought to the Coleville cult focus by a peyotist uncle. Joe Ryder, who significantly was also a shaman, took up the cudgels for his brother. John Mack and Martinez Kyser were close political allies of Steve Earl. Although most vehement in their opposition to peyote, no reasons other than affiliation with Earl were brought to light.

32. Stewart was invited to this conference (1944:83).

33. In August 1939 the number of Washo attending Sam Dick's meetings was reduced to seven. Ten patronized Ben Lancaster's meetings. Dick's devotees were:

Susie Dick	— Dick's mother
Harrietta Charlie	— Dick's father's sister
Leonard Moore	— Dick's father's sister's son
Leola Charlie	— Dick's father's sister's daughter
Salina Charlie	— Dick's father's sister's daughter
Spotty George Dick	— Dick's mother's brother
Oliver John	— Dick's mother's sister's son's son

The close kinship existing in Dick's group should be noted. This was not true of Lancaster's. His faithful followers were Hansen Pete, Winnie Simpson (Hansen Pete's wife), Visalia Cornbread, Emory Arnot, Seymour Arnot (Emory's son), Morrison Walker, Edwin Peter, Johnson Walker, Mary Walker (Johnson's wife), and Streeter Dick. It should be remembered that by 1939, meetings, which were then being held only on the farthest boundaries of Washo territory or beyond it, were attracting far more non-Washo than Washo.

34. Sapir 1934:411; Kardiner 1939:8.

35. Stewart 1944.

36. Evidently no rare phenomenon wherever peyote diffused (cf. La Barre 1975:147n.37).

37. Sam Dick one day produced a copy of a Jehovah's Witness tract entitled, "Riches." ("Information which will enable every person to realize in fullness the greatest desire and fondest hopes of humankind," by J. F. Rutherford.) On a colored plate (the third opposite page 193) is pictured "The Great Multitude (Rev. 7:9–17)." Among the assembled throng standing before God, Dick pointed out a single Indian in feather headdress. He told how he had purchased the volume for

twenty-five cents from a "peddler" after a peyote meeting. "Of course I can't read, but I help him out a little bit."

38. La Barre 1975:148–50.
39. Hallowell 1938:45–46.

Chapter 5. THE CLASH BETWEEN SHAMANISM AND PEYOTISM

1. Spier 1921, 1935; Radin 1914; Nash 1937; Du Bois 1939.

2. Mooney 1896:719–20; Lesser 1933a:115; Nash 1937:377; Du Bois 1939:137; Linton 1940:502–3, 517–19. Messianic movements, which have recurred at intervals throughout Jewish history, afford an example of the same correlation on a different cultural level. Goldenweiser (1937:266–67) has described similar phenomena in nineteenth-century Russia.

3. Frémont's second expedition passed through the heart of Washo terrain. The entries January 19–February 20 in his narrative (1846:134–44) relate the daring thrust through the high Sierras in midwinter snows. His guides were Washo (cf. also Nevins 1939:152–58). The ill-fated Donner party (1846–47) came to grief in the mountains on the northern shore of Lake Tahoe—Washo territory (Houghton 1920:54–122). The Sierra Nevada passes were accessible only through Washo territory.

4. Bancroft 1875, vol. 1:440–42. This opinion is shared by Mark Twain, who in his *Roughing It* depicts the Indians of Nevada generally and of Carson Valley particularly in the same unflattering terms (1872, vol. 1:131–35, 260–61).

Billington (1981:117) has pointed out that by mid-nineteenth century, the Indian, no longer conceived as the Rousseauian noble savage living in a pure Eden, was now imagined a devil, "treacherous, vindictive, cruel, many of them cannibalistic . . . scalping travelers, abducting heroines, battling with white hunters, and devising torture techniques that would have shocked the Marquis de Sade" (1982 addition).

5. Hopkins 1883:60–65; cf. Park 1938:11.
6. Lowie 1939:303; d'Azevedo 1973:4–5.
7. Dollard et al. 1939:10.
8. Du Bois 1939:7.
9. Radin 1914:7; Shonle 1925:59; Petrullo 1934:26, 131; M. E. Opler 1936a:143; M. K. Opler 1940a: 192, 1940b:476; La Barre 1975:7, 117, 121.
10. Goldenweiser 1912:600–607; Wallis 1941:251–52; Wissler 1912:100–106, 1915:120–23; Lowie 1912:68–71.
11. Park 1938:44; Eggan 1941:13.
12. Murdock 1937:450–51.
13. Du Bois 1939:135–36.
14. Linton 1940:205; Mandelbaum 1941a:26.
15. Du Bois 1939:4–11, 130–34; Nash 1937:414.
16. Mooney 1896; Lesser 1933b:60–76; Petrullo 1934:78–86; La Barre 1975: 151–61.
17. La Barre 1975; Stewart 1941:305–6.
18. See La Barre (1975:123) on Jonathan Koshiway and Mandelbaum (1941b) on Sulli.
19. M. E. Opler 1936a:109; Kluckhohn 1941:109.
20. Comparable phenomena in ambivalence have been described by M. E. Opler (1936b) and Hallowell (1940).
21. M. K. Opler 1940b:194.
22. Dollard 1938:15.

23. Cf. Dollard et al. 1939:45–46.

24. Nash 1937:377–78.

25. Kardiner 1939:8; cf. also Murray 1938:609–10; Sapir 1938:9; Linton 1936:464.

26. Murray 1938:609.

27. Murray 1938:722; Horney 1937:16.

28. Schultes 1938:712; Radin 1914:12; La Barre 1975:43, 97–98; Shonle 1925:59; Parsons 1936; 67–68.

29. Kardiner 1939:9.

30. La Barre 1975:93.

31. La Barre 1975:97, 100; Sapir 1936:127.

32. Kardiner 1939:129.

33. Radin 1926:136–38, 168, 188–90; Hallowell 1938:45; Benedict 1934:24.

34. Mundelbaum 1941b.

35. Sapir 1934:408, 411–12; Dollard 1935:287.

36. Hallowell 1940; La Barre 1975:120n.72; Stewart 1944:69; Kardiner 1939:8.

37. Geertz 1969:176–77; Firth 1981:595 (1982 addition).

38. Du Bois 1939:7–9.

39. Du Bois 1939:7, 9.

40. Du Bois 1939:9.

41. Parsons 1936:66–68, 1939.

42. M. E. Opler 1936a; Parsons 1939:1094–97.

43. M. K. Opler 1940a; 1940b.

44. Mandelbaum 1941b:236; Sapir 1932:242.

45. M. K. Opler 1940b:194.

EPILOGUE

1. Deloria 1981:13; Dorris 1981:63.

2. *Nevada Appeal* 3 June 1974.

3. Price 1980:68; Dorris 1981:59; d'Azevedo 1978:xi.

4. Nevers 1976:89–91.

5. Fortes has described a parallel phenomenon which has taken place in South Africa over the past half-century: "In spite of restrictions, frustrations and privations the educational level and standard of living among the Blacks, as well as the Indian and Colored communities, have risen markedly in the past fifty years" (1981:159).

6. Downs 1963:130.

7. Downs 1963:127; Hinkle 1949:135; d'Azevedo 1963:2.

8. Downs 1963:130; d'Azevedo 1966:318; Siegel and Beals 1960; Lieber 1972:387.

9. Num. 13:33.

10. d'Azevedo 1978:29; Downs 1963:130–31.

11. Hopkins 1883:60–65.

12. Gigli 1974.

13. Leis 1963:60.

14. Price 1980.

15. Downs 1961:373; Leis 1963:60.

16. Turner 1967:113.

17. Stewart 1956, 1980c:17; cf. Anderson 1980:7.

18. Olofson 1979:18; Bean 1975; Bean and Vane 1978b:128.

19. Much of the information on Henry (Moses) Rupert is drawn from the writings of Don Handelman (1967a, 1967b, 1972), from the unpublished notes and manuscript material of Grace Dangberg, and from conversations with both. Rupert was one of my informants in 1938.

20. Handelman 1967a:447.

21. Handelman 1967a:451.

22. Handelman 1967b:151.

23. Handelman 1967a:452.

24. Handelman 1967b:151.

25. Eliade's views on the role of the shaman do not take into account the character of the shaman among many American Indian tribes, including the Washo. "What is fundamental and universal," he writes, "is the shaman's struggle against what we could call 'the powers of evil' "(1964:509). In their manipulation of witchcraft, the old Washo shamans, far from struggling against the powers of evil, could be said to have been in league with them. Eliade calls shamans "anti-demonic champions," although he cites Park's testimony for the Northern Paiute that "the practice of witchcraft may be as important a part of shamanism as curing a disease." He claims that the shamans "combat not only demons and disease, but also black magicians," despite instances found in primitive societies where healer and "black magician" are one and the same. Eliade also errs in stating that spirit possession is not an essential characteristic of shamanism. Among the Washo, as among most American Indian tribes, it is (Lewis 1971:49-50).

26. Handelman 1972.

27. Merriam and d'Azevedo 1957:615-16.

28. Stewart 1944; Merriam and d'Azevedo 1957:616.

29. Stewart 1944:127-32; Downs 1966:104.

30. Price 1980:45.

31. d'Azevedo 1978:xi.

32. The amoral cast of shamanism was not a narrowly localized phenomenon. The case of the Northern Paiute has been cited. Power to the California Indians is a "mixture of both good and bad essences," and humans with power are "potentially amoral toward others" (Bean 1975). Don Juan, Carlos Castaneda's celebrated Yaqui shaman, has been described as amoral. In common with Washo shamans, his teachings reveal little concern for the norms of Western morality. His revelations and admonitions float in a universe of amoral relativism (Harris 1974:208-22).

33. Stewart 1980b:2.

34. d'Azevedo 1978:30, 40, 41, 48.

35. Stewart 1980b:16.

36. d'Azevedo 1978:34.

37. Stewart 1944:64; La Barre 1975:165, 202.

38. Handelman 1967a:448.

39. Merriam and d'Azevedo 1957:618.

40. d'Azevedo 1978:14-15.

41. d'Azevedo 1978:36-37.

42. d'Azevedo 1978:32.

43. d'Azevedo 1978:37-38.

44. Berlin 1979:266.

45. Yinger 1970:324.

46. Barber 1941; La Barre 1975:43n.85, 1970:281; Spindler 1952;155.

47. La Barre has referred to similar behavior as "propaganda for the ethnographer's benefit" (1975:163n.9).

48. Downs 1966;102-3.

49. La Barre 1970:300.

50. d'Azevedo 1978:21.

51. Downs 1966:104.

52. Downs 1963:133.

53. La Barre 1975:195, 200; Barber 1941:675; Stewart 1944:86.

54. Stewart 1944:98.

55. Shonle 1925:59.

56. Downs 1966:55–56; Price 1980:41.

57. Merriam and d'Azevedo 1957:617; Downs 1966:109.

58. Price 1980:33.

59. The tales were taken down by Brooke D. Mordy and are now part of the archival collection.

60. History discloses several examples of a break with the past resulting from a religious controversy. The Reformation in sixteenth-century Europe was a notable instance. Luther and Calvin did more than reform the church, they revolutionized Christianity. "The Reformation was a revolution," writes Elton, the English historian (1963:274). It marked a break with traditional Christianity.

61. Bean and Vane 1978b; Bean 1975; Downs 1961:372-73.

62. Dorris 1981:63–65.

BIBLIOGRAPHY

Abbreviations signify the following:

A	Anthropos
AA	American Anthropologist
AAA-M	American Anthropological Association, Memoirs
AMNH-AP	American Museum of Natural History, Anthropological Papers
AMNH-B	American Museum of Natural History, Bulletin
AMNH-M	American Museum of Natural History, Memoirs
AQ	Anthropological Quarterly
BAE-B	Bureau of American Ethnology, Bulletin
BAE-R	Bureau of American Ethnology, Annual Report
CU-CA	Columbia University, Contributions to Anthropology
EL	Ethnology
ES	Ethnos
GSA	General Series in Anthropology
JAFL	Journal of American Folklore
JASP	Journal of Abnormal and Social Psychology
JCA	Journal of California Anthropology
JRP	Journal of Religious Psychology
JSP	Journal of Social Psychology
M	Man
NSM-AP	Nevada State Museum, Anthropological Papers
NSM-OP	Nevada State Museum, Occasional Papers
NU-SSS	Northwestern University, Studies in the Social Sciences
P	Psychiatry
PMM- B	Public Museum of the City of Milwaukee, Bulletin
SF	Social Forces
T	Tomorrow; Quarterly Review of Psychical Research
TLS	Times Literary Supplement
UC- AR	University of California, Anthropological Records
UC-PAAE	University of California, Publications in American Archaeology and Ethnology
UUP-AP	University of Utah Press, Anthropological Papers
UW-PA	University of Washington, Publications in Anthropology
W	Wassaja; The Indian Historian
YU-PA	Yale University, Publications in Anthropology

Aberle, David F.
1966   *The Peyote Religion among the Navaho.* Chicago.

Anderson, Edward F.
1980   *Peyote: The Divine Cactus.* Tucson.

Bancroft, Hubert H.
1875–   *The Native Races of the Pacific States of America.* 5 vols. New York.
1876

Barber, Bernard
1941   A Socio-cultural Interpretation of the Peyote Cult. AA 43:673–75.

Barrett, Samuel A.
1917   *The Washo Indians.* PMM–B 2:1–52.

Barrett, Samuel A., and Edward W. Gifford
1933   *Miwok Material Culture.* PMM–B 2:117–376.

Beals, Ralph L.
1933   *Ethnography of the Nisenan.* UC—PAAE 31(6):335–414.

Bean, Lowell J.
1975   Power and Its Application in Native California. JCA 1:117–29.

1976   California Indian Shamanism and Folk Curing. In *American Folk Medicine: A Symposium*, ed. Wayland D. Hand, pp. 109–23. Berkeley.

Bean, Lowell J., and Sylvia B. Vane
1978a   Cults and Their Transformations. In *Handbook of North American Indians*: Vol. 8, *California*, ed. Robert F. Heizer and William C. Sturtevant, pp. 662–72. Washington, D.C.

1978b   Shamanism: An Introduction. In *Art of the Huichol Indians*, Kathleen Derrin, pp. 177–28. New York.

Benedict, Ruth F.
1922   The Vision in Plains Culture. AA 24:1–23.

1923   *The Concept of the Guardian Spirit in North America.* AAA–M 29.

1924   A Brief Sketch of Serrano Culture. AA 26:366–92.

1934   *The Patterns of Culture.* Boston.

Bennett, Wendell C., and Robert M. Zingg
1935   *The Tarahumara: An Indian Tribe of Northern Mexico.* Chicago.

Berlin, Isaiah
1979   *Russian Thinkers.* New York.

Billington, Ray Allen
1981   *Land of Savagery, Land of Promise.* New York.

Clements, Forrest E.
1932   *Primitive Concepts of Disease.* UC–PAAE 32(2).

Culin, Stewart
1907   *Games of the North American Indians.* BAE–R 24.

Curtis, Edward S.
1907–   *The North American Indian.* 20 vols. Cambridge, MA.
1930

Dangberg, Grace
nd   Washo Field Notes. Unpublished MS.

1927   *Washo Texts.* UC–PAAE 22(3):391–443.

1972   *Carson Valley Historical Sketches of Nevada's First Settlement.* Carson Valley
       Historical Society, Carson City.

d'Azevedo, Warren L.
1966   Comments on Tribal Distribution. In *The Current Status of Anthropological
       Research in the Great Basin: 1964*, ed. Warren L. d'Azevedo, Wilbur A.
       Davis, Don D. Fowler, Wayne Suttles, pp. 315–34. Reno.

1973   *The Delegation to Washington: A Washo Peyotist Narrative.* W 6:4–6.

1978   *Straight with the Medicine.* Reno.

(comp. and ed.)
1963   *The Washo Indians of California and Nevada.* UUP–AP 67.

Deloria, Vine, Jr.
1970   *Custer Died for Your Sins.* New York.

1981   Identity and Culture. In *Daedalus* (Spring issue):13–27.

de Mille, Richard
1976   *Castaneda's Journey: The Power and the Allegory.* London.

Densmore, Frances
1922   *Northern Ute Music.* BAE–B 75.

1932   *Yuman and Yaqui Music.* BAE–B 110.

Dixon, Roland B.
1905   *The Northern Maidu.* AMNH–B 17(3).

1907   *The Shasta.* AMNH–B 17(5):381–498.

1908   Notes on the Achomawi and Atsugewi Indians of Northern California.
       AA 10:208–20.

Dollard, John
1935   *Criteria for the Life History, with Analyses of Six Notable Documents.* New
       Haven.

1938   Hostility and Fear in Social Life. SF 17:15–26.

Dollard, John, et al.
1939   *Frustration and Aggression.* New Haven.

Dorris, Michael A.
1981   The Grass Still Grows, the Rivers Still Flow: Contemporary Native
       Americans. In *Daedalus* (Spring issue):43–69.

Downs, James F.
1961   *Washo Religion.* UC–AR 16(9).

1963   Differential Response to White Contact: Paiute and Washo. In *The Washo Indians of California and Nevada*, ed. Warren L. d'Azevedo, pp. 115-37. UUP-AP 67.

1966   *The Two Worlds of the Washo*. New York.

Du Bois, Cora
1932   Tolowa Notes. AA 34:248-62.

1935   *Wintu Ethnography*. UC-PAAE 36(1).

1939   *The 1870 Ghost Dance*. UC-AR 3(1).

Eggan, Fred
1941   Some Aspects of Culture Change in the Northern Philippines. AA 43:11-18.

Eliade, Mircea
1964   *Shamanism: Archaic Techniques of Ecstasy,* trans. Willard R. Trask. Princeton.

Ellis, Havelock
1898   Mescal: A New Artificial Paradise. *Contemporary Review* 73:130-41.

Elton, G. R.
1963   *Reformation Europe, 1517-1559*. London.

Firth, Raymond
1981   Spiritual Aroma: Religion and Politics. AA 53:582-601.

Forde, C. Daryll
1931   *Ethnography of the Yuma Indians*. UC-PAAE 28(4):83-278.

Fortes, Myer
1981   The Sociopathology of the Afrikaner. TLS 4063:159.

Fowler, Don D.
1966   Great Basin Social Organization. In *The Current Status of Anthropological Research in the Great Basin: 1964*, ed. Warren L. d'Azevedo, Wilbur A. Davis, Don D. Fowler, Wayne Suttles, pp. 57-74. Reno.

Freed, Stanley A.
1960   *Changing Washo Kinship*. UC-AR 14(6):349-418.

Freed, Stanley A., and Ruth S. Freed
1963   A Configuration of Aboriginal Washo Culture. In *The Washo Indians of California and Nevada*, ed. Warren L. d'Azevedo, pp. 41-56. UUP-AP 67.

Frémont, John C.
1846   *Narrative of the Exploring Expedition to the Rocky Mountains in the Year 1842 and to Oregon and N. California in the Years 1843-44*. New York.

Gayton, A. H.
1930   *Yokuts-Mono Chiefs and Shamans*. UC-PAAE 24(8).

Geertz, Clifford
1969   Religion in Java: Conflict and Integration. In *Sociology of Religion*, ed. Roland Robertson. New York.

Gifford, Edward W.
   1932a *The Northfork Mono.* UC–PAAE 31(2):15–65.

   1932b *The Southeastern Yavapai.* UC–PAAE 29(3):177–252.

   1933   *The Cocopa.* UC–PAAE 31(5):257–334.

Gifford, Edward W., and Robert H. Lowie
   1928   *Notes on the Akwa'ala Indians of Lower California.* UC–PAAE 23(7).

Gigli, Jane Green
   1974   *Dat So La Lee, Queen of the Washo Basket Makers.* NSM–AP 16:1–27.

Goddard, Pliny Earl
   1903   *Life and Culture of the Hupa.* UC–PAAE 1(1).

Goldenweiser, Alexander A.
   1912   Origin of Totemism. AA 14:600–607.

   1937   *Anthropology: An Introduction to Primitive Culture.* New York.

Greenberg, Joseph H., and Morris Swadesh
   1953   Jicaque as a Hokan Language. *International Journal of American Linguistics*
           19(2):216–22.

Günther, Erna
   1926   *Klallam Ethnography.* UW–PA 1(5):171–314.

Hallowell, A. Irving
   1938   Fear and Anxiety and Cultural and Individual Variables in a Primitive
           Society. JSP 9:25–47.

   1940   Aggression in Saulteaux Society. P 3:395–407.

Handelman, Don
   1967a The Development of a Washo Shaman. EL 6(4):444–64.

   1967b Transcultural Shamanic Healing: A Washo Example. ES 32:149–66.

   1972   Aspects of the Moral Compact of a Washo Shaman. AQ 45(2):84–101.

Harris, Jack S.
   1940   The White Knife Shoshoni of Nevada. In *Acculturation in Seven American
           Indian Tribes*, ed. Ralph Linton, pp. 39–116. New York and London.

Harris, Marvin
   1974   *Cows, Pigs, Wars, and Witches: The Riddles of Culture.* New York.

Herskovits, Melville J.
   1940   *The Economic Life of Primitive Peoples.* New York.

   1941   Some Comments on the Study of Cultural Contact. AA 43:1–10.

Hinkle, George H., and Bliss M. Hinkle
   1949   *Sierra-Nevada Lakes.* Indianapolis and New York.

Hooper, Lucille
   1920   *The Cahuilla Indians.* UC–PAAE 16(6):315–80.

Hopkins, Sarah Winnemucca
    1883   *Life among the Piutes*, ed. Mrs. Horace Mann. Boston.

Horney, Karen
    1937   *The Neurotic Personality of Our Time.* New York.

Houghton, Eliza P. Donner
    1920   *The Expedition of the Donner Party and Its Tragic Fate.* Los Angeles.

Huxley, Aldous
    1954   *The Doors of Perception.* New York.

Jacobsen, William H., Jr.
    1966   Washo Linguistic Studies. In *The Current Status of Anthropological Research in the Great Basin: 1964*, ed. Warren L. d'Azevedo, pp. 113–36. Reno.

Kardiner, Abram
    1939   *The Individual and his Society.* New York.

Kelly, Isabel T.
    1932   *Ethnography of the Surprise Valley Paiute.* UC–PAAE 31(3):67–210.

    1936   Chemehuevi Shamanism. In *Essays in Anthropology Presented to A. L. Kroeber in Celebration of His Sixtieth Birthday*, ed. Robert H. Lowie, pp. 129–42. Berkeley.

Kluckhohn, Clyde
    1941   Patterning as Exemplified in Navaho Culture. In *Language, Culture, and Personality: Essays in Memory of Edward Sapir*, ed. Leslie Spier, A. Irving Hallowell, Stanley S. Newman, pp. 109–30. Menasha, WI; reprinted 1960, University of Utah Press, Salt Lake City.

Kroeber, Alfred L.
    1906–   *The Washo Language of East Central California and Nevada.* UC–PAAE
    1907   4(5).

    1907   *The Arapaho.* AMNH–B 18.

    1925   *Handbook of the Indians of California.* BAE–B 78.

    1939   *Cultural and Natural Areas of Native North America.* Berkeley.

(ed.)
    1935   *Walapai Ethnography.* AAA–M 42.

La Barre, Weston
    1970   *The Ghost Dance: Origins of Religion.* New York.

    1975   *The Peyote Cult.* 4th ed., enlarged. Hamden, CT.

Leis, Philip E.
    1963   Washo Witchcraft: A Test of the Frustration-Aggression Hypothesis. In *The Washo Indians of California and Nevada*, ed. Warren L. d'Azevedo, pp. 57–68. UUP–AP 67.

Lesser, Alexander
    1933a   The Cultural Significance of the Ghost Dance. AA 35:108–15.

    1933b   *The Pawnee Ghost Dance Hand Game: A Study of Culture Change.* CU–CA 16.

Lewis, I. M.
1971   *Ecstatic Religion.* New York.

Lieber, Michael D.
1972   Opposition to Peyotism among the Western Shoshone: The Message of Traditional Belief. M 7(3):387–96.

Linton, Ralph
1936   *The Study of Man.* New York.

(ed.)
1940   *Acculturation in Seven American Indian Tribes,* New York and London.

Loeb, Edwin M.
1926   *Pomo Folkways,* UC-PAAE 19(2).

Lowie, Robert H.
1909   *The Northern Shoshone.* AMNH-AP 2(2).

1912   Some Problems in the Ethnology of the Crow and Village Indians. AA 14:68–71.

1922   *The Religion of the Crow Indians.* AMNH-AP 25(2).

1924   *Notes on Shoshonean Ethnography.* AMNH-AP 20(3).

1939   *Ethnographic Notes on the Washo.* UC-PAAE 36(5):301–52.

Lumholtz, Carl
1898   *The Huichol Indians of Mexico.* AMNH-B 10:1–14.

1902   *Unknown Mexico.* 2 vols. New York.

Mandelbaum, David G.
1941a Culture Change among the Nilgiri Tribes. AA 43:19–26.

1941b Social Trends and Personal Pressures: The Growth of a Culture Pattern. In *Language, Culture, and Personality: Essays in Memory of Edward Sapir,* ed. Leslie Spier, A. Irving Hallowell, Stanley S. Newman, pp. 219–38. Menasaha, WI; reprinted 1960, University of Utah Press, Salt Lake City.

Mason, J. Alden
1912   *The Ethnology of the Salinan Indians.* UC-PAAE 10(4):97–240.

Merriam, Alan P., and Warren L. d'Azevedo
1957   Washo Peyote Songs. AA 59:615–41.

Montgomery, G. Edward
1965   Washo Health and Disease. Unpublished MS. lent by author.

Mooney, James
1896   *The Ghost Dance Religion and the Sioux Outbreak of 1890.* BAE-R 14(2): 641–1110.

Murdock, George Peter
1937   Correlations of Institutions. In *Studies in the Science of Society,* ed. George Peter Murdock, pp. 445–70. New Haven.

Murray, Henry A.
    1938   *Explorations in Personality*. The Workers at the Harvard Psychological Clinic, New York.

Nash, Philleo
    1937   The Place of Religious Revivalism in the Formation of the Intercultural Community of Klamath Reservation. In *Social Anthropology of North American Tribes*, ed. Fred Eggan, pp. 377–442. Chicago.

Nevers, Jo Ann
    1976   *Wa She Shu: A Washo Tribal History*. Reno.

Nevins, Allen
    1939   *Fremont: Pathmaker of the West*. 2 vols. New York.

Nomland, Gladys Ayer
    1935   *Sinkyone Notes*. UC–PAAE 36(2):149–78.

Olofson, Harold
    1979   Northern Paiute Shamanism Revisited. A 74:11–24.

Opler, Marvin K.
    1940a   The Character and History of the Southern Ute Peyote Rite. AA 42:463–78.

    1940b   The Southern Ute of Colorado. In *Acculturation in Seven American Indian Tribes*, ed. Ralph Linton, pp. 119–203. New York and London.

Opler, Morris E.
    1936a   The Influence of Aboriginal Pattern and White Contact on a Recently Introduced Ceremony, the Mescalero Peyote Rite. JAFL 49:143–67.

    1936b   An Interpretation of Ambivalence of Two American Indian Tribes. JSP 7:82–115.

    1938   The Use of Peyote by the Carrizo and Lipan Apache Tribes. AA 40:271–85.

Park, Willard Z.
    1938   *Shamanism in Western North America*. NU–SSS 2.

Parsons, Elsie Clews
    1936   *Taos Pueblo*. GSA 2. Menasha, WI.

    1939   *Pueblo Indian Religion*. 2 vols. Chicago

Petrullo, Vincenzo
    1934   *The Diabolic Root: A Study of Peyotism, the New Indian Religion among the Delawares*. Philadelphia.

Price, John A.
    1980   *The Washo Indians: History, Life Cycle, Religion, Technology, Economy and Modern Life*. NSM–OP 4.

Radin, Paul
    1914   A Sketch of the Peyote Cult of the Winnebago: A Study in Borrowing. JRP 7:1–22.

    1926   *Crashing Thunder: The Autobiography of a Winnebago Indian*. New York.

1937   *Primitive Religion: Its Nature and Origin.* New York.

Ray, Verne F.
1932   *The Sanpoil and Nespelem, Salishan Peoples of Northeastern Washington.* UW–PA 5.

Russell, Frank
1908   *The Pima Indians.* BAE–R 26:3–389.

Sanchez, Thomas
1973   *Rabbit Boss.* New York.

Sapir, Edward
1907   Religious Ideas of the Takelma Indians of Southwestern Oregon. JAFL 20:33–49.

1932   Cultural Anthropology and Psychiatry. JASP 27:229–42.

1934   The Emergence of the Concept of Personality in a Study of Culture. JSP 5:408–15.

1936   The Application of Anthropology to Human Relations. In *The American Way,* ed. Newton Diehl Baker, Carlton J. H. Hays, Roger Williams Strauss, pp. 121–29. Chicago.

1938   Why Cultural Anthropology Needs the Psychiatrist. P 1:7–12.

Schultes, Richard Evans
1938   The Appeal of Peyote *(Lophophora williamsii)* as a Medicine. AA 40:698–715.

Shonle, Ruth
1925   Peyote: The Giver of Visions. AA 27:53–75.

Siegel, B. J., and A. R. Beals
1960   Pervasive Factionalism. AA 62:394–417.

Siskin, Edgar E.
1938   Washo Territory. *In* Tribal Distribution in the Great Basin, Willard Z. Park et al. AA 40:625–27.

Spier, Leslie
1921   *The Sun Dance of the Plains Indians: Its Development and Diffusion.* AMNH–AP 16:453–522.

1923   *Southern Diegueno Customs.* UC–PAAE 20:297–358.

1925   *The Distribution of Kinship Systems in North America.* UW–PA 1(2).

1928   *Havasupai Ethnography.* AMNH–AP 29(3).

1930   *Klamath Ethnography.* UC–PAAE 30.

1933   *Yuman Tribes of the Gila River.* Chicago.

1935   *The Prophet Dance of the Northwest and Its Derivatives: The Source of the Ghost Dance.* GSA 1. Menasha, WI.

Spier, Leslie, and Edward Sapir
1930   *Wishram Ethnography.* UW–PA 3(3):151–300.

Spinden, Herbert J.
    1908   *The Nez Percé Indians.* AAA–M 2(3).

Spindler, George
    1952   Personality and Peyotism in Menomini Indian Acculturation. P15:
            151–59.

Steward, Julian H.
    1933   *Ethnography of the Owens Valley Paiute.* UC–PAAE 33(3):233–250.

Stewart, Omer C.
    1938   Northern Paiute. *In* Tribal Distribution in Eastern Oregon and Adjacent
            Regions, Verne F. Ray et al. AA 40:405–7.

    1939   *The Northern Paiute Bands.* UC–AR 2(3):127–49.

    1941   The Southern Ute Peyote Cult. AA 43:303–8.

    1944   *Washo–Northern Paiute Peyotism: A Study in Acculturation.* UC–PAAE 40(3):
            63–141.

    1956   Three Gods for Joe. T 4(3):71–76.

    1973   Anthropologists as Expert Witnesses for Indians: Claims and Peyote
            Cases. In *Anthropology and the American Indian*, ed. James Office, pp.
            35–42. Indian Historical Press, San Francisco.

    1980a   The Native American Church. In *Anthropology on the Great Plains*, ed. W.
            Raymond Wood, Margot Liberty, pp. 188–96. Lincoln, NB, and Lon-
            don.

    1980b   Economics of Peyotism in the Great Basin. Unpublished MS.

    1980c   American Indian Religion: Past, Present, Future. W 13(1):15–18.

Strong, William Duncan
    1929   *Aboriginal Society in Southern California.* UC–PAAE 26.

Teit, James
    1900   *The Thompson Indians of British Columbia.* AMNH–M 2(4).

    1906   *The Lillooet Indians.* AMNH–M 4(6).

    1909   *The Shuswap.* AMNH–M 4(7).

Thomas, William I.
    1937   *Primitive Behavior.* New York.

Turner, Victor
    1967   *The Forest of Symbols: Aspects of Ndembu Ritual.* Ithaca, NY, and London.

Twain, Mark
    1872   *Roughing It.* 2 vols. New York.

U.S. Department of the Interior, Office of Indian Affairs
    1936   *Constitution and By-Laws of the Washoe Tribe, Nevada and California.*
            Washington, D.C.

    1937   *Corporate Charter of the Washoe Tribe of the States of Nevada and California.*
            Washington, D.C.

Wallis, Wilson D.
   1941   Alexander A. Goldenweiser. AA 43:250-55.

Wissler, Clark
   1912   *Ceremonial Bundles of the Blackfoot Indians.* AMNH-AP 7:100-106.

   1915   The Material Cultures of the North American Indians. In *Anthropology in North America*, Franz Boas et al., pp. 76-134. New York.

Yinger, J. Milton
   1970   *The Scientific Study of Religion.* New York and London.

INDEX